Holistic Discourse Analysis

Second Edition

Series Editor
Mike Cahill

Volume Editor
Lynn Frank

Production Staff
Bonnie Brown, Managing Editor
Mary Huttar, Copy Editor
Lois Gourley, Compositor
Barbara Alber, Cover Design

Holistic Discourse Analysis

Second Edition

Robert E. Longacre
and
Shin Ja J. Hwang

SIL International®
Dallas, Texas

© 2012 by SIL International®
Library of Congress Catalog No: 2011941350
ISBN: 978-1-55671-329-3

Printed in the United States of America

All rights reserved

No part of this publication may be reproduced, stored in a retrieval system, or transmitted in any form or by any means—electronic, mechanical, photocopy, recording, or otherwise—without the express permission of SIL International®. However, short passages, generally understood to be within the limits of fair use, may be quoted without written permission.

Copies of this and other publications of SIL International® may be obtained from:

SIL International Publications
7500 W. Camp Wisdom Road
Dallas, TX 75236-5629

Voice: 972-708-7404
Fax: 972-708-7363
publications_intl@sil.org
www.ethnologue.com/bookstore.asp

Contents

Preface ix
Acknowledgments xiii
Abbreviations and symbols xv

Chapter 1 Why Discourse Analysis? 1
   1.1 Word order 1
   1.2 Functions of different forms of the verb 3
   1.3 Participant reference in discourse. 4
   1.4 Definitivization and deictics 6
   1.5 Temporal and locational expressions; adverbial clauses 7
   1.6 Sequence signals and conjunctions 8
   1.7 Mystery particles 9
   1.8 The length of syntactic units. 11
   1.9 Conclusion 13
   1.10 Exercises 14

Chapter 2 A Layman's Introduction to Discourse Analysis 15
   2.1 What different forms of verbs contribute to a story 17
   2.2 What nouns and pronouns do within a story 20
   2.3 How verbs and referents interplay
       in the structure of this paragraph 22
   2.4 Internal relations in the text: Cohesion and coherence 23
   2.5 Marking a great moment within a story. 26
   2.6 What part does each sentence play in the plan of the whole? 27
   2.7 The resultant constraints on interpretation 29
   2.8 Exercise 30
   Appendix 2A. Paragraph analysis: Tree diagram. 31
   Appendix 2B. Paragraph analysis: Indentation diagram 33

Chapter 3 Text Typology 35
   3.1 An etic scheme of discourse types 35
   3.2 An emic scheme of discourse types in Aguacatec (Mayan). 39
   3.3 Sample texts from English 42

3.4 Exercises	44

Chapter 4 Approaching a Narrative: Constituent Charting and Macrosegmentation 45
   4.1 Constituent charting of a text 46
      4.1.1 The basic charting 46
      4.1.2 Tracking by colors 52
      4.1.3 Making notes 53
   4.2 Macrosegmentation of a text 53
   4.3 Comparative charting as a translation check 60
   4.4 Conclusion 61
   4.5 Exercises 61
   Appendix 4. Constituent chart of "Hans" 63

Chapter 5 How the Listener/Reader Follows a Story 71
   5.1 Salience scheme for English 72
   5.2 Salience scheme in chaining languages 76
   5.3 Conclusion 79
   5.4 Exercises 79

Chapter 6 Participant Reference: Discourse Operations and Ranking 81
   6.1 Three variable factors 82
      6.1.1 Participant reference resources 82
      6.1.2 Ranking 83
      6.1.3 Discourse operations affecting participant reference 83
   6.2 "Hans" 85
   6.3 "The Three Little Pigs" 88
   6.4 Summary for English participant reference 90
   6.5 Conclusion 92
   6.6 Exercises 92

Chapter 7 Clause Combining in Discourse 93
   7.1 Co-ranking and chaining structures 94
   7.2 Clause combining devices 95
   7.3 Distribution and functions of clause combining devices in English 96
      7.3.1 Juxtaposition 99
      7.3.2 Coordination 99
      7.3.3 Chaining or participial clauses 100
      7.3.4 Adverbial clauses 101
      7.3.5 Relative clauses 102
      7.3.6 Complement clauses 103
   7.4 Distribution and functions of clause combining devices in chaining structures 103
      7.4.1 Migabac chaining 103
      7.4.2 Korean chaining 107
   7.5 Conclusions 115
   7.6 Exercises 116
   Appendix 7A. Notional structure combinations of propositions 117

Appendix 7B. English sentence types by nuclei 123
Appendix 7C. English sentence margins 125
Chapter 8 Drafting Trees for Discourses and Paragraphs **127**
    8.1 Representations of extensive sections
        including whole discourses 132
    8.2 Representations of paragraph structures 135
    8.3 Concluding remarks 148
    8.4 Exercise 148
    Appendix 8A. Paragraph types 149
    Appendix 8B. Dialogue and similar paragraph types. 151
Chapter 9 Procedural Discourse **153**
    9.1 Segmentation of English procedural discourse 154
    9.2 Characteristics of a Korean recipe 162
    9.3 Toward a characterization of procedural discourse 163
    9.4 Conclusions 167
    9.5 Exercises 168
Chapter 10 Hortatory Discourse **169**
    10.1 The hortatory template 170
    10.2 Text organization 171
    10.3 Peak 173
    10.4 Mainline and supportive information 174
        10.4.1 Mainline of exhortation. 174
        10.4.2 Salience ranking scheme of verb forms 175
        10.4.3 The importance of sociolinguistic dynamics 176
    10.5 Sample text analyses 176
        10.5.1 English texts 177
        10.5.2 A Korean text 180
    10.6 Conclusions 184
    10.7 Exercises 185
    Appendix 10. Paragraph structure of "The Working Person" 187
Chapter 11 Expository Discourse. **189**
    11.1 Analysis of Psalm 23 in tree structure 190
    11.2 Analysis according to the structure of information 193
    11.3 Conclusion 205
    11.4 Exercises 205
    Appendix 11A. Ephesians 1:3–14 (NIV) 207
    Appendix 11B. Alzheimer disease text. 209
Glossary 211
References 227
Language Index 239
Index 241

Preface

This book is meant to be a manual for discourse analysis under field conditions everywhere. While it can be used as a textbook for classroom instruction, it is the fervent hope of its authors that it can and will be used by anyone desiring to do discourse analysis without the benefit of an organized classroom with a teacher.

The title *Holistic Discourse Analysis* is chosen to highlight the conviction that linguistic analysis properly deals with wholes and not with fragments. Discourse analysis, properly developed and practiced, implies analysis of the lower-level concerns that may be collectively referred to as the morphosyntax. Discourse analysis cannot be carried out in any language without knowledge of the morphosyntax. On the other hand, the morphosyntax itself demands the insights discoverable in discourse analysis as its rationale. We claim that the whole determines the part and that most of the whys are found in consideration of discourse context. So the title *Holistic Discourse Analysis* simply affirms this mutual dependency of grammatical structure from morpheme to discourse. What our title specifically denies is that discourse analysis can be bundled off and shifted to an area of semi-autonomous concerns such as pragmatics, with the implication that it is a good thing to do some day if one ever gets around to it. This conviction is explained and justified in chapter 1 "Why Discourse Analysis," where we argue that much of grammar as traditionally defined needs insights from broader context, that is, from discourse, to be fully understood.

Long before the close of the past century, Harald Weinrich (1964) in Germany and Emile Benveniste (1974) in France affirmed the relevance of tense-aspect systems to discourse. In summarizing their work some ten years later, Paul Ricoeur reaffirmed the work of Weinrich and Benveniste in insisting that tense-aspect systems exist to expedite discourse. Thus Ricoeur cites with approval Weinrich's assertion that "the function of the syntax is to guide the reader's attention and expectation. This is precisely what occurs in French in the tense that is particularly suited for putting into relief in the narrative domain, the preterite; whereas the imperfect signals the receding into the background of the narrated contents; as is frequently observed at the beginning of folktales and legends" (Ricoeur 1985:71). Assuredly, the time is well past when tense-aspect systems can be myopically analyzed as autonomous structures relating simply to the speaker's time of utterance.

Discourse analysis may be applied in several areas, such as translation, preparation of literacy material, code switching in sociolinguistics, and ESL composition, to name a few. We are particularly interested in the application to translation and to the training of translators. We believe we must adapt the writing of the original author to the conventions of another language; the translator must skillfully exploit the conventions of the second language to express something similar to the original text. After a workshop in Mexico years ago a fieldworker expressed such a successful adaptation in the words "Now that we have taught St. Paul to talk Mixtec…"

A less happy outcome ensued in another part of the world where translators were enjoined to do comparative discourse analysis by charting both a text in their language about a cultural hero and also their translation of the story of Joseph—a cultural hero of the Hebrews (Longacre 1998). In this case the TARGET[1] LANGUAGE was a language characterized by CHAINING in narrative, that is, by linking an indefinite number of non-final clauses with dependent verbs (gerunds, participles, medial verbs, co-verbs,) culminating in a fully inflected verb at the end. SWITCH REFERENCE all along the line kept track of subject reference. Having charted the native text and his own translation of the Joseph story, one translator volunteered the information that the two differed in several ways which he did not at all find difficult to state: The translation contained shorter sentences than the native text and contained more final verbs. At the same time it used many more pronouns than the native text. It was apparent that for the most part, the peculiar structures of his native language were not being plugged in, namely, clause chaining and switch reference. When asked what changes he was prepared to make in his translation, he replied that he couldn't change anything because it was the Word of God! He assumed that a good translation would not so much employ the target language structure as reflect the structure of the SOURCE LANGUAGE that he was acquainted with. This is an assumption this book attempts to overcome.

This new book is an attempt to put discourse analysis in such simple terms that it can guide the national translator even in the absence of a tutor. If we have not wholly succeeded in reaching this goal, it is at least believed that the book is an improvement over extant materials. In any case, this overall goal has been a useful constraint in writing this manual.

As to the theoretical framework of *Holistic Discourse Analysis*, we assume that there is a valid distinction between SURFACE STRUCTURE and NOTIONAL STRUCTURE. Common messages in the notional structure may surface

---

[1] Words that appear in small caps are technical terms that occur for the first time in this book. These terms can also be found in the glossary.

differently in the same language as well as in different languages. There may be SKEWING between surface and notional structures, that is, there is no one-to-one correspondence. The conjunction *and* in English, for example, may be used to express CONTRAST as well as COUPLING and TEMPORAL SUCCESSION. When skewing occurs, there is added meaning, such as playing down the contrast in the use of *and* rather than *but*.

We also assume that there is more to the whole than the sum total of its parts. Thus, a holistic approach is needed in order to see how the parts, such as the word, phrase, clause, and sentence, function in the whole text. We believe that comprehension of a text results from multiple simultaneous processing, including top-down (e.g., use of preexisting SCHEMAS and TEMPLATES) and bottom-up (use of words, grammatical structures, and contextual cues from the text).

We further assume that there are hierarchical levels in the grammar of language from morpheme and stem to word, phrase, clause, sentence, paragraph, and discourse. Each level has its own unique constituent structure, such as SOV (subject, object, and verb) at the clause level, the THESIS and paraphrase in a paraphrase paragraph at the paragraph level, and the STAGE, EPISODES, and CLOSURE in a story at the discourse level. A linguistic unit at any level of the grammatical hierarchy is like a coin with two sides. One side is the slot or function in the larger structure, such as subject or episode. The other side is the class or set, identifying the construction that fills the function, such as a noun phrase, a transitive clause, a coordinate sentence, or a result paragraph. We believe that discourse analysis should be carried out along with a solid analysis of the morphosyntax of the text, as well as the cognitive and socio-cultural concerns.

Another of our assumptions is that there is no free variation or randomness in the surface structure of grammar. Any form in a text represents the author's choice, whether conscious or automatic. We ask different types of questions: *what* (forms and constructions), *how* (how a form is structured or formulated), and *why* (why the form is used). Especially important is the last type of question; that is, for what purpose and function is a form used in discourse context?

This model can be described as a broad descriptive approach with interests in the functions of grammatical forms and the typology of cross-linguistic variations.

Beyond chapter 1, which addresses the question as to why such a study as this is necessary, the volume unfolds as follows: Chapter 2 presents a study in miniature, a sort of "everything you might want to know about discourse analysis," illustrated on a small scale. Chapter 3 then addresses the problem that not all discourses are of the same type and presents a typology of discourse types. This is a necessary caution lest we try to analyze a food recipe as if it were a story. Rules for one type may be different from those for another type. Chapter 4 finally gets down to the nuts and bolts of doing narrative analysis, a how-to-do-it chapter. It presents a constituent-based charting method and analyzes a short story in terms of PEAK and profile.

Chapter 5 has to do with the "followability" of a story and attendant matters; but mainly the different sorts of verbs and clauses that contribute to shaping the story. This, in turn, necessitates chapter 6, which tells us what nouns, pronouns, and the like contribute to shaping the story: who is on stage, who is backstage, who is waiting in the wings, and who is interacting with whom, and who does what to whom. Special focus is on discourse operations and ranking of PARTICIPANTS. Chapter 7 deals with how the elemental units, the clauses with verbal and nominal parts, combine and cluster into bigger wholes. It discusses clause combining devices and their functions in CO-RANKING and chaining structures. Chapter 8 graphically presents ways of representing combinations of sentences in a paragraph with extensive illustration in relation to a contemporary novel. Finally, chapters 9, 10, and 11, deal with non-narrative discourses: procedural, hortatory, and expository.

The reader interested in the intellectual history of this volume will find Longacre's second edition of *The Grammar of Discourse* (1996) of interest. While our work is not dependent on it, the advanced student will want to refer to it. The present volume is less concerned with theories or formalism than the earlier work and is more manual-like with practical hands-on instructions with sample text examples. New material not covered in *The Grammar of Discourse* includes "Why discourse analysis?" (chapter 1); an introductory application of discourse analysis to a short passage in its varied concerns, for example, nouns and verbs (chapter 2); a charting method and narrative text analysis (chapter 4); participant reference (chapter 6); and three non-narrative discourse types, each in its own chapter dealing with specific issues pertaining to the discourse type with sample texts (chapters 9–11). Finally, a glossary of technical terms is added for quick reference.

In addition, exercises are added at the end of each chapter for translators. The purpose of these exercises is to get the user of this book to be not just a reader but rather to plug in what he reads to the analysis of a target language—whether his own mother tongue or another language. Since the answers are not likely to be final or complete at this stage of the reader's competence, "guess and check" is the order of the day, making hypotheses from day one, but being prepared to modify or abandon them in the light of future research.

This book does not present discourse features of individual languages. We refer the readers interested in Bible translation to other studies, such as Black (1992) and Levinsohn (2000) for New Testament Greek; Bergen (1994), Longacre (2003a), and Longacre and Bowling (to appear) for Biblical Hebrew. Wiesemann and Spielmann's (2002) book may be helpful for those working in African languages. Levinsohn's (2007) self-instruction materials for work on narrative texts incorporate African language examples as well as others.

Acknowledgments

The idea for this book started about twenty years ago. We wanted to have a textbook that is relatively easy to understand for the native and nonnative speakers of English both in the classrooms and on the field.

We are grateful to many people, students and colleagues, for their creative ideas and input into this textbook and field guide. We express our thanks to over a thousand students who took the discourse analysis course and tried to learn and apply the model in class and later on the field. Their questions and suggestions helped us clarify the concepts and methodology in the study of discourse which can easily be opaque. Some of our colleagues have helped us teach the discourse model that is discussed in this book over the last twenty plus years and provided valuable inputs. We specially thank Rhonda Thwing, Clyde Whitby, and Marlin Leaders, who taught the course for several years and helped develop the model further. We are grateful to Bob Dooley, who read earlier versions of all the chapters. As a discourse specialist himself, his comments were especially instructive and helpful. We also thank those in attendance at the Bible Translation 2007 conference, where we presented the synopsis of the book and our motivation for writing, under the title "*Holistic Discourse Analysis* as a New Resource for Training Translators." In addition to their comments at the conference, some have chosen to read and comment on the written versions of the chapters. Our thanks also go to Steve McEvoy for providing and checking the Migabac textual data from Papua New Guinea included in chapter 7 and to Johanna Fenton for copyediting an earlier version of chapter 10. We are especially grateful to Lynn Frank for editing the entire book, Mary Huttar for copy editing, and Lois Gourley for typesetting. We express our thanks to all those who have helped us in many different ways. We regret that we cannot name all here.

There is one special person who deserves our sincere gratitude in several aspects. Marlin Leaders has not only taught the course for a number of years but also edited and commented on the whole book. Over a period of twenty years, he compiled the attached glossary, painstakingly explaining many technical terms as well as terms that are often taken for granted but may be unclear. His computer expertise and its application to linguistics was what enabled us to see the light at the end of the tunnel in this project. Thank you, Marlin!

Fall 2010

Robert E. Longacre
Shin Ja J. Hwang

Abbreviations and symbols

1	first person
3	third person
(E)	expository
(H)	hortatory
(N)	narrative
(P)	procedural
¶	paragraph
A	answer
ACC	accusative
ALT	alternative
AMPL	amplification
AO	agent orientation
BENEF	benefactive
BEN.O	benefactive object agreement
c-	counter (in dialogue)
CAUS	causative
Comm	comment
Coor	coordinate
CTS	contingent temporal succession
CU	continuing utterance
DECL	declarative
DS	different subject
D	dual
DUR	durative
Ep	episode
ET	equivalent thesis
EVAL	evaluation
IMP	imperative
INST	instrument
IU	initiating utterance
LI	lead-in

NAP	negated antonym paraphrase
NEG	negative
NOM	nominative
NOMZ	nominalizer
NP	noun phrase
NRRC	nonrestrictive relative clause
NS	notional structure
O	(1) object; (2) object agreement (in gloss)
P	projection
P / PL	plural
P.M	past modifying ending
PASS	passive
POSS	possessive
PR.M	present modifying ending
PRESUM	presumptive
PRO	proposal
PROG	progressive
Q	question
QF	quote formula
QUOT	quotative
REM	(1) remote; (2) remark
RES	response
RESULT	resultative
RU	resolving utterance
S / SG	singular
S	(1) subject; (2) sentence (as in S1 for sentence 1)
SEQ	sequence (¶ type)
Seq.Thesis	sequential thesis
Simul	simultaneous
SS	(1) same subject; (2) surface structure
SUB	subject marker
TAM	tense, aspect, modality
TOP	topic
TU	terminating utterance
V	verb
VP	verb phrase

Chapter 1

Why Discourse Analysis?

Doesn't the linguist have enough to do without having to analyze texts? Why add to an agenda that is already very full? Our answer here is that DISCOURSE analysis is a means of gaining further insight into the linguist's everyday research, a rationale of all that is being done, a set of wings rather than a burden to be borne. To the butterfly emerging from the cocoon the wings droop on both sides like damp weights, but as soon as the wings dry out and stiffen they provide the butterfly with flight. And flight equals power and enhanced range and perspective. So the linguist equipped with knowledge of the discourse structure of language, which is the object of research, attains more control over the data and increased perspective and insight.

We want to discuss here some grammatical issues, such as word order variation, tense/aspect/modality of verb forms, and nominal forms in PARTICIPANT REFERENCE, that are not adequately described within the domain of the sentence but require a holistic discourse perspective to understand the variable forms.

1.1 Word order

Discourse concerns affect clause structure. Myopic concentration on the structure of the clause itself to the exclusion of broader contextual concerns can therefore be self-defeating. All too often, claims that word order (or constituent order) is free, or something to that effect, are proffered to gloss over the analyst's ignorance of the situation.

In attempting to ascertain the normative word order of a language, perhaps the best place to begin is in narratives with sentences/clauses that seem to carry the MAINLINE INFORMATION of the story, that is, the temporally sequential events on the STORYLINE. Avoid questions, exclamations, and emotion-packed sentences, all of which may for various reasons not exhibit the basic word order.

The most common three word orders found in languages around the world are SOV, SVO, and VSO, all with S before O. If one order is strongly preferred, you, the investigator, should discover this in the data being inspected. If the subject is initial in its clause, it will soon become evident that the language is either SOV or SVO. A further inspection to determine the position of the V can then serve to decide between SOV and SVO. If a clause most commonly begins with the V, then the basic word order of the language is probably VSO.

After discerning normative word order, you ask: "Is there any way to recognize the subject other than by its position?" If only word order and lexical probability (e.g., it is more probable that the lion ate the man than that the man ate the lion) identify the subject, we can say that the language has GRAMMATICAL WORD ORDER (Thompson 1978). The other non-subject noun is the object, complement and the like; these can conveniently be lumped together under "object."

On the other hand, if the subject is in some way morphologically marked and if a basic word order is difficult to establish, the language very probably has PRAGMATIC WORD ORDER. In such circumstances, the investigator has to resort to the context, that is, discourse concerns, to understand the rationale of differing word orders. Is something on the order of old versus new information, thematic versus non-thematic information, responsible for the variation in word order? Czech is one language that employs pragmatic word order; in the early twentieth century Mathesius pioneered in Prague a method of analysis, which came to be called *functional sentence perspective* (Firbas 1966). According to this way of viewing a discourse, the noun that encodes RHEME (relatively new information) comes final or near final in the sentence and is rotated (as THEME, relatively old information) to sentence initial in the following sentence with a new noun occurring as rheme. Thus, in a kind of gigantic cross-stitching, old and new information bind the discourse together with newer information becoming old or given, and further new information being introduced sentence by sentence. In this model relatively old or given information appears in sentence-initial position, and new or non-given information occurs later in the sentence.

Roger Van Otterloo (2011) tells of a situation in Kifuliiru, a Bantu language of the Democratic Republic of the Congo, where sentence-final is the FOCUS (the main point of the whole sentence). In such a situation the sentence *Don't steal from widows* is somewhat ludicrous, since it implies that it is all right to steal from someone who isn't a widow. Van Otterloo solved this problem by permuting the word for 'widow' to somewhere earlier in the clause. This insight, in turn, proved to be relevant in many other passages in the draft of the Kifuliiru New Testament.

Even sentence-medial position is not always free of concerns of word order variation. Thus, a mutual switching of the positions of S and O should be studied with great attention to text context. Sometimes proximity to the verb can have significance, as in Hungarian where the focus must immediately precede the verb (Comrie 1989:63), rather than being clause-initial or clause-final.

Whether the word order is grammatical or pragmatic in a language, it is only in context that questions of word order in a given clause can be fully solved. In fact, grammatical and pragmatic word order can both be relevant in the same language where the basic word order helps identify subject versus object but where deviations from the basic word order have pragmatic import. Since discourse concerns affect clause structure, the analyst should concentrate not only on the structure of an individual clause, but also on the broader context.[1]

1.2 Functions of different forms of the verb

Analysis of the various verb forms of a language can be a formidable task. A verb system may appear to be disarmingly simple or may involve long stem-affix strings in an AGGLUTINATIVE language. Even in a language of inflected structure, such as Latin or Greek, or a modern language such as French or German, questions as to the appropriateness of one form of the verb rather than another can be perplexing. Witness the typical confusion that a beginning French student has as to the use of the French IMPERFECT (*imparfait*) versus the past tenses (*passé composé* or *passé simple*).

In a workshop held in a South American country, a participant (Linda Howard) entered the office and slapped on the desk a manuscript of some ninety pages in which the morphology of the Camsa language of Colombia was analyzed with great care, morpheme-by-morpheme and allomorph-by-allomorph. Her problem was that, although she controlled the rules for forming the long verb strings, she had little idea how to use the resultant complex verb units. Out of frustration she said, "Here it is; what do I do with it?" Unless we accept the analysis of morphological structures as an end in itself, a further perspective is clearly needed.

In regard to the French problem, the analysis of a few simple stories provides the main clue to the usage of verb tenses, subject to further refinements (Rand 1993). In a traditional story the stage is laid in the opening PARAGRAPH or two: time, place, and circumstances are sketched, and maybe a participant or two is introduced; nothing is happening as yet. In these paragraphs the French *imparfait* is the prevalent verb form. When the action line of the story begins, there is a shift to the *passé composé* or the *passé simple*, depending on the relative informality or formality of the style in which the story is told (since the *passé simple* is a literary tense). In the interior of the story the *imparfait* may reappear wherever staging rather than narration is in order. The *imparfait* can occur in a SUBORDINATE clause in a sentence whose main verb is, for example, *passé simple*: 'While Jack was cleaning his room, Jill arrived.' Ricoeur (1985), in discussing the functions of various tenses in French, states that the tenses are distributed in a narrative in such a way as to

---

[1] For information structure involving word order variation with topic and focus, see Lambrecht (1994), Van Valin (1993), and Levinsohn (2007).

enhance the "followability" of the story. In fact, in a language such as French, where one particular tense form carries the storyline, a tolerably adequate abstract of the story may be put together by jotting down all clauses that have the appropriate tense.

In analyzing the functions of the various forms of the Camsa verb, we enter a non-Indo-European world of agglutinative languages. Furthermore, the discourse types that are distinguished lead us onto unfamiliar ground. In Camsa narrative, it is necessary to distinguish three types: legend, historic, and contemporary. We quote Howard (1977:280) here: "Legend narratives are stories of the old people; historic narratives are the records of actual happenings in the past; and contemporary narratives are the records of actual happenings in the immediate or recent past." In a preliterate society such as the Camsa were at that time, historic narrative is confined to events within the memory of the oldest people now living, or immediately handed down from those who witnessed them.

The important thing to note here is that among the many affixes that occur on the verbs certain affixes are diagnostic of each narrative discourse type. Thus, verbs in clauses which are on the storyline in legend narrative have the prefix *yoj-*; verbs in clauses on the storyline of historic narrative have the affix combination *toj...an*; while verbs in clauses on the storyline of contemporary narrative have *toj-* (Howard 1977:285). Howard considers that procedural discourses are a further type of narrative, whose mainline is marked by the affix combination *j...na* 'infinitive'. While some subanalysis is possible (Howard calls *y-* vs. *t-* discourse markers), these affix combinations serve to distinguish the four narrative discourse types and at the same time contribute to the followability of the story/procedure. The full analysis of Camsa verb morphology can integrate around these discourse insights. We might summarize: Not all affixes are created equal.

1.3 Participant reference in discourse

While the verb morphology of a language contributes to the movement and delineation of discourses of various types, participants and themes are kept track of by noun phrases, nouns, pronouns, and personal endings on the verbs. We even have to add to these tracking devices a further device sometimes called ZERO ANAPHORA, that is, in certain languages (noticeably in Chinese) a participant/theme once identified can be assumed in certain contexts to be the referent even though no formal reference is subsequently made to that person/theme.

In English a person once identified is tracked in the immediate context (roughly the structural paragraph) by pronouns which act as placeholders. Often, when a paragraph boundary is crossed the noun is repeated and the noun-pronoun chain begins anew. This is necessary when a new participant is introduced and made thematic. There is even a cross-play in English between reference to a participant in an initial ADVERBIAL CLAUSE and in the main clause. Robert Kantor years ago (1976) pointed out the distinction between *When Augustus came to power, he...* and *When he came to power, Augustus...* In the latter case, we proceed in the succeeding sentences to treat Augustus as THEMATIC. But in the former case, when the name Augustus occurs in the initial *when* clause and the pronoun in the main clause, we proceed in the subsequent sentences not to make Augustus himself thematic but rather his works, his programs, the progress of the empire under him, etc. The thematic participant is anticipated by a pronoun in the initial subordinate clause but announced by name in the following main clause. Such are some of the conventions regarding pronouns in English.

Why is it that in a bilingual Spanish-English storybook with Spanish on one page and English on the facing page, there are roughly four times as many subject pronouns in the English as in the Spanish version? The answer is that Spanish has an inflected verb whose personal pronominal endings serve well to track a participant, so pronouns are not so frequently needed. Pronouns can be reserved for more emphatic or contrastive use in Spanish. But in looking at a story in Totonac (a language of Mexico), pronouns are even scarcer. Totonac has an intricate system of verb affixes that index both the subject and the object. Thus, where object pronouns are needed in Spanish they are not so necessary in Totonac. In fact, in a story in Totonac, the most frequent use of pronouns is in the context of direct quotations where they reflect dialogue between two participants. The situation in Biblical Hebrew is somewhat similar to that in Spanish. Thus, in the text of the Joseph story in the latter part of Genesis there is no occurrence of a subject pronoun with a finite verb; verb affixes handle participant tracking. In verbless clauses that are EQUATIVE, pronouns find their natural use, as in a sentence such as, 'he Ø good man'.

In a chaining structure with switch reference that marks subjects as same or different from clause to clause within the sentence, there is little call for pronouns; so the latter are reserved for more special uses. Thus, in examining a text in Aguaruna (South America) or Fore (Papua New Guinea), we find that there is little use for pronouns. A frequent error in translation is, in fact, to sprinkle unneeded pronouns throughout such sentences.

An extreme instance of non-English use of pronouns is found in Konda, a Dravidian language of India (Jacob and Susan George 1990). In stories in this language pronouns are reserved for what is almost an honorific usage, that is, the main participant of a story when he/she has vanquished his foes or risen above difficult circumstances can then, near the end of the story, be referred to by a pronoun! What a source of confusion it would be in Konda to sprinkle in pronouns like the placeholders of English!

Chinese is famous for zero anaphora. But the rules for zero anaphora in Chinese are as complicated as the rules for overt pronouns in some languages (Li and Thompson 1981, Pu 1997, Chu 1998).

1.4 Definitivization and deictics

The use of the English definite article is notoriously difficult for a person learning English. Furthermore, even native speakers of English differ somewhat in usage at this point. Larry Jones (1983) has done some excellent work in this regard. FIRST MENTION of an entity in an English text can be by means of the indefinite article upgrading to a definite article in subsequent references. But if the first mention of an entity is implied in previous mentions of another entity or situation, then the implied entity in the FOREGROUNDED FRAME can take the definite article on first mention (Prince 1981 refers to such information as inferable, and Chafe 1994 as accessible). Thus, in a paragraph about sailboats, the first mention of a sail is *the sail* since it is surely implied by the sailboat. Likewise, oars are employed in the context of rowboat, while mast is implied for most vessels. If a policeman is in the foreground, it is implied that he has a badge. Therefore, in these varied contexts, *the sail, the oars, the mast,* and *the badge* all can be expected to take the definite article on first mention. Jones' arguments are quite detailed and elaborate at this point, but the obvious lesson for us is that contextual concerns dictate the choice of indefinite and definite articles in English.

Languages that have definite articles do not necessarily have parallel uses across languages. It is of some interest here that Greek, another Indo-European language, also has a definite article, but it is not used exactly like the English definite article. In Greek, the definite article occurs before proper names, for example, 'the Cyrus'. Current European languages differ in the use of the article; some years ago a sign appeared in English denouncing 'the Communism' even though English does not take the definite article before a noun which names an abstraction. Keats did not write *the beauty is the truth, the truth the beauty* but rather "Beauty is truth; truth beauty..." ("Ode on a Grecian Urn" ca 1820).

Other sorts of items come in for concern as well, such as proper nouns, possessive pronouns, and DEICTICS (pointing to extralinguistic properties of person, place, and time, Anderson and Keenan 1985). These are part of a broader concern, participant/thematic reference in discourse, and are therefore discussed no further here, except to mention that systems of deictics can be extremely varied across languages and culture areas. Spanish has two near deictics, *aqui* 'right here' and *aca* 'here, in this general vicinity', and two far deictics, *alli* 'right over there' and *alla* 'over there'. Previously mentioned entities can be referred to as *aquel* or *este*. The Trique language has three deictics covering the same range: *nanh3* 'here', *manh3* 'there', and *danh3* 'out of sight', 'mentioned in previous context'. But this is nothing compared to languages which have deictics referring to such parameters as 'up hill' versus 'downhill' (in a culture in mountainous terrain) or 'toward the ocean' or 'away from the ocean' (in an island or coastal culture) or 'up river' and 'down river' (in a jungle river culture). Here linguistic parameters intersect with concerns of geography.

Another consideration has to do with DEIXIS broadly conceived, that is, the establishment of a base relative to motion. Thus, in American English if a person is in an apartment and there is a knock on the door, the person may yell out *I'm coming!*, but in the same situation in Spanish a person would yell out *Ya voy* meaning 'I'm going' or a Korean *Naka-yo* 'I'm going out'. In English the use of the verb *come* implies that the speaker takes the perspective of the one knocking on the door, that is, 'you're there and I'm coming to where you are'. In Spanish and Korean, the use of the verb 'go' implies the opposite perspective, that is, 'I'm here and I'm leaving where I am to go to you'.

As a broad notion, deixis affects general motion verbs. In textual context the uses of motion verbs can be perplexing in a language with which one is not familiar until one "stakes out," so to speak, the parameters of the situation: toward the speaker, away from the speaker, toward the hearer, away from the hearer, toward home, away from home, first trip, return trip, etc. Such parameters as these are basic to understanding the use of motion verbs in Mixtec and Trique.

1.5 Temporal and locational expressions; adverbial clauses

Some years ago, it was in fashion to set up formulas for clauses in various languages, with a grouping of S, V, and O (in whatsoever order was appropriate) as nuclear and sometimes obligatory, while temporal and locational expressions were labeled *optional*. It has since become evident that even if such expressions can be regarded as locally optional—when we are thinking only of clause structure, they are far from optional in terms of the context. Certainly in a narrative text, specification of time and location are quite necessary to staging and continuing a story. They are broadly speaking obligatory although in what particular clause they surface has its own discourse constraints.

Temporal expressions structured as clauses are used frequently in narrative texts as a BACKREFERENCE to a clause in a previous sentence. *John went right home.* **When he got there** *he found things in a far worse condition than he had feared.* Here, the temporal clause, *when he got there*, in the second sentence is a backreference to *John went right home.* It progresses along a semantic EXPECTANCY CHAIN in which 'go' is followed by 'arrive/get somewhere'. This kind of linkage has been referred to as TAIL-HEAD LINKAGE since the tail of one sentence (or paragraph) is RECAPITULATED as the head or the beginning of the following sentence (or paragraph). In some parts of the world, including most languages of Papua New Guinea, such backreferences between sentences are very regular. The backreference clause can be equivalent to a conjunction *and then* between the sentences. Actually, in English a nominalized backreference is often preferred, so that a temporal phrase occurs rather than a temporal clause: *John went right home.* **On arrival**, *he found things in a worse condition than he had feared.*

In non-narrative texts, locational clauses or expressions can also serve a similar connective function. Thus, in the following hortatory discourse in which an older man advises a younger man, we find a locational clause in the second sentence with backreference to the first sentence: *Perhaps in such circumstances the wisest thing to do is to get out of the house. But **wherever you go**, let your absence be brief and don't think that flight per se ever solves many problems.* Or consider the following fragment of an expository discourse in which a PARTICIPIAL CLAUSE in the second sentence harks back to the first sentence: *The flower most sought for has six petals. **Nestled among the rich petals** you may sometimes find a honeybee too overcome with nectar to fly home.* Of course, temporal clauses can serve for backreference here as well as in narrative. Thus, in the hortatory discourse fragment above, we might find *when you do that* rather than *wherever you go*. Likewise, in the expository discourse fragment above, we might find *when you look down deep among the petals* instead of *nestled among the rich petals*.

There are other uses of adverbial clauses in providing textual connection. To mention only one more, note that *if* clauses find a natural function in setting up contrasting situations or options: ***If you sell your house as is**, you will have less fuss and bother getting rid of it, but will clear less on the deal. **If, however, you make even a few repairs**, it may up the salability of the house and increase its value.*

1.6 Sequence signals and conjunctions

Besides textual connections established by adverbial clauses, SEQUENCE SIGNALS and conjunctions serve cohesive functions. While we could summarily speak of conjunctions, there are many sequence signals that are phrasal in nature, and usually are not simply called conjunctions. Instructive analyses of sequence signals and conjunctions in English are found in Halliday and Hasan (1976) and Rudolph (1987).

In English, not only are simple conjunctions such as *but*, *and*, and *for* found, but also such GRAMMATICALIZED conjunctions as *furthermore*, *nevertheless*, and *moreover* which are obviously frozen composites, and *on the other hand* and *to the contrary* which are still phrasal in structure. Regardless of their possible morphological breakdown, all of these and still others serve to contrast or connect sentences with each other within the paragraph, and paragraph with paragraph within larger recursive wholes. Even in a language with not near the wealth of sequence signals as English, a similar range of structures may be found. Thus, while *ni4* 'and' and *sa3ni4* 'but' are simple conjunctions in Trique, we also find *we2 dan3 ni4*, a stronger sequence signal meaning something on the order of 'consequently', 'whereupon', and the like. This is really a short clause consisting of *we2* 'attention calling verb' plus *dan3* 'that' and the conjunction *ni4* 'and'. The morphological complexity of such a frozen combination either in English or Trique seems to make little, if any, difference in the function of the signal. Thus, in English, *but, on the other hand, conversely, nevertheless,* and *to the contrary* are not markedly different in that all indicate an adversative relation, although shades of lexical meaning and appropriateness to context have to be sorted out. Thus, while we probably could say, *He's tall but not handsome*, we probably wouldn't say, *He's tall, on the other hand, not handsome*. This is probably because *but* can express either contrast or frustrated expectancy, while *on the other hand* is more limited to contrast. Conjunctions and sequence signals have to be sorted out according to the rhetorical relations that they reinforce.

1.7 Mystery particles

MYSTERY PARTICLES are particles that occur in a text but neither the analyst nor the native speaker can readily gloss. The native speaker, however, knows where to use them even if translation proves elusive. To the outsider these particles appear to be salt-and-peppered through a text without any rhyme or reason.

We cite here again (Longacre 1976) a long but instructive example from the Guajiro language of Colombia and Ecuador (data from Richard and Karis Mansen 1976). The problem encountered in this language had to do with particles used as auxiliary verbs, that is, they occur following the main verb in the verb phrase and their meaning and function are not immediately evident. Some of these auxiliaries have quasi-modal meanings. Thus, the Mansens described *tata* as indicating 'action viewed as in stages or actors viewed as units' which we are inclined to dub 'distributive'; *wala* 'action represents the retention of some elements in the narrative, such as an action repeated again or an action done in addition to another action'; *laa* 'action considered to be as transformation of the actor'; *paa~waa* 'action considered as a single temporal unit'; and *yaa* 'action unreal or subjunctive', plus a couple of other auxiliaries still not well defined at the time they wrote their article. But three further auxiliaries proved clearly to have meaning-functions relevant to discourse. One, *maa* was quickly disposed of as a discourse connector, either cross-referencing a discourse to a previous one (when occurring in discourse stage), connecting a closure explicitly to the text which it closes, or connecting related bases in a coordinated paragraph. But two further auxiliaries, *calacá* and *taa*, proved a bit more recalcitrant to analysis.

The auxiliary *calacá* proved to be a prominent EVENTLINE marker. It occurs with the verbs that mark successive storyline events in a paragraph but not with sentences that are merely paraphrases or explanation of such an event. A further feature of this auxiliary is that it is partially or wholly phased out at the peak of a narrative.

With reported speech, in which direct quotations occur, the situation is a bit intricate. A QUOTE FORMULA, such as 'he said', has a verb marked with *calacá* which binds the speech act onto the mainline. But the quotation itself has its own world and may mark a mainline with *calacá* within the quotation. Furthermore, dominance of one speaker in an exchange or lack of such dominance is also indicated by that same auxiliary. Here we quote the Mansens (1976:156): "In a Dialogue Paragraph in which one speaker has control of the Exchange…the Quote Formula of only that speaker is the one marked by the auxiliary *calacá*. In a Dialogue Paragraph in which control of the exchange is balanced, that is, neither speaker has full control, the Quote formulas of both speakers are marked by *calacá*." In exemplifying these two possibilities they give an example of a spirit speaking to a boy as the first situation, and a wife and a husband talking as the second situation. Here the structure of the whole narrative, of reported speech within a narrative, and even some indication of who is in control in a dialogue, are all relevant to the distribution of this auxiliary verb.

A further auxiliary *taa* relates not to prominence on the mainline but to the topicality of the subject of the verb. We again quote the Mansens (156): "The verb auxiliary *taa* marks the paragraph topic in Narrative Discourse where it obligatorily occurs... [We] define topic as that participant which the speaker wishes to make prominent." Here, again, the consideration of reported speech comes in. The quotation presents a world of its own with not only its own eventline as seen above but its own topic. Therefore, *taa* occurs within the quotation to mark the topic within it. But this necessitates a re-marking of the topic of the main narrative once we get on the other side of the quotation. Across paragraph boundaries the continuing topic is often re-marked with *taa*. And even within the paragraph, coordinated sentences may mark the continuing topic on each.

What emerges from a study of the two auxiliaries *calacá* and *taa* in Guajiro is that these two mystery particles cannot be analyzed without consideration of two important features of narrative discourse: its mainline (storyline) and its topicality structure. The Mansens' study also illustrates nicely the way in which reported speech functions within narrative: (1) as part of the whole narrative, but (2) as introducing encapsulated worlds within the narrative.

Stephen Levinsohn's (1976) analysis of Inga (a Quechuan language of Colombia) presents what appears at first blush to be a simpler situation that involves only one mystery particle, the suffix -*ca*. But here the multifunctional nature of this suffix makes its analysis anything but simple. To begin with, this suffix occurs on nouns, verbs, temporals, locatives, and certain conjunction-like uses. On a noun this suffix marks the referent of that noun as the main participant of the narrative. On verbs it marks progress down the storyline of a narrative. In these uses the suffix -*ca* apparently combines the functions of both *calacá* and *taa* in Guajiro. But there are further uses of the suffix. For one thing, -*ca* can occur on temporals in the quasi-conjunction function mentioned above. Here it helps mark a trajectory through time: and then, and then, and then, etc. But in a travelogue discourse, -*ca* can occur on locational elements in a similar quasi-conjunction usage, and marking a trajectory through space. But -*ca* may also mark an instrument that figures in an action. Levinsohn dubs this an "inappropriate use" of the suffix and says that it marks focus on the instrument, presumably in a digression from the main eventline. But when the eventline is resumed, the next verb is appropriately marked with -*ca*. Thus, it can be claimed that the suffix in Inga discourse marks both progression and digression along the storyline.

As a final example in this section we cite some data from the Ica language, also from Colombia. In Ica (Tracy and Levinsohn 1977) an early analytical problem arose as to how the subject of a clause is encoded. Subjects were more often than not covert in the text, yet the native speaker always knew who did what to whom. What cues were available to the native speaker that eluded the analyst? Here the analysis of two mystery particles provided the key. The suffix *-ri* was found to mark the first occurrence of a noun marking the thematic participant in the first sentence of the paragraph. Once marked in this way, the participant indicated by that noun was understood to be the subject of all clauses in the paragraph—unless otherwise indicated. The occurrence of the suffix *-se'* on a noun indicates that the participant thus indicated, although not the thematic participant of the paragraph, was nevertheless the subject of the clause in which it occurred. A provision is also made for switching the thematic participant of a paragraph. For example, when two participants are contrasted, *-se'ri* is added to the noun to indicate the new thematic participant within the paragraph. This is a somewhat simplified presentation of a complex situation, but this is basically how it works. The moral here is that we find that the grammar of the clause, for example, the indication of the subject, is inextricably tied into the grammar of the paragraph and discourse.

1.8 The length of syntactic units

We need to go no further than English to illustrate the dramatic way in which the length of sentences and clauses is sometimes tied into discourse-level concerns. For example, Hemingway is famous for his short crisp sentence structure. But he could, on occasion, indulge in a long, loose sentence of considerable length when the discourse called for such a unit. We reproduce here a one-sentence paragraph from *The Short Happy Life of Francis Macomber*, which was previously cited (Longacre 1996:44):

> The car was going a wild forty-five miles an hour across the open and as Macomber watched, the buffalo got bigger and bigger until he could see the gray, hairless, scabby look of one huge bull and how his neck was a part of his shoulders and the shiny black of his horns as he galloped a little behind the others that were strung out in that steady plunging gait; and then, the car swaying as though it had just jumped a road, they drew up close and he could see the plunging hugeness of the bull, and the dust in his sparsely haired hide, the wild boss of horn and his outstretched wide-nostrilled muzzle, and he was raising his rifle when Wilson shouted, "Not from the car, you fool!" and he had no fear, only hatred of Wilson, while the brakes clamped on and the car skidded, plowing sideways to an almost stop and Wilson was out on one side and he on the other, stumbling as his feet hit the still speeding-by of the earth, and then he was shooting at the bull as he moved away, hearing the bullets whunk into him, emptying his rifle into him as he moved steadily away, finally remembering to get his shots forward into the shoulder, and as he fumbled to reload, he saw the bull was down. (Hemingway 1938:126–127)

This sentence is found at the CLIMAX of the story where Macomber shoots his first bull. The very rhythm of the sentence is iconic of the mad career of the car, its sudden stop, and the plunging gait of the buffaloes. A similar, but shorter, rollicking sentence occurs at the denouement of the story, where Macomber's wife (accidentally?) shoots him in the head as he is leveling with another bull. The sentence structure and length at both the climax and denouement of this story are responsive to their positions within the story.

For the marking of a great moment of a story by short sentences we turn to Arthur Hailey's *The Final Diagnosis*. We quote here a passage out of the denouement of the story.[2] The hospital has suffered an outbreak of typhoid. Right as the health officials are in the process of advising that the hospital must be shut down—lest the typhoid outbreak extend itself into the city—a young lab assistant says, "I have it," namely, the identification of the fecal specimen of a person who proves to be the carrier. From here on, the sentences get short and crisp as the demonstration moves down a row of test tubes:

> Pearson picked up the first of the ten tubes. He called out "Glucose."
> Checking the list, Alexander answered, "Acid formation, but no gas."
> Pearson nodded. He replaced the tube and selected a second. "Lactose."
> "No acid, no gas," Alexander read.
> "Right." A pause. "Dulcitol."
> Again Alexander read, "No acid, no gas."
> "Sucrose."
> "No acid, no gas." Once more the correct reaction for typhoid bacilli. The tension in the room was mounting.
> Pearson took another tube. "Mannitol."
> "Acid formation, but no gas."
> "Correct." Another. "Maltose."
> "Acid, but no gas."
> Pearson nodded. Six down, four to go. Now he said, "Xylose."
> Once more Alexander read, "Acid, but no gas."
> Seven.
> "Arabinose."
> John Alexander said, "Either acid but no gas or no reaction at all."
> Pearson announced, "No reaction."
> Eight. Two more.
> "Rhamnose?"
> "No reaction."
> Pearson looked at the tube. He said softly, "No reaction."
> One to go.
> From the last tube Pearson read, "Indole production."
> "Negative," Alexander said, and replaced the book.
> Pearson turned to the others. He said, "There's no question. This is the typhoid carrier." (Hailey 1959:295)

---

[2] This extensive citation and quotation from the Hailey novel is by permission of the author and copyright holder, as follows: *The Final Diagnosis* (chapter 3) © 1959 Arthur Hailey. Used by permission.

In this example, the use of sentence fragments at denouement contributes to the suspense of the passage, and provides a way of marking a great moment of the story.

It is of interest, however, that a broader principle is at work: that of marking a peak (a great moment of a story marked by unusual surface structure features) by varying the sentence length radically from the norm. In the Hemingway example, the variation was to a sentence of much greater length than is normally found in this author. In the Hailey selection, the variation is to sentence fragments. Similar purposes are accomplished by each. Examples of such purposeful variation in sentence length could be given from a variety of languages around the world.

While the two previous examples illustrate marking a great moment of a story by variation of sentence length, a related distinction can be found in clause structure per se. In Aguaruna (Peru), length considerations that involve paragraph, sentence, and clause are relevant to the distinguishing of the four discourse types that are EMIC in that language. We quote here Longacre's summary of Larson (1984):

> Aguaruna is a chaining language in which several relatively uninflected medial verbs and the clauses of which they are the head may precede a fully inflected final verb in the final clause... In narrative discourse, the chains that occur are so long that the sentence tends to be coterminous with the paragraph in the realization of episodes—although paragraphs that consist of more than one such sentence-chain are found. In procedural discourse, the chains are somewhat shorter, the component clauses are more internally complex (e.g., they often specify the instrument), and adverbial clauses occur as margins which specify temporal, conditional, and causal relations. In expository (typically descriptive) discourse, clause chaining is replaced by coordination: sentences consist of one clause or two or three coordinated clauses. In hortatory discourse, there likewise is no chaining; the clause and the sentence tend to be coterminous, with imperative and interrogative structures occurring as well as the declarative structures which, in the main, characterize the other discourse types. (Longacre 1996:17)

In this section we have illustrated how variation in sentence and clause length can be influenced by high level discourse concerns relating not only to placement on the overall structure of a discourse but to discourse typology as well.

1.9 Conclusion

The grammatical features that are discussed in this chapter require a holistic discourse perspective for an adequate analysis. Many details of linguistic structure are dependent on the analysis of discourse, so discourse analysis is not a luxury but a necessity. What have been described in the past simply as free variation are often found to be dependent on discourse structure, socio-cultural factors, and cognition. If we want to produce a natural translation or good literacy material, discourse analysis will enable us to have wings to fly and help prevent misunderstandings at the higher message levels of paragraph and discourse.

1.10 Exercises

Can you list some ways in which you anticipate that discourse studies may enhance your translation work? Are there any problems that come to mind in your work as a translator that discourse analysis might help you resolve?

Chapter 2

A Layman's Introduction to Discourse Analysis

Any utterance that is longer than a sentence cannot fully be analyzed in terms of any variety of grammar that studies only what is going on within the sentence. The linguistic study of any multi-sentential production, whether oral or written, requires a type of linguistics called discourse analysis (or TEXTLINGUISTICS).

Texts (discourses) vary considerably in type. One very frequently encountered text type is the story. In this presentation we choose one paragraph from a story by Mark Twain, *A Connecticut Yankee in King Arthur's Court*. We propose to illustrate from this paragraph several crucial concerns of discourse analysis: (1) What verbs (words of action, being, state, etc.) contribute to a discourse; (2) What nouns and pronouns (words which refer to persons, places, abstractions, and things) contribute to a discourse; (3) How the two interplay with each other in the ongoing structure of a discourse; (4) The various kinds of COHESION and coherence that hold a discourse together; (5) How a discourse builds to one or more peaks (or climaxes); (6) How all this determines precisely what part each sentence plays in the fabric of the whole; and (7) How all this constrains how we may interpret a discourse.

Before taking up these various concerns in detail, we call the reader's attention to some basic assumptions that underlie all that we will do. First of all, the discourse analyst rejects the assumption that variety simply occurs for variety's sake. The counter assumption is that variation in form is a choice made by the speaker or writer with a certain end in view. Even when a speaker/writer wants to inject more variety into an ongoing composition, his particular choices reflect such goals. Therefore, any variation in form can be studied with a view to what it implies. Secondly, it is assumed that the discourse as a whole, and the parts, greater and smaller, of which it is composed are in living interplay with each other. The thrust or outline of the whole, as the hearer/reader begins to grasp it, affects his understanding of the parts. But, just as surely, it is information gleaned from each successive part of the discourse that facilitates the understanding of the whole. The whole constrains the parts; the parts explain the whole. Thirdly, the hearer's/reader's interpretation of the discourse is dependent on not only the objective structure of the discourse but on the subjective contribution of the interpreter. If the knowledge bank and experiential background of the hearer/reader were exactly the same with the knowledge bank and experiential background of the speaker/writer, interpretation should not present great problems—unless the text is inadvertently or purposely ambiguous at one or more points. But at least to some degree the knowledge banks of speakers/writers and hearers/readers do not coincide. Therefore, some disparity of interpretation will result in many discourses. Fourthly, a discourse is an ongoing thing. That the analysis given here is necessarily static should not be construed to be a denial of the dynamic nature of discourse.

The discourse fragment that we are analyzing is presented in tabular form in (1):

(1) Mark Twain passage from *A Connecticut Yankee in King Arthur's Court*

1. In a minute a third slave was struggling in the air.
2. It was dreadful.
3. I turned away my head a moment, and when I turned back I missed the king!
4. They were blindfolding him!
5. I was paralyzed;
6. I couldn't move.
7. I was choking,
8. my tongue was petrified.
9. They finished blindfolding him,
10. they led him under the rope.
11. I couldn't shake off that clinging impotence.
12. But when I saw them put the noose around his neck, then everything let go in me and I made a spring to the rescue—
13. and as I made it I shot one more glance abroad—
14. by George! here they came, a-tilting—five hundred mailed and belted knights on bicycles!
15. The grandest sight that ever was seen.
16. Lord, how the plumes streamed,
17. how the sun flamed and flashed from the endless procession of webby wheels!

Mark Twain's story, *A Connecticut Yankee in King Arthur's Court*, is a satire on medieval England, on chivalry, on the people's popular superstitions, and other such matters. The narrator, a man from modern America (late nineteenth century), falls into some sort of time warp and finds himself in England in the time of King Arthur. After various adventures he becomes a confidante of the king and sets about to introduce various anachronistic innovations from his own (forward) time, such as printing and the making of bicycles. This paragraph comes from a sizeable part of the story where the king and some of his court, dressed in ordinary non-regal dress, are encountered out in the countryside by a group of hostile people, and—after an unsuccessful jail break from a city jail (London)—are sentenced to be hung.

In the analysis of this paragraph from Mark Twain's (1964:240) story, we use the sentence numbers (S) for ease of reference, but they do not necessarily correspond to Twain's sentence divisions. He was inordinately fond of the comma splice (see S7–8, and 9–10, 16–17). We also consider that S5–6 (where a semicolon joins two simple sentences) and S12–13 (where a dash appends one sentence to the other) can likewise be separated for our analytical purposes. This paragraph in tabular form is presented several times over the following pages with colorcoding to illustrate various phases of the analysis.

2.1 What different forms of verbs contribute to a story

The verb forms of a language typically constitute a system consisting of different forms popularly called tenses, but distinguished by the linguist as tense (time), aspect (type of action, for example, ongoing versus completed), and mode (real, unreal, probable, etc.). English has only a few differing forms of the verb: a present tense, a past tense (marked with -*t*/-*d* as well as in many irregular ways), an -*n* form or its equivalent (commonly called a past participle), and an -*ing* form (commonly called a present participle). These forms plus or minus forms of *be* and *have* make up several complex forms (*is running, had run, have run, has been run,* etc.).

In accordance with the central assumption of discourse grammar that variety of form is motivated, we assume that within a discourse, in this case a story, variations in the form of verbs have something to tell us about the shading and highlighting of various successive parts of the story.

1) S3, 9, 10, 12, and 13 contain simple past tense forms that refer to actions or COGNITIVE EVENTS (e.g., *I missed the king.*) on the part of participants in the story. The actions are presented as simply PUNCTILIAR (without reference to duration) and as successive. We exclude here past progressives (see 2 below) and simple past tense forms that refer to PROPS (inanimate) and may properly be considered to be DESCRIPTIVE (*streamed, flamed,* and *flashed* in S16 and 17). Subject to these exclusions, the sentences with simple past tense forms— non-progressive and non-descriptive—are highlighted in red. They constitute the most dynamic part of the paragraph. The reason for the red font instead of the red highlights in S3, 12, and 13 is explained in section 2.4.

2) S1 and 4 contain regular past PROGRESSIVE forms, which consist of a form of the verb *be*, plus an *-ing* form of the verb. By resorting to this form the writer tells us that he regards what he reports not as simple punctiliar actions but as ongoing activities, which are conceived of as having certain duration. Activities reported in this fashion are not given a precise placement in the successive actions reported in simple past forms. Thus, the third slave's death throes do not necessarily terminate before what is reported in S3, while the process of blindfolding the king presumably begins before what is reported in S3 and does not terminate until S9. We highlight these sentences in orange.

We also highlight S14 in orange since *came, a-tilting* is an archaic form of the progressive. We do not thus underline S9 because the phasal verb *finished* is simple past, and *blindfolding* is used as a verbal noun instead of as a past progressive.

3) S2, 5, 7, and 8 contain a form of the verb *be* plus an adjective or participle (a kind of verbal adjective). They report neither an action nor an activity but are descriptive, either of a situation (S2), or of the narrator's feelings (S5, 7, 8). S7 is somewhat ambiguous in that English has two synonymous constructions: *be* + *-ing* form as a progressive verb form (see 2 above) or *be* + *-ing* form as a participle (adjectival). Thus, a few years ago *Time* magazine had a caption *Old people are revolting* in which the progressive form of the verb seems to have been intended (i.e., 'old people are in the process of revolt') but which could have been taken as *be* + participle (i.e., 'old people are repulsive'). Similarly, we take S7 *I was choking* to be semantically DEPICTIVE rather than simply progressive. As such, it depicts not a voluntary activity on the part of the narrator, but a state of physical impairment brought about by the shock of what he saw.

We take S15 to be somewhat similar. Here by means of the verb *be* (although the subject and the verb are omitted in the text) the narrator depicts how the changed situation looks to him (e.g., *It was the grandest sight that ever was seen*).

S16 and 17 contain verbs with inanimate subjects. Certainly, neither actions nor activities are represented; the sentences are semantically depictive. We highlight all these sentences in yellow.

4) Finally, there are forms in S6 and 11 that are both negative and modal (e.g., *I couldn't move, I couldn't shake off*). These sentences describe things that don't happen, events that don't get off the ground of possibility into the orbit of actuality; they are unrealized (IRREALIS). They round off the actions/cognitive events (red), overlapping activities (orange), and descriptions (yellow) by further picturing the impotence of the narrator in regard to what he couldn't do. We highlight these sentences in green.

The choice of colors in our coding has not been random. We have invoked here the analogy of the optical spectrum and the artist's palette to symbolize the progression from the most dynamic elements to the least dynamic elements in the structure of a narrative. Table 2.1 shows the parallels in rank and color. The sentences that are highlighted in red are the most dynamic part of the paragraph; they are the action-line or storyline. The sentences that are

2.1 What different forms of verbs contribute to a story

highlighted in orange do not represent actions/cognitive events in the main sequence of the paragraph, but activities that overlap with the sequential actions. They are still dynamic, but represent a first degree departure from the storyline of punctiliar, sequential actions with perfective meaning (Comrie 1976:5). The sentences that are highlighted in yellow represent an even further departure from the storyline and are descriptive rather than dynamic. In this paragraph, such sentences report the narrator's EVALUATION or depiction of the situation (S2, 15, 16, 17) or his own feelings (S5, 7, 8). The sentences that are highlighted in green are still further removed from the storyline because of their irrealis nature. See section 2.4 for use of the color blue.

Table 2.1. Spectrum colors for rank in discourse

Rank	Color
1	Red
2	Orange
3	Yellow
4	Green
5	Blue

The following example (2) presents the text, the paragraph from Mark Twain, with the colored highlights. It suggests a SIMILE: the text compositor is at work like an artist with his palette filling his canvas with the various verb forms and the clauses which contain them so as to round out the picture, which is his discourse.

A story can contain other forms than those illustrated in this paragraph, for example, a FLASHBACK such as *They had already hung two slaves*. While such further elements can be added to the spectrum of verb forms found in the story, they simply take their place in an enlarged scheme built in the same way (Longacre 1989, 1996).

(2) What Different Forms of Verbs Contribute to a Story with colorcoding.

1. In a minute a third slave was struggling in the air.
2. It was dreadful.
3. I turned away my head a moment, and when I turned back I missed the king!
4. They were blindfolding him!
5. I was paralyzed;
6. I couldn't move.

7. I was choking,
8. my tongue was petrified.
9. They finished blindfolding him,
10. they led him under the rope.
11. I couldn't shake off that clinging impotence.
12. But when I saw them put the noose around his neck, then everything let go in me and I made a spring to the rescue—
13. and as I made it I shot one more glance abroad—
14. by George! here they came, a-tilting—five hundred mailed and belted knights on bicycles!
15. The grandest sight that ever was seen.
16. Lord, how the plumes streamed,
17. how the sun flamed and flashed from the endless procession of webby wheels!

2.2 What nouns and pronouns do within a story

While verb forms refer to HAPPENINGS or states within a story, nouns and pronouns refer to participants (usually human or animate) and props (usually inanimate). Here we assume a hierarchical structuring of the participant references according to their placement and function within the discourse: the narrator; the king and his party; the hostile villagers; the props. This hierarchy is based on the assumption that participants outrank props and that participants are ranked according to relevant nearness to the main participant. In this case the narrator relates first of all to the king (and his party), secondarily to the hostile populace around them, and lastly to the various props that are mentioned in the scene.

REFERENCES to the narrator (*I, my, me*) are highlighted in red in (3). This is a first person narrative in which the narrator himself is the principal participant.

(3) What Nouns and Pronouns Contribute to a Story

1. In a minute a third slave was struggling in the air.
2. It was dreadful.
3. I turned away my head a moment, and when I turned back I missed the king!
4. They were blindfolding him!
5. I was paralyzed;
6. I couldn't move.
7. I was choking,

2.2 What nouns and pronouns do within a story 21

8. my tongue was petrified.
9. They finished blindfolding him,
10. they led him under the rope.
11. I couldn't shake off that clinging impotence.
12. But when I saw them put the noose around his neck, then everything let go in me and I made a spring to the rescue—
13. and as I made it I shot one more glance abroad—
14. by George! here they came, a-tilting—five hundred mailed and belted knights on bicycles!
15. The grandest sight that ever was seen.
16. Lord, how the plumes streamed,
17. how the sun flamed and flashed from the endless procession of webby wheels!

References to the king are highlighted in orange in (3). Next in importance to the narrator himself is the king. References to the king's party are marked with an orange font. Clearly the knights that come to the rescue are of the king's party. The third slave, whose execution is referred to in the first sentence, is temporarily of the king's party by virtue of being jailed with the king's party.

References to the crowd who are trying to execute the narrator along with the king and his party are highlighted in yellow in S4, 9, 10, and 12. Notice that the *they* in S14 does not have the same referent as the *they* in S4, 9, and 10. The *they* in S14 is identified as the knights on bicycles who are coming to the rescue.

References to props are highlighted in green. As we shall see in section 2.4, these references have a function in reinforcing the coherency of the paragraph. Here we note that reference to a *blindfold* is found incorporated in a verbal form in S4 and 9, while S10 refers to a *rope*, and S12 to a *noose*. Likewise, there is a predicative use of the noun *mail* in *mailed* and of the noun *belt* in *belted* in S14, as well as in the reference to the *plumes* (of the knights' helmets) in S16. The noun *bicycles* occurs in S14 and a reference to their *wheels* in S17. A natural object, the sun, is referred to in S17. The cross-references between these nominal references are discussed in section 2.4.

A few nouns and pronouns indexing various phases of the situation are highlighted in blue. In S2 *it* refers to the situation that is depicted in S1, the previous sentence. In S11, *that clinging impotence* refers to the narrator's shocked inaction as pictured in S4–8; it relates rather directly to the *I couldn't* … in S6 and in S11, and comes down with summary force at the end of the first half of the paragraph. Likewise, the noun *the rescue* in S12 marks the change in mode from impotence to action. The noun phrase *the grandest sight (that ever was seen)* in S15 is evaluative of the changed situation just as *it*, in S2, refers to distress of the original situation. In S12 *everything* is simply part of the idiomatic phrase *everything let go in* ('I was no longer unable to act'), while *spring* is part of the idiom *made a spring*, which could have been expressed as a simple past tense verb 'sprang'. Even *I shot one more glance* equals 'I glanced up once more'.

We see here a considerable hierarchical range of noun/pronoun uses. The first three ranks are clearly participants; the props are used by the participants, or characterize them; the lowest range of noun references indexes phases of the situation and is quasi-verbal in several instances. The lowest range of noun usage does not, in fact, involve participant reference at all. These highlights are found in (3).

2.3 How verbs and referents interplay in the structure of this paragraph

In this paragraph verbs of the highest dynamic rank, the storyline verbs, which are highlighted in red co-occur with nouns of the two highest ranks which are highlighted in red or orange, that is, sentences with mainline verbs include participant references to the narrator and/or the king and his party. If we write down the sentences with the highlighted red verbs and with at least one red or orange noun or pronoun, we obtain in fact a tolerably good abstract of the paragraph (but we will have to summarize S14–17):

(4)   3a   I turned away my head for a moment.
      3b   I missed the king.
      9   They finished blindfolding him.
      10   They led him under the rope.
      12a   Everything let go in me.
      12b   I made a spring to the rescue [of the king].
      13   I shot one more glance abroad.
      14-17 [= 'I saw help coming for myself and the king.']

Nouns/pronouns of rank one occur in S3a, 3b, 12a, 12b, and 13; nouns of rank two in S3b, 9, 10, and implied in S12b, that is, he sprang to the rescue of the king. Likewise the summary implies a verb of cognition ('I saw' as implied in *the grandest sight*) and implies help for both the narrator and the king.

If we add to the above, the sentences that have verbs of BACKGROUND activity (highlighted in orange), we further round out the story. It happens that the three such sentences in this paragraph all contain participant references of rank two (the king and his party).

(5) In a minute a third slave was struggling in the air. I turned away my head for a moment. I missed the king. They were blindfolding him. They finished blindfolding him. They led him under the rope. Everything let go in me and I made a spring to the rescue. I shot one more glance

abroad—by George, here they came, a-tilting—five hundred mailed and belted knights on bicycles.

We have carried out the above exercise of obtaining an abstract in two stages to demonstrate that the clauses whose verbs are of the highest dynamic ranking are also clauses that refer to the more CENTRAL PARTICIPANTS. It should not be surprising if the more important developments in a story relate to the more important participants.

We can now further round out the abstract of the story by adding the sentences whose (descriptive or depictive) verbs are highlighted in yellow, that is, S2, 5, 7, 8, 15, 16, and 17. Finally, we can add the green coded sentences, that is, the irrealis-negative ones. These do not add much to the content of the paragraph. *I couldn't move* is clearly a NEGATED ANTONYM PARAPHRASE of S5 *I was paralyzed*—since paralysis and motion are antonyms and a negation of motion equals paralysis. S11 is a summary and echo of S5–8. Rounding out the abstract in this fashion approximates closely the Mark Twain text itself. In fact, it is mainly some connective material that needs to be added.

All this illustrates how verbs/sentences of various dynamic rankings and participants of varying centrality to a story interrelate in a systematic way to give us a text. The text can be therefore visualized as a kind of double helix, one strand verbal and one strand nominal, with the individual clauses (simple sentences) functioning as bridges between the two strands of the helix.

2.4 Internal relations in the text: Cohesion and coherence

We distinguish cohesion and coherence as follows: Cohesion is the EXPLICIT linkage found in a text or some part of it, while COHERENCE has to do with lexical associations and is more implicit.

To begin with, the actions-in-sequence noted in section 2.1 and the strands of participant references noted in section 2.2 are themselves highly cohesive. What we describe here are types of cohesion and coherence not already subsumed above.

We consider that overt connectives are of the highest possible rank in a possible system of internal relations in the text. Thus, *But* in S12 articulates the paragraph into two halves that picture horror and impotence in S1–11 and action and rescue in S12–17. The connectives *and* and *then*, in S3, 12, 13 mark temporal sequence and reinforce the time line of the story.

Two sequence signals in paragraph initial positions suggest that this paragraph is part of a larger unit: *in a minute*, and *(a) third (slave)*. Presumably, the events of this paragraph follow immediately on events described in the preceding paragraph(s), hence *in a minute*. That the slave that is hung in S1 is called *a third slave* makes it probable that two slaves have already been mentioned in the preceding context—and presumably hung.

In S2 an initial *it* refers to the situation described in the first sentence, thus making S2 a comment on S1.

In (6), all these overt cohesive elements we highlight in red, as overt cues of the highest order in the cohesion and coherence of the paragraph.

Another scarcely less important cohesive element is the role of adverbial clauses in S3, 12, and 13—elements that we highlight here in orange but which are in red font in (2). Consider first of all *I made a spring to the rescue* in S12 along with *as I made it* in S13. Here the adverbial clause *as I made it* serves to relate the clause *I shot one more glance abroad* in S13 to the previous main clause *I made a spring to the rescue* in S12. In somewhat less direct fashion *when I turned back* in S3 recapitulates *I turned my head away* earlier in the same sentence by stating the next probable sequence in the head movements. This adverbial clause *when I turned back* relates *I missed the king* to the preceding clause *I turned away my head for a moment*. Finally, in S12 *when I saw them put the noose around his neck* relates sequentially to *they led him under the rope* in S10 so as to relate the ensuing main clauses of S12 to S10. Indeed recapitulation of this sort by means of an adverbial clause is much similar to *and then* between sentences or between parts of the same sentence. As S12 shows, such a recapitulatory clause and *then* can be used together.

A text also employs paraphrase and parallelism as cohesive devices. We have highlighted in yellow the elements that are in a paraphrase relation. As already discussed, S5 and 6 are in such relation. Broadly speaking, however, S5–8 are all loose paraphrases, summarized as impotence in S11. Likewise, *I shot one more glance abroad* in S13 is loosely paraphrastic to the reference to *the grandest sight that ever was seen* in S15. PARAPHRASE is saying (more or less) the same thing in different words.

The elements that we have highlighted in green are parallel statements rather than paraphrases. Thus, S4 and S9 are parallel as are also S6 and S11. In S16 *how the plumes streamed* is parallel to *how the sun flamed and flashed...* in S17. PARALLELISM is saying different things in more or less the same mold of sentence structure.

The perception of paraphrase and parallelism requires judgment on the part of the reader. The perception of a paraphrase is clearly a semantic judgment. The perception of parallelism requires a judgment as to structural similarity between two elements.

Finally, there is a type of coherence relation that very clearly depends on the knowledge bank and experiential background of the text interpreter, that is, hearer or reader. This type of coherence relation, indicated in blue, is dependent on a FRAME (set of related concepts) or SCRIPT (sequence of related concepts or events). Note the reference to the *blindfold* in S4 and 9, plus the *rope* in S10 and the *noose* in S12. Furthermore, note the accompanying uses of these props: S4 to blindfold, S9 to finish blindfolding, S10 to lead under the rope, and S12 put the noose around the neck. This clearly is a hanging script, the successive steps of which are well known to contemporary readers. Besides, the context has already reported two hangings. Here the reader's knowledge of the script leads us to recognizing these various doings as preliminary steps to executing

2.4 Internal relations in the text: Cohesion and coherence

the king. The reader therefore perceives the storyline as moving rapidly, in spite of the narrator's turning aside from the storyline to describe his subjective feelings in S5–8 and 11. And thus the paradox of suspense in which one focuses on enough minor details to live a lifetime in a moment. But the hanging script turns into a rescue-from-hanging script in S12 with the clause *I made a spring to the rescue,* thus turning an "execution script" into a "stay of execution." Fortunately for both the narrator and the king, the real rescue shows up in S14ff.

In S14 through 16, two frames, each alien to the other, are JUXTAPOSED in a fashion characteristic of the whole book. The frame juxtaposition is seen in the phrase *five hundred mailed and belted knights on bicycles.* Presumably, the contemporary reader has a knowledge frame for knights: that they were armored medieval warriors who rode on horseback, carried lances, dressed in mail or plate armor, were of the nobility, etc. In S14 *a-tilting* refers to knights charging with leveled lances, *mailed and belted* refers to their armor. Furthermore, in S16 the *plumes* are presumably attached to the knights' helmets. So far so good. But medieval knights did not ride bicycles—and here comes the clash in frames. Once, however, bicycles are mentioned in S14, we are prepared for the reference to *webby wheels* in S17. Our bicycle frame contains the information that bicycles have wheels.

All these script and frame connected elements add greatly to the coherence of the discourse. They are dependent, however, on the reader's sharing the same scripts and frames as the writer. Thus, a reader unacquainted with a contemporary hanging script might not cue in early enough in this paragraph to the threat to the king's life, unless the previous context in Mark Twain's novel was sufficient to teach the script itself. Likewise a person unacquainted with the institution of medieval knighthood might find that references in S14 to *a-tilting, mailed* and *belted* are obscure as well as the reference to *plumes* in S16 (*plumes* of what?). The person who had never seen a bicycle would not understand the reference to wheels in the last sentence. And finally, a person who naively assumed that bicycles were used hundreds of years ago would miss entirely the humor and satire of the passage! The contribution of the interpreter is indeed very large and indispensable here. The author, however, has evidently written in the confidence that in such matters his readers will have these same frames and scripts in their knowledge banks.

We have colorcoded (see table 2.1) these various elements of cohesion and coherence so as to distinguish them one from the other and to suggest a possible overt-to-covert ranking (with greater reader contribution required as we go from top to bottom in the scheme) in (6).

(6) Cohesion and Coherence

1. In a minute a third slave was struggling in the air.
2. It was dreadful.
3. I turned away my head a moment, and when I turned back I missed the king!
4. They were blindfolding him!
5. I was paralyzed, [paraphrase of 6–8 and 11]
6. I couldn't move. [paraphrase of 7–8; parallel of 11]
7. I was choking,
8. my tongue was petrified.
9. They finished blindfolding him,
10. they led him under the rope.
11. I couldn't shake off that clinging impotence.
12. But when I saw them put the noose around his neck, then everything let go in me and I made a spring to the rescue—
13. and as I made it I shot one more glance abroad—
14. by George! here they came, a-tilting—five hundred mailed and belted knights on bicycles!
15. The grandest sight that ever was seen.
16. Lord, how the plumes streamed,
17. how the sun flamed and flashed from the endless procession of webby wheels!

2.5 Marking a great moment within a story

Most discourses are not spoken/written at a uniform level of excitation. Rather, a discourse typically has a spike or peak. When a story is given orally, phonological parameters of increased volume, accelerando, and heightened key can come into play. Written texts usually have features that compensate for the absence of such phonological parameters.

The first half of this paragraph pictures graphically the impotence of the narrator in the face of the threatened execution of the king. Features of parallelism and paraphrase are used to mark time, so to speak, even while the hanging script proceeds with rapid movements.

With the onset of the word *But* in S12 everything changes. Not only does the narrator ('the Connecticut Yankee') make a desperate effort to thwart the hanging, but—more to the point—he looks up and sees adequate help coming. From this point onward there is a dramatic change in the nature of the paragraph.

To begin with, two expletives or mild oaths occur: *by George* in S14 and *Lord* in S16. Secondly, there is a shift to exclamatory sentences in S15–17. Here, undoubtedly—as indeed already probable in S14—oral style would resort to the phonological parameters indicated. Exclamatory sentences, by their suggestion of incompleteness (e.g., *the grandest sight that ever was seen,* and the *how* sentences), are meant to mirror such phonological features. Finally, assonance and alliteration are resorted to in a fashion more characteristic of poetry. We have not tried to indicate these features in a color plate, since features of this sort do not lend themselves well to such marking.

Consider the two long and sonorous noun phrases in S14 (*five hundred mailed and belted knights on bicycles*), and S17 (*the endless procession of webby wheels*). In the former phrase note the *l*'s in *mailed and belted,* as well as the initial bilabials. Note also the alliteration (use of similar consonants) of *b*'s in *belted* and *bicycles.* There is considerable resort to *s*'s in S15 plus the vowel similarity between *grandest* and *ever.* Medial *m*'s occur in S16 in *plumes* and *streamed,* plus *s*'s at the word boundary. There is initial similarity in S17 in *flamed* and *flashed* which builds on the many uses of *fl-* words which refer to light and fire. Both words are also two syllable past tense verbs which end in *-d.* Finally, there are the *s-* sounds which are final in *endless,* and occur twice in *procession,* and the alliteration of *w*'s in *webby wheels.*

2.6 What part does each sentence play in the plan of the whole?

In answering this question, all the features discussed in the sections above prove relevant: (1) Relative rank of each sentence on the dynamic-static scale as seen in section 2.1, (2) participant/prop/abstract noun reference as seen in section 2.2, (3) devices of cohesion and coherence that relate one sentence to another as seen in section 2.4, and (4) suspense versus peak marking as seen in section 2.5.

S1 and S2 belong together. The initial *it* in S2 must be accounted for; it appears to introduce a summary comment on S1. Furthermore, the static nature of S2 requires that it be backgrounded to some other sentence. Finally, in terms of participant reference only S1 and S2 refer to the hanging of the third slave.

S3 and S4 also belong together. It seems a fair inference that S4 gives the reason that the narrator at first couldn't spot the whereabouts of the king. In terms of dynamic verb ranking, the verbs of S3 outrank as perfective/sequential actions (or cognitive events) the verb of S4, which pictures a backgrounded activity. Both sentences, furthermore, have to do with the king.

S5 and S6 belong together in that, as observed in section 2.4, S6 relates as a negated antonym paraphrase to S5.

The block of four sentences, S5–8, all in somewhat the same range on the dynamic-static scale, belong together by virtue of this factor plus the further consideration of participant reference, that is, all refer to the narrator (or a part of his body) as subject.

In relating S1–8, we assume that S3, 9, and 10, whose verbs are the most dynamic, dominate this part of the paragraph. S3 dominates over S4 as just seen. We believe that the block of S5–8, which is relatively low in the scale, express the result on the narrator of S3–4, that is, perceiving that the king has shifted position on the stage and is being blindfolded shocks the narrator into something approaching paralysis. The block of S3–8, plus 9, plus 10 relate then sequentially with S3 dominating its block, and S9 and 10 following on in storyline sequence. By contrast, S1–2 seem to be preparatory (and transitional from previous context), while S11 seems to be some sort of summary or terminus.

That a major new part of the paragraph starts in S12 can be argued from the occurrence of *But...* in that sentence. Furthermore, in terms of action sequence the narrator is impotent and a mere spectator in S1–11, but springs into action in S12 and at the same time sees effective help coming (S13ff). Just as S1–11 dwells considerably on the narrator's helpless perception of the danger to the king, so the second half of the paragraph dwells considerably on the glad sight of the arrival of the rescue party.

In placing the function of the various sentences in part two of the paragraph, we start at the end and work backwards. S16 and 17 are very parallel structurally (*how...*) and semantically. We consider both of these sentences to be, however, some sort of comment or elaboration on S15 *The grandest sight that ever was seen*. But in turn the three sentences, S15–17, are a very pictorial comment on S14 whose verb *came a-tilting* is also more dynamic than the static elements in S15–17. Finally, all these sentences (S14–17) tell what the narrator saw when *he shot one more glance abroad* (S13). We relate S14–17 to S13 by making the latter the AWARENESS FORMULA (says that the narrator saw something); and the former (S14–17), the awareness (the field of vision, i.e., what the narrator saw).

Thus, S13–17 record the last event of the paragraph, a cognitive event: [the narrator perceives that] rescue is coming. The preceding sentence, S12, records the narrator's immediate attempt to effect a personal rescue.

All these relations are summarized in the accompanying tree diagram in appendix 2A. An indentation diagram with text material is found in appendix 2B.[1] The paragraph as a whole is labeled a *narrative contrast paragraph*. It is labeled a *contrast paragraph* because several features already discussed and argued indicate that essentially the paragraph has two contrastive parts. It is labeled a *narrative contrast paragraph* because a contrast paragraph need not be narrative in structure (as here) but can be, for example, expository or hortatory. The two halves of this paragraph are labeled *thesis* and ANTITHESIS.

The thesis part of the paragraph embraces S1–11, which, as we have seen, belong together. They are considered here to constitute an embedded narrative sequence paragraph, which has a SETTING (S1 and 2) and sequential theses one through three (Seq.Th 1–Seq.Th 3). Of these only sequential thesis 1 is internally complex. It consists of a result paragraph, whose thesis is S3–4 and whose result is S5–8. The former chunk, S3–4, constitutes a reason paragraph, of which S3 is the thesis and S4 is the reason. The latter chunk, S5–8, constitutes a coordinate paragraph, of which S5–6 (internally a

---

[1] See chapter 8 for a discussion of different diagrams as notational variants and for detailed discussions of paragraph analysis.

negated antonym paraphrase paragraph) constitutes thesis 1, while S7 and S8 are thesis 2 and thesis 3, respectively.

The second half of the paragraph, S12–17, also constitutes another embedded narrative sequence paragraph, whose sequential thesis 1 is S12 and whose sequential thesis 2 is a nest of embedded paragraphs, which must be peeled off one by one. Thus S13–17 are an awareness paragraph, which tells us what the narrator saw. S13 is the thesis and is an awareness formula (it tells us that the narrator saw something). S14–17 constitute the awareness, that is, it tells us what the narrator saw. Internally, S14–17 is a comment paragraph, of which S14 is the thesis and S15–17 the comment. Internally, S15–17 is also a comment paragraph, of which S15 is the thesis and S16–17 the comment. Finally, S16–17 constitute a coordinate paragraph, the two parts of which are thesis 1 and thesis 2.

The intent of such a representation is to specify precisely what each sentence does in the linear sequence of the paragraph. A tree or indentation diagram of this sort attempts to fit each sentence into its functional context.

2.7 The resultant constraints on interpretation

In the preceding sections we have attempted, by various analytical strategies, to get at the question of text meaning—or, if one prefers to put it another way—the matter of how the structure of the text constrains possible interpretations of it.

That the paragraph is broadly satirical can be imputed from the frame juxtaposition, which was discussed in section 2.4, where references to medieval knighthood and modern bicycles are juxtaposed. Furthermore, we can assume that the normal reader who has read the preceding context would have the clue to several further anachronisms that occur due to the inventive ingenuity of the Connecticut Yankee himself.

Mark Twain is, however, not simply writing a satire but telling a story. As with any storyteller in any language and culture, his linguistic medium allows him to foreground some sentences at the expense of others. Or, to put it more accurately, the verbs and nouns of the language (in this case English) allow him both to mark the storyline and to distinguish various degrees of departure from the storyline. The resultant texture can be compared to a tapestry composed of different threads.

In foregrounding his action line, the writer treats the death of the third slave and the narrator's reaction to it as setting for the main action: the threat on the life of the king. Even here, Mark Twain interweaves the storyline with an account of the narrator's horrified reaction to what he saw happening, so as to paint a striking picture of the narrator's impotence in the face of the threat.

The word *But* prepares us for some kind of reversal—and indeed it is followed with a rescue attempt on the part of the narrator and a perception of real rescue coming. The narrator takes time to let us see through his own eyes the welcome sight of the oncoming rescue party. He even plays on our poetic inclination to help us sense that it was indeed *The grandest sight that ever was seen.*

Frames and scripts are skillfully used by the author in both parts of the paragraph so as to cue in our interpretation. The assumption is made that there will be very few readers indeed who do not have such frames and scripts to guide them in the interpretation of the text. If such readers do exist, their interpretations must be discounted. Interpreters are not all of the same quality. The deficiency of the required frames and scripts would amount, in our contemporary culture, to a cognitive handicap.

In summary, while the paragraph is satirical, it also is part of an absorbing story that portrays a threat to the life of the king and the circumstances of the rescue as well as the subjective emotions of the narrator himself.

2.8 Exercise

Can you think of some ways in which your knowledge bank as a translator (with its frames and scripts) may differ from the knowledge banks of the potential readers of your translation?

Appendix 2A. Paragraph analysis: Tree diagram

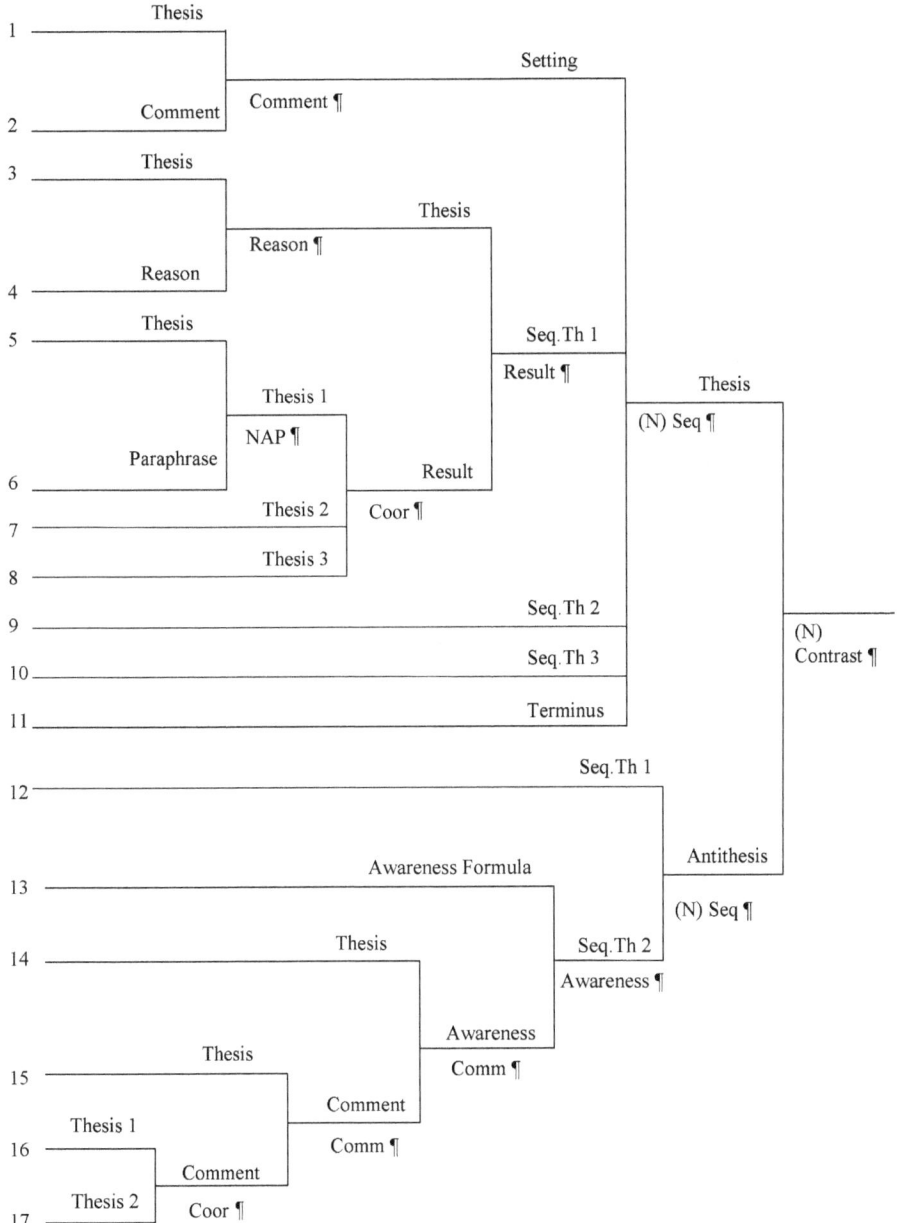

Appendix 2B. Paragraph analysis: Indentation diagram

(N) Contrast ¶

Thesis: (N) Sequence ¶
   Setting: Comment ¶
        Thesis: 1 *In a minute a third slave was struggling in the air.*
        Comment: 2 *It was dreadful.*
   Seq.Th 1: Result ¶
      Thesis: Reason ¶
         Thesis: 3 *I turned away my head a moment, and when I turned back I missed the king!*
         Reason: 4 *They were blindfolding him!*
      Result: Coordinate ¶
         Thesis 1: Negated Antonym Paraphrase ¶
           Thesis: 5 *I was paralyzed;*
           Paraphrase: 6 *I couldn't move.*
         Thesis 2:   7 *I was choking,*
         Thesis 3:   8 *my tongue was petrified.*
   Seq.Th 2: 9 *They finished blindfolding him,*
   Seq.Th 3: 10 *they led him under the rope.*
   Terminus: 11 *I couldn't shake off that clinging impotence.*
Antithesis: (N) Sequence ¶
   Seq.Th 1: 12 *But when I saw them put the noose around his neck, then everything let go in me and I made a spring to the rescue—*
   Seq.Th 2: Awareness ¶
      Awareness Formula: 13 *and as I made it I shot one more glance abroad—*
      Awareness: Comment ¶
         Thesis: 14 *by George! here they came, a-tilting—five hundred mailed and belted knights on bicycles!*
         Comment: Comment ¶
            Thesis: 15 *The grandest sight that ever was seen.*
            Comment: Coordinate ¶
               Thesis 1: 16 *Lord, how the plumes streamed,*
               Thesis 2: 17 *how the sun flamed and flashed from the endless procession of webby wheels!*

Chapter 3

Text Typology

Before analyzing a text in detail we need to have a preliminary identification of the text type to which the text belongs. Otherwise, we cannot make specific statements about such matters as the following: the distribution of verb tense/aspect/modality, anaphoric reference ranging from noun to pronoun to personal endings on the verb to zero anaphora, devices of topicalization and thematization, and distribution of connectives and mystery particles, and many others which are mentioned in chapter 1. Without identification of text type we are left with the familiar dilemma of traditional grammar writing: how can we give, for example, a general statement of the use of tense/aspect/modality in the verb structure of a given language when our grammatical statements attempt to cover all uses of verbs in all discourse types with examples culled willy-nilly from the various types?

In this chapter, we want to first go over an ETIC scheme of discourse types that has already been presented elsewhere (Longacre 1982, 1996). In section 3.2 we illustrate how an emic description of text types can eventually be evolved for a given language and replace the etic scheme which is useful for a starting point. The scheme of discourse types that we present again here must not be taken as an indication of the finished analysis of discourse types in a given language but rather as a convenient starting point. In section 3.3 we present a few sample texts with regard to text types.

3.1 An etic scheme of discourse types

The etic scheme initially posits two parameters: (1) CONTINGENT TEMPORAL SUCCESSION and (2) AGENT ORIENTATION (see fig. 3.1). Narration (stories of all sorts) is positive in regard to both these parameters. A story is not a story without successive perfective events (at least in partial causal connection) nor without a slate of participants who engage in voluntary actions as well as things happening to them. PROCEDURAL or how-to-do-it discourses are plus in regard to contingent temporal succession (procedures must be ordered and causally connected) but minus in regard to agent orientation. The minus value is seen in that procedures are goal-oriented rather than agent-oriented; any qualified agent may implement them in regard to the intended goal. BEHAVIORAL discourse (a pep talk, a hortatory sermon, a eulogy, a political speech) is minus contingent temporal succession but plus in regard to agent orientation. Finally, EXPOSITORY discourse is minus in regard to both parameters. It has logical rather than temporal connections, and themes rather than agents.

These four notional etic discourse types can be multiplied to eight by the addition of a further parameter, PROJECTION, for projected time. Projection, when plus, indicates actions or states which are future, anticipated, or irrealis, rather than present, accomplished, or realis. For example, most narrative discourse is minus projection; the events described are conceived of as already having taken place. But occasionally we are confronted with a discourse that purports to recount courses of action before they occur. If this discourse otherwise meets the requirements plus temporal succession and plus agent orientation, then it can be considered to be a kind of projected narrative, or what is commonly called prophecy. Procedural discourse is commonly plus projection but there clearly exists a kind of procedural discourse which is minus projection, for example, an account of the way something was built or some rite carried out before contact with Western civilization. This is a how-it-was-done text rather than a "how-to-do it" text. Behavioral discourse in one of its most common forms is the exhortation (wherein the speaker tries to change the conduct of the hearers). It is likewise plus projection, as are the command forms that are the backbone of such a discourse. A eulogy, however, is clearly behavioral in terms of minus contingent temporal succession and plus agent orientation but is minus projection. Finally, expository discourse, while explaining or describing some phase of reality, is normally minus projection, but plus projection expository discourse can occur as well, as in a futuristic text, "This is the kind of world we will be living in, in the year 2050 A.D."

Still a further parameter, TENSION, is posited as well. This parameter has to do with whether or not a text affects a struggle or polarization of some sort. Narratives commonly are plus tension, that is, they have a plot structure that builds up to a confrontation (whether overt and violent or very restrained and urbane) and a denouement (release). But certainly discourses which are plus temporal succession and plus agent orientation but minus tension also exist, for example, a recital of what one did and said on a particular morning—whether for an interested spouse or as a witness in a court room. In the latter, the very purpose of the narrative may be to portray the recounted course of events as if they were completely routine and insignificant (an alibi). Likewise, a course of procedures may not have a perceptible build-up (minus tension) or may clearly build up to a target

3.1 An etic scheme of discourse types

procedure (plus tension). A behavioral (HORTATORY) discourse, if it is to be effective, is quite predictably plus tension; this often involves a build-up from highly mitigated forms of request to an outright command form (imperative) at the end. We can find, however, hortatory discourses that are intentionally low-geared throughout and are therefore minus tension (the soft sell). Even expository or DESCRIPTIVE discourse can so select its sequence of presentation as to present the most interesting and gripping material at the end and therefore qualify as plus tension.

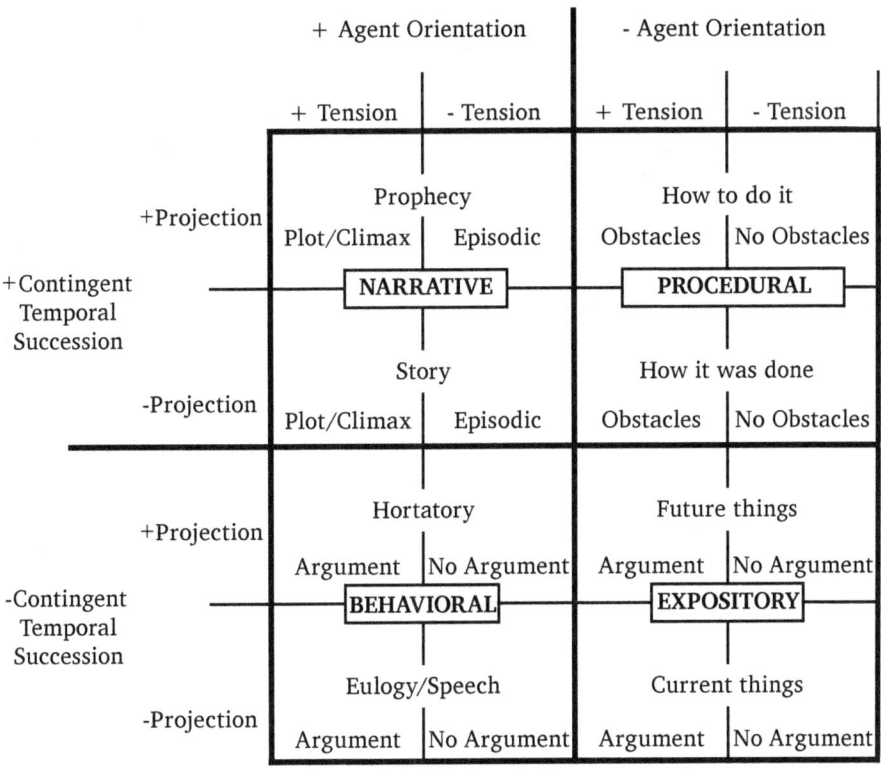

Figure 3.1. Notional discourse types

The resultant scheme is presented in figure 3.1. This diagram covers a considerable variety of possible notional structures. How comprehensive is such a system? There are a few apparent omissions: (1) drama; (2) persuasion/argument aimed at influencing beliefs and values (rather than primarily at changing conduct); (3) description as opposed to expository discourse; (4) an indictment. DRAMA is, we believe, a surface structure discourse type in which a story is told entirely through reported speech—whether intended simply to be read, or, as is much more common, to be enacted. We subsume drama under narrative, although the reenactment feature sets it somewhat apart. PERSUASIVE discourse as opposed to hortatory is aimed more at the hearer's values and beliefs than at his conduct, although the two are ultimately inseparable. We subsume this sort of discourse rather uncomfortably under behavioral. Description and expository discourse are closely related. To description pertains the special feature of descriptive order—whether spatial (front-back, panoramic view, head to toe), part-whole, etc. Again, we leave this discourse type somewhat uncomfortably aligned with expository. An INDICTMENT is not so difficult; presumably it is minus temporal succession and plus agent orientation and therefore clearly a kind of behavioral discourse.

In comparing these notional text types with surface structure discourses we need further specifications and adjustments. Further specifications should proceed along the lines congenial to a given language in terms of contrasting backbone structures, systems of participant/theme reference, and types of linkage—almost equivalent to saying "account for what verbs, nouns, and particles do in a given discourse type." Ultimately, such an investigation should lead to positing a system of emic discourse types as suggested in section 3.2 of this chapter.

One must recognize that notional types are not necessarily in one-to-one correspondence with the surface specifications. A general problem here is the presence of hortatory motivation underlying diverse surface forms. Thus, in African folk cultures, a story commonly has a moral slot at its end. The general impression is that stories are told to reinforce values and norms of conduct. But even here, the presence of a trivial moral may be a clue that the aim of a particular story is entertainment rather than edification. It seems best to classify all such stories as surface structure narratives while recognizing that the presence of a moral slot compromises it somewhat in the direction of a hortatory discourse.

There are other, however, more transparent cases of one notional discourse type cast in the surface structure form of a somewhat differing type. Thus, a narrative may gain a certain poignancy by being cast as a procedural (this-could-also-happen-to-you) discourse, while a procedural discourse can gain concreteness by being cast into a narrative (you asked me how to do X, but I'll tell you how a real craftsman did X once). We quote from the 1996 work which is a companion to the present volume:

> There may be occasions on which it is stylistically effective to present notional narration in the surface structure form of procedural discourse. An example of this occurred in a news story in the *Dallas Morning News* (Davenport 1973). Its notional intent was to give a first person account of an apartment fire in Dallas, but it is cast in the form of procedural discourse, i.e., the pronoun *you* is used through most of the account, *you go to bed, you wake up, you smell smoke*, etc., and cast into the present tense which is characteristic of procedural discourse in English. The thrust of it is, 'This is how you might act if you were to find yourself in the same circumstances in which I found myself.' Or, conversely, procedural discourse may be given as narrative. Thus our colleagues Jannette Forster and Myra Lou Barnard elicited Dibabawon texts relating to game procurement (Longacre 1968, Part 3). While several of their texts are clearly surface structure procedural texts, there are a few in which we are told how a certain capable hunter or trapper procured game. Here we have the story of how a master of the art behaved in implementing his art. They are surface structure narratives, which run somewhat as follows: *So*

and so (by name) built a fishtrap on a certain bend of a certain river a certain year. He was highly successful. He caught so and so many fish in his trap, etc. Although this is surface structure narrative, the purpose is to inform us how to build a successful fish trap; and of course we can learn this quite well from being told how a master trapper of fish built his trap. (Longacre 1996:14–15)

Some have asked: Do we not find mixed types in the real world of text material?[1] Several things need to be said in response to this query: (1) Skewing of notional and surface types, as just discussed and illustrated can lead to the impression of 'mixture'. (2) EMBEDDED discourses within a main overall discourse can lead to the same impression, since an embedded discourse may not be of the same type as the main discourse. Thus, very commonly stories embed more or less extensive expository or descriptive discourses, especially in the staging of a whole narrative or one of its episodes. A piece of REPORTED SPEECH can be of any discourse type and can be very extensive. Frequently the narrator puts persuasion, or hortatory discourse, into the mouth of one of the participants in his story. Just as frequently, however, a hortatory discourse can embed more or less extensive patches of narrative, while even a piece of expository discourse can have an illustrative narrative. Thus, the presentation of a new scientific discovery or hypothesis can embed a piece of the investigator's autobiography as discoverer.

What then? The main discourse is of classifiable structure and so is each embedded discourse. Our analysis may give the impression of a mosaic of diverse discourse types, but the mosaic is hierarchically structured and is certainly not a mixture. If we are to analyze successfully the various EMBEDDING and embedded pieces of discourse we must know the discourse type at the very turn of the analysis. It won't do to try to analyze a story as if it were an essay, or an essay as if it were a story! To attempt either is to fail to account for the textlinguistic surface features.

3.2 An emic scheme of discourse types in Aguacatec (Mayan)

At this point we discuss the Aguacatec language to illustrate how an emic scheme that is evolved for a given language can be at once similar to and

---

[1] Longacre and Bowling (to appear) state: "We assume that the discourse types which we posit are discrete and contrast with each other in a system of discourse types. We also assume that a discourse type may have variants consistent with its contrast with other types. And we further assume that a given type or variant of a type has distribution relative to other types, whether by embedding or juxtaposition—a sort of collage. In these respects, we follow the theoretical framework of K. L. Pike as argued in detail in Pike's massive work of 1967, and stated succinctly in terms of contrast, variation, and distribution being basic to the delineation of an emic unit (Pike 1982, but current before then). Furthermore, the framework allows for neutralization of contrast at certain points in a system. It could be argued, of course, that this is not the only theoretical framework according to which discourse types could be posited. It would be possible, for example, to posit a theory of discourse types based on something analogous to the 'cardinal vowels' as developed in Great Britain and passed down orally to successive generations of disciples." One could argue that there are certain cardinal or prototypical discourse types and various degrees of adherence to or departure from them (see also Hwang 2005).

distinct from the general etic scheme. We refer the reader to Longacre (1996:16–21) for emic schemes of discourse types in Aguaruna (Peru), Camsa (Colombia), and Biblical Hebrew.

For discourse types of Aguacatec, McArthur (1979:100) states: "The role of aspect is very significant in distinguishing the various types of discourse in Aguacatec. Although the presence or absence of any one of the various aspect markers is not the only distinguishing feature, it is certainly one of the most important." He describes four main types: narrative, procedural, hortatory and expository, with additional subtypes for narrative and hortatory. He also adds one hybrid type called descriptive-narrative, making a total of seven types.

We will now sketch briefly the characteristics of these various discourse types in Aguacatec as labeled and grouped by McArthur, with special attention to his hybrid type.

1) Narrative 1 (definite-event)

This type of narrative conforms more to what we customarily think of as stories, such as historical events, legends, and folktales. These are event sequences which are conceived of as having actually occurred until outside contact destroys the belief system of a folk community. Its storyline consists of verbs unmarked for aspect; such verbs are described as the 'completed-definite' aspect (McArthur 1979:115). A secondary storyline is marked by verbs with the past participle suffix *-e'n*, whether in PREPOSED dependent clauses or in independent clauses. A pivotal action/event is marked with the *-tz* affix on the verb nucleus; the representation for such a pivotal event can be built onto the zero aspect or onto the form marked with *-e'n*. Backgrounded material is reported in clauses with other constructions, especially EXISTENTIAL and topic-comment clauses. When a verb that reports background information is marked with *-tz*, it reports "more crucial background than the rest" (1979:100).

2) Narrative 2 (immediate past)

McArthur describes this narrative as recountings of events that took place on the same day as that on which they were recounted (1979:104). The mainline of this discourse type does not distinguish primary and SECONDARY STORYLINES but marks both with *n-/m-*, the 'completed-indefinite' aspect marker. These are anecdotal accounts, for example, "how we went swimming (earlier that day)." McArthur describes such narratives as having weak chronological linkage; many sentences in such accounts begin with *nin* 'and'. Here again, pivotal events are marked with *-tz* on the verb.

3) Descriptive narrative

McArthur posits this as a hybrid type rather than a further subtype of narrative. Its distinguishing formal characteristic is the use of the preverbal particle *ja*, the 'completed-descriptive' aspect. While this marks primary

3.2 An emic scheme of discourse types in Aguacatec (Mayan)

action/events, secondary actions/events are marked in one of two ways with *-e'n* (participle) marking the more definite events, while *n-/m-* "signals transitional or introductory events, and functions as weak chronological linkage between the episodes of the discourse" (1979:107).

Essentially, this discourse type has a weak narrative line and a wealth of descriptive content. In the example of this text in the McArthur article (107–108), *ja* occurs on main verbs which are largely motion and perception verbs: "we arrived at so and so place...we saw such and such." The *n-/m-* aspect occurs in pseudo-cleft structures: "The first thing we did (*n-* verb) was X.... The second thing we did (*n-* verb) was Y...." The *-e'n* form is used in purpose clauses: 'in order to our arriving (*-e'n*) as far as Q' (=in order to arrive at Q).

Our personal preference is to make even a weakly narrative discourse a kind of narrative. What is instructive about Aguacatec discourse types 1, 2, and 3 is the total distinctiveness of their primary storylines: zero aspect, *n-/m-* aspect, *ja* aspect—with the latter especially used in a "we went and saw..." narrative with a large quantity of description.

4) Expository

The mainline of this discourse type is marked with the preverbal particle *na*, 'continuous or customary action' (108). There is no secondary information given in independent clauses, but dependent clauses also marked with *na* are considered to convey secondary information. There is a wealth of logical connectives in this discourse type: *na* 'because', *cha's tzun te* 'for that reason', and *ya's tzun* 'that's what'/'that's why'.

5) Procedural

McArthur posits only one type of procedural discourse which is characterized by *tz'-* 'incomplete-definite' aspect on the mainline verbs of the discourse, *-l/ l-* 'incomplete-indefinite' aspect on verbs in secondary steps or in dependent clauses, and *n-/m-* 'completed-indefinite' aspect in the target procedure (i.e., "when the target, or goal, of a set of procedures has been reached," McArthur 1979:111).

6) Hortatory 1 (presumably the normative hortatory discourse)

This surface form is used in a social situation of superior to inferior. Imperatives are used (second person) or first person plural including the hearers (slightly mitigated). McArthur calls this "action-oriented imperative."

7) Hortatory 2 (polite-exhortation)

McArthur reports that this discourse type is used in social situations where request or advice is the order of the day instead of outright command, such as in giving advice to a young married couple. While the discourse is second-person oriented, commands give way to mainline verbs which are marked with *tz'*-, the 'incomplete-definite' aspect. Here, apparently the Aguacatec speaker modifies his exhortation by moving toward the surface form of the procedural discourse (see 5). This is somewhat parallel to what happens in Biblical Hebrew (see also Longacre 1996:19–20).

Our overall etic scheme for discourse types is seen to provide a general framework for discourse types in Aguacatec. We believe that McArthur's hybrid discourse type, the descriptive narrative, can be considered a variety of narrative, but the fact remains that the three narrative types, definite-event, immediate past, and descriptive narrative, are as distinct from each other as are expository, procedural, and hortatory. There is no special structural basis for grouping together the three narrative types. The mitigation of hortatory discourse in certain social situations leads to a partial substitution of the features of procedural discourse.

3.3 Sample texts from English

To illustrate how one can go about analyzing a text type, we conclude this chapter by presenting some sample texts from English. Two one-paragraph texts appear below (from the August 1988 *Reader's Digest*).

(7) Time is the coin of your life. It is the only coin you have, and only you can determine how it will be spent. Be careful lest you let other people spend it for you (by Carl Sandburg on p. 112).

(8) Never mistake knowledge for wisdom. One helps you make a living; the other helps you make a life (by Sandra Carey on p. 101).

Both texts are minus contingent temporal succession but have logical succession. They are plus agent orientation in that they are directed toward the audience (expressed by the second person pronoun *you*). The third parameter, projection, is plus, pointing toward the anticipated behavior of the audience, which is reflected in the use of the present and future tense forms. The tension, however, is not marked specially in these short texts, so they can be described as minus tension. The text type for these texts is therefore hortatory. They try to infuence your thinking and behavior.

(9) After hearing me talk about my job, my young son looked forward to spending the day with me at the office. Although usually shy, he seemed eager to meet each co-worker I introduced. On the way home, however, he appeared sullen. I couldn't see the reason for his disappointment until he complained, "I never got to see the clowns you said you worked with" (contributed by Marvella McDill on p. 121).[2]

---

[2] Reprinted by permission from the August 1988 *Reader's Digest*. Copyright 1988 by The Reader's Digest Assn., Inc.

3.3 Sample texts from English

This four-sentence text in (9) is a short story, of course, with agent orientation (mother and son) and contingent temporal succession with events occurring in sequence as shown in simple past tense forms, which also reflect minus projection. A slight tension can be detected in the second half, where the misunderstanding about the clowns makes it an interesting story with a climax.

The next text comes from "Words to Grow on" by Iron Eyes Cody, who introduces himself as the Indian actor well-known to TV viewers by a single tear rolling down his cheek while looking at the polluted waters. Then he says, "Now I have another story to tell, an old legend, with a warning as potent as that tear." Then he tells a story of an Indian youth who trusted a snake's words only to be bitten by the snake. The last part of the story follows in (10):

(10) The youth resisted a while, but this was a very persuasive snake with beautiful markings. At last the youth tucked it under his shirt and carried it down to the valley. There he laid it gently on the grass, when suddenly the snake coiled, rattled and leapt, biting him on the leg. "But you promised...," cried the youth. "You knew what I was when you picked me up," said the snake as it slithered away. (Cody 1988:32–33)[3]

It is a climactic story with agent orientation (two participants, the youth and the snake), contingent temporal succession (events in succession which are partially contingent on previous ones), and tension, but with minus projection. Although the story itself ends there, the author adds some more words.

(11) And now, wherever I go, I tell that story. I tell it especially to the young people of this nation who might be tempted by drugs. I want them to remember the words of the snake: You knew what I was when you picked me up.

This paragraph in (11) is expository on the surface but notionally a hortatory text. With this additional material, the overall text may now be classified as hortatory, explicitly warning the reader against the temptation from drugs. The story itself, which consists of twenty-eight sentences, is lengthy relative to the expository/hortatory material, but this poignant story is embedded within the hortatory text to provide the motivation to heed the advice.[4] The embedded story is what makes the whole text more memorable and vivid in the minds of the reader. Thus, embedding achieves

---

[3] Copyright 1988 by *Guideposts*. All rights reserved. www.guideposts.com
[4] An alternative analysis is possible when one takes this three-sentence paragraph in (11) to be a trivial addition to the story (i.e., not enough to change the overall text type), similar to a moral slot.

a higher degree of vividness and a stronger impact on the reader (see also Hwang 1993).

3.4 Exercises

(1) Consider Joseph's speeches to his brothers before (Gen. 42:18–20) and after (Gen. 45:9–13) he reveals himself to them as their long-lost brother. What resources does the target language have to convey this difference in Joseph's attitudes?

(2) Consider also Gen. 29:2–3. In verse 2, Jacob encounters a well in a field with three flocks of sheep nearby. Verse 3 pictures a daily routine of gathering the flocks, rolling the stone from the mouth of the well, watering the flocks, and finally replacing the stone. How can you indicate that this is a routine procedure and not simply something done on the occasion when Jacob arrived there?

Chapter 4

Approaching a Narrative: Constituent Charting and Macrosegmentation

Among the four basic types of text—narrative, procedural, behavioral, and expository—our primary concern here is with narratives, although the same sort of principles and methodology would apply to other types as well. No culture is without some kind of narratives, such as legends, folktales and first-person accounts, like what-happened-to-me-today. In addition to being a cultural universal, narratives prove to be the best text type for a field linguist to approach initially. They usually deal with concrete topics and participants in well-delineated situations and report specific sequences of events and actions. Narratives give information regarding *who, what, when, where, why,* and *how* usually more explicitly than other types.

The first step in the analysis is to chart the text in some workable presentation format. Then, utilizing the display on the chart, the initial analysis can be done in terms of the major divisions within the text. This MACROSEGMENTATION, or gross CHUNKING, is done into surface structure constituent slots at the discourse level, such as stage, episodes, and closure, and the schematic slots in the notional plot structure, such as EXPOSITION, INCITING INCIDENT, climax, denouement, and CONCLUSION. These slots are specific to the narrative type.

The first part of this chapter describes a charting method, which was originally presented in Longacre and Levinsohn (1978) but is adapted here to deal with more complex examples. The second part of the chapter discusses the macrosegmentation of a narrative text. The third part of the chapter presents a method of comparative charting—comparing a translation with a native text—as a translation check.

4.1 Constituent charting of a text

One may chart a text in different ways depending on one's purpose at hand. The focus may be, for example, on the semantic types of information as in the Thurman chart (Grimes 1975), or on the grammatical and syntactic constituents, or on the plot or thematic structure. The focus of the charting method presented here is the grammatical structure of the text as a whole. Our purpose is not so much to make an exact detailed analysis of each word or phrase but to put the constituents of a text in big groups in order to reveal its discourse-level characteristics in the chart.

It is assumed that the text to chart is well formed and that the analyst controls to a large extent the grammatical structure of the language and the facts of the text, such as who did what to whom, when, where, why, and how.

4.1.1 The basic charting

The basic unit in our charting method is the sentence, which can be established based on morphological, syntactic, and phonological criteria.[1] Each sentence is further divided into clauses, which are in turn divided into phrases. Using large-size columnar paper or a computer (e.g., excel program), we chart a text in four major columns: *introducer, preposed dependent clause, main/independent clause,* and *postposed dependent clause*. On the left of the chart we enter the sentence numbers and, on the far left or right, set up a notes column, in which we enter on-going observations and analytical notes regarding any unusual features.

The columns for dependent clauses include adverbial clauses, which are as much constituents of the sentence as are the independent clauses. That is, independent (or interdependent) clauses and adverbial clauses form a CLAUSE COMBINATION in the sentence structure (see Matthiessen and Thompson 1988; Thompson, Longacre, and Hwang 2007). In contrast, complement and RELATIVE CLAUSES reflect an embedding relationship. Prototypical COMPLEMENT CLAUSES function as arguments within another clause (Horie 2000), while relative clauses modify the head noun of a noun phrase and are embedded in that phrase.

The chart is read from left to right and from top to bottom. Thus, when there is not enough space in the column for a given constituent, we go down to further lines in the same column.

The introducer column includes vocatives, exclamations, time/locative phrases, and coordinate conjunctions like *and, but,* and *or,* which may start the sentence or clause. The column is divided into two sections: *sentence-initial* and *sentence-medial*, with the sentence-initial column carrying elements that occur initially in the sentence and the sentence medial column carrying conjunctions that connect two independent clauses within a sentence.

---

[1] The sentence, thus established, may not necessarily look like a 'sentence' in English. For example, in Trique (Mexico), conjunctions characteristically mark sentence boundaries and occur sentence-initial, while in English many conjunctions occur sentence medially.

Within each of the three major clause columns, the order of the sub-columns reflects the basic and most frequent word (constituent) order of the language, for example, Subject-Verb-Object for English and SOV for Korean. When a constituent is not overtly expressed but is implied, it is marked by a dash (–) or zero (Ø) in the appropriate column. Since there may be other constituents than S, V, and O in a clause, the labels of these sub-columns are often to be interpreted broadly, for example, V may include not only the verb but also many prepositions functioning as verbal particles, as in *set off*. When adverbs occur before or within the verb phrase, they are entered in the V column as well. The O column, in particular, includes a wide range of constituents from direct/indirect objects and complements to time and locative phrases, practically anything other than S and V that occurs after the verb (or before the verb in OV languages). It is, therefore, best to leave a wide column for the O.

The space for each column reflects the relative size of each constituent in the language. It is usually best to leave the most space for the independent clause since not every sentence in the text may have a dependent clause. In HEAD-FINAL chaining languages, however, there may be several preposed clauses before the final clause with its verb, justifying giving space to dependent clauses equal to (or sometimes even larger than) the independent clause. If POSTPOSED dependent clauses do not normally occur in the language, as in the case of Korean, we do not need to set up this column. Any occasional occurrence may be entered in the independent clause column with appropriate comments in the notes.

In the case of dependent clauses (both pre- and postposed if both occur in the language), an additional sub-column for conjunctions is necessary within the dependent clause column for languages like English, where most (adverbial) dependent clauses are headed by a subordinate conjunction like *when, before, because,* and *since*. In this way all the elements of a dependent clause are grouped together. If the conjunctions are suffixed to verbs (as in Korean), they may best be left with the verbs of which they are a part or add a subcolumn for conjunctive elements.

Types of clause combination and embedding need to be distinguished in charting. In English, for example, it is possible for *that*-clauses to be in different grammatical relations with the main clause:

(12) a. complement clause which functions as an argument in the main clause
(***That** Jack missed the plane is incredible*),
b. adverbial (purpose) clause with *so* immediately preceding it
(*They inspected the site carefully **so that** no one would be injured*), or
c. coordinate sentence with two independent clauses with *so* and an adjective in front (*They were so tired **that** they all fell asleep as soon as they went to bed*).

The complement clause in (12a) is charted as the subject in the independent clause column; the *so that* (purpose) clause in (12b) is charted as a postposed dependent clause; and the *(so)...that* clause in (12c) as another independent clause on the next line. Relative clauses are a part of the noun phrase describing and delimiting the head noun they modify, so they are charted with their head noun.

In English there are also other types of dependent clauses:

(13) a. those not headed by subordinate conjunctions but marked by *-ing* as participial clauses
   (*Looking at the screen, I found out that the plane had already departed* or
   He had great fun, riding swings and roundabouts), and
   b. those marked by *to* as purpose clauses
   (*I came to Dallas [in order] to attend the conference*).

These are treated as pre- and postposed dependent clauses and are distinguished from complement-type clauses that form a CLOSE-KNIT combination (called MERGED SENTENCES in Longacre 1970), for example, *I kept on reciting the poem, He saw the wolf coming up the hill*, and *I want to see Paris one more time*.

In other languages as well, an analysis of clause combination and embedding in a similar manner will clarify the grammatical structure of the language and will enable charting the text material in a systematic, revealing way. When an analysis of clause combination and embedding has been done even only tentatively, the process of charting may prove to be helpful in arriving at a more definite analysis by looking at recurrent structures in dependent versus independent clauses. The parts, such as sentence, clause, phrase, and word may be known better through the study of the whole (the text), while the whole is known through the study of both its parts and the whole by itself holistically.

In the study of narrative discourse it is important to distinguish quoted material from regular narration as the former usually has the "I-thou-here-now" perspective among the participants while the latter retains the perspective of the narrator and the hearer/reader. Instead of setting up another column to handle quotations or of treating them as objects of verbs, we suggest that they be distributed as sentences/clauses in the regular columns as appropriate. But clearly mark them as quotations by some means such as using double angle brackets around the quoted material. In this way, we are able to see the grammatical structure of the quoted material better and not assume erroneously that the quoted material, which is often extensive, is a direct object of a speech verb. In a sentence like, *John said, "I will be late tonight,"* our position is that the sentence is a combination of two clauses (rather than a clausal embedding), a quote formula (*John said*) and a quotation, and they are charted on two separate lines in the independent clause column (see Longacre 1996:86–89; Matthiessen and Thompson 1988).

4.1 Constituent charting of a text

Indirect quotations are also a combination of clauses: a clause identifying the source of speech, like *John said*, or cognition, like *John realized* (and other similar verbs such as *know, see, hear,* and *find*), and another clause providing the content of speech or cognition. They are charted in the same way as a direct quotation, on two separate lines. In certain texts it may be easier to chart them as objects of verbs since indirect quotations are generally shorter and simpler and more restricted in use than direct quotations. Whether we chart the content of speech or cognition as a separate clause or as an object of the complement-taking verb,[2] it is helpful to mark them with single angle brackets.

The most important characteristic of this method of charting is its preservation of the linear order of text material. No words or phrases are turned around to fit the column label in the chart. Any irregularity in word order may be conditioned by the surrounding text and the study of discourse should include the discovery of such conditioning. Therefore, we clearly mark the unusual order by directly inserting analytical notes in the chart in brackets such as [in O] in the S column when the subject occurs after the verb as in: *...said the man* and put the postposed subject in the O column. The element out of its normal order, for example, *the man*, may be highlighted such as with boldface. Additional analytical comments or hypotheses may be made in the notes column to draw our attention to them later. This method is thus surface or morphosyntax oriented rather than semantics or notion oriented.

Other characteristics of this charting method are:

1. The sentence (not the clause) is treated as the basic unit.
2. The grammatical constituents are largely kept together (such as a whole noun phrase even including a relative clause, and an adverbial clause with its subordinating conjunction).
3. Any unusual word order stands out.
4. Independent clauses are clearly separated from pre- and postposed dependent clauses.
5. Introducers are grouped together in the first column where they stand out in their function as sequence signals and boundary markers for paragraphs and episodes.
6. The text in its entirety is recoverable from the chart, so we may work directly with the chart in analyzing the text.

The passage from *A Connecticut Yankee in King Arthur's Court* by Mark Twain, which is dealt with in chapter 2, is charted in table 4.1. As the passage does not have any occurrence of postposed dependent clause, the chart has only three major columns, namely, introducers, preposed dependent clauses, and independent clauses. Notice that the chart is adapted not only

---

[2] See Noonan (2007:120–145) for a discussion of thirteen classes of complement-taking predicates, such as propositional attitude predicates (e.g., *think, believe*) and immediate perception predicates (e.g., *see, hear, watch, feel*).

to the structure of the particular language but also to the structure of the particular text. We modify the basic charting method to fit our purpose, text, and language. When we modify, however, we have to be consistent and systematic. The chart is a tool that we use to reveal the structure of a particular text and language. It can help us do gross chunking into larger units by showing certain correlations between the use of introducers and the paragraph divisions. It may help us understand why there is an inversion of word order from the customary order, and indicate what different forms of participant reference are used to refer to the same individual and for what reason.

Table 4.1. Constituent charting of the Mark Twain passage

	Introducer		Preposed Dep Clause				Independent Clause		
	S-in	S-med	Conj	S	V	O	S	V	O
1	In a minute						a third slave	was struggling	in the air.
2							It	was	dreadful.
3							I	turned	my head away a moment,
			and	when I	turned back		I	missed	the king!
4							They	were blindfolding	him!
5							I	was	paralyzed;
6							I	couldn't move,	
7							I	was	choking,
8							my tongue	was	petrified.
9							They	finished blindfolding	him,
10							they	led	him under the rope.
11							I	couldn't shake off	that clinging impotence.
12	But			when I	saw	them put the noose around his neck,			

4.1 Constituent charting of a text

	Introducer		Preposed Dep Clause				Independent Clause		
	S-in	S-med	Conj	S	V	O	S	V	O
		then					everything	let go	in me
		and					I	made	a spring to the rescue—
13		and	as	I	made	it	I	shot	one more glance abroad—
14	By George!								
		here					they	came, a-tilting!—	500 mailed and belted knights on bicycles!
15							∅	∅	The grandest sight that ever was seen.
16	Lord,	how					the plumes	streamed,	
17		how					the sun	flamed	
		and					∅	flashed	from the endless procession of webby wheels!

This passage[3] includes three sentence-initial introducers: *In a minute* in S1, *But* in S12, and *Lord* in S16. There are three preposed dependent clauses, each of which is headed by a conjunction *(when* or *as)* and, interestingly, is preceded by a coordinate conjunction *(and* or *But).* It is because of this possibility of having a coordinate conjunction before a subordinate clause that we position the sentence-medial conjunctions in the introducer column rather than in the independent clause. The exclamation *by George!* in S14 is treated as an introducer, as is the adverb *here,* both introducing the content of the narrator's vision/awareness, which stretches in fact to S17.

The phrase *500 mailed and belted knights on bicycles!* in S14 is a right dislocated subject clarifying the pronoun *they.* S15 consists only of the noun phrase, *The grandest sight that ever was seen,* and may be charted as a complement in the O column, as there is an ellipsis of the subject and verb *(it was).*[4] The ellipsis is indicated in the chart by a dash or zero in each sub-column.

---

[3] The numbers 1–17 are given following the divisions in chapter 2 for ease of reference. Orthographically, there are actually ten sentences, which are shown in the chart by capitalization and punctuation. For example, S13 is part of S12, so the conjunction *and* is treated as a sentence-medial introducer.

[4] Bob Dooley (personal communication) suggests an alternative analysis for S15, as a second right-dislocation to the main predication of S14, in addition to *500 mailed and belted knights on bicycles!*

Two occurrences of *how* in S16 and S17 are charted in the sentence-medial introducer column as they occur before the subject after *Lord.*

4.1.2 Tracking by colors

After the preliminary charting is done, check through the whole chart for consistency and systematicity. Did we chart the same sort of grammatical construction in two different ways, perhaps once as a dependent clause and at another time as an independent clause? Did we divide V and O elements in a consistent manner? Did we enter all implicit information (such as zero anaphora) with a dash or zero? Did we include all needed analytical notes like [in O] and mark << >> for quoted material and < > for indirect quotations? Notice that the chart reflects our analysis of the grammatical structure of the text.

When the checking is done, decide which element to focus on for the first stage of analysis. In the analysis of narrative, one might focus on the uses of (1) noun phrases, especially the participant and prop reference system; (2) verb phrases, to see the pattern in the storyline and other forms of departure from the storyline; or (3) introducers, such as conjunctions, to study cohesion.

In order to highlight some elements in the text, colors or some special symbols or lines may be utilized. We may colorcode specific elements directly on the chart to see the pattern in the text. We could, for instance, focus on participant reference and colorcode different participants. Starting with red in the spectrum, all references to the narrator could be colored in red, references to the king and his party in orange, etc. In tracking participant references we need to color the whole noun phrase (including the article and the relative clause describing the participant), not just the head noun. The purpose is to discern which forms of reference are used to refer to the same individual at different points in the text. Perhaps at the introduction, a person may be referred to by a long noun phrase with descriptive information, and later by a pronoun or by zero anaphora (e.g., **John, who was one of the students,** didn't come on Monday. **He** was sick and **Ø** missed the class).

In order to discern the storyline verb scheme, we colorcode the tense, aspect, and modality forms in the verb phrase. For example, we could color in red all simple past tense verbs or all preterite or perfective aspect verbs. Of course, we may not know which tense/aspect is associated with the storyline. We will proceed in a guess-and-check manner by consistently coloring a given tense in one color and another one in another color. These colors will stand out in our chart to reveal some system. One color might be predominantly used at the beginning stage of the discourse but not much in the subsequent independent clauses, while another color might be associated with the event/action sequences, mostly in the independent clauses in the body of the text. Again, the chart with notes and colorcodes is a tool for the analyst to discover the patterns in the language used at the discourse level.

When there is one or more mystery particles in the text, whose meanings at the sentence level are either unclear or variable, colorcoding or marking each occurrence of the particle(s) will clearly show its position of occurrence in discourse and greatly enhance the analyst's ability to detect its possible functions and meanings at the discourse level.

Often it is good to make copies of the chart to focus on particular aspects of the discourse one at a time, as it is easy to clutter the chart with too many colors and marks to reveal any structure.

4.1.3 Making notes

The notes column is used for any analytical comments regarding specific elements and lines in the chart. These comments may be entered while charting or colorcoding, or after charting and colorcoding are done.

Any discontinuity in time and location is marked in the notes column. They are often indicated by time and locative phrases in the introducer column such as *The next day* and *In Mexico,* or by a preposed dependent clause such as *When we arrived at home.* They are very helpful in determining the paragraph boundaries, and eventually in segmenting the text. We make intuitive divisions of the text, roughly guided by these introducers and thematic unity along with changes in time, location, participants, and action. These should be substantiated by MORPHOSYNTACTIC and semantic features later. Sometimes the boundary may be altogether unmarked, having no explicit linking element. The absence of linkage may be indicative of two opposite possibilities: either the two sentences are closely related to each other or there may be a major break between them.

Tentative divisions into stage, episode 1, episode 2, etc. may be made in the notes column, as well as any speculations regarding the storyline verb scheme and the functions of each tense, aspect, and modality. Any unexpected pattern in the text is also noted. For example, we may note the usage of a noun phrase where a pronoun is normally expected as a form of reference immediately after the introduction of the participant. We may speculate the reason why the noun phrase is used instead of the pronoun in that case and write down our hypothesis in the notes column, which thus includes tentative observations and analytical comments made by the analyst.

4.2 Macrosegmentation of a text

The display on the chart is used to do macrosegmentation of a narrative text into discourse-level slots. As Longacre (1996:34–36) shows, a narrative text may have the surface slots of title, APERTURE, stage, prepeak episodes, peak episode, postpeak episodes, closure, and FINIS, and the notional schema (or template) slots of exposition, INCITING MOMENT, developing conflict, climax, denouement, final suspense, and conclusion.

The peak, as described by Longacre in his various writings (1981, 1985, 1989, 1990, and 1996), is an episode-like unit corresponding to the notional climax or denouement, which is set aside as a zone of turbulence in the flow of the discourse by unusual surface features. There are positive features that often occur at this zone such as rhetorical underlining by repetition and heightened vividness by person and/or tense shift (Longacre 1996: chapter 2), but the key to the concept is a break from the norm, that is, there is a shift and change from the expected and normal features. This "gear shift" is the surface reflection of the notional tension and excitation.

The concept of peak is very useful to the analyst for making hypotheses regarding features of discourse like the storyline verb scheme and the participant reference system, independent of the zone of turbulence, the zone of irregularities, and the zone of analytical difficulties. That is, we try to establish the "normal" discourse features and observe how they are broken at the high point of the story.

Once the turbulent zone of peak episode is identified, we can draw a profile of the story as a visual representation of its horizontal structure. A bell curve-like profile reflects a text which starts low at the beginning but reaches its highest point at peak episode and then comes down to a closure at the end. (See Longacre 1981 for three types of shapes of the profile. There may be a profile with one peak, a profile with two action peaks, or a profile with one action peak and one thematic peak.)

The seven notional structure slots of a story are described in Longacre (1996:34–35) and listed here as follows:

1. Exposition, "Lay it out." Here crucial information of time, place, local color, and participants is given.
2. Inciting moment, "Get something going." The planned and predictable is broken up in some manner. Thus a certain man has plodded faithfully to work for twenty-five years, passing certain points at hours so exact that people could have set their watches by him, but today he is one hour late—and thereby hangs a tale.
3. Developing conflict, "Keep the heat on." The situation intensifies—or deteriorates—depending on one's viewpoint.
4. Climax, "Knot it all up proper," is where everything comes to a head. Here is where the author gets untidy, brings in contradictions, and adds all sorts of tangles until confrontation is inevitable.
5. Denouement, "Loosen it." A crucial event happens which makes resolution possible. Things begin to loosen up. We see a way out—even if not to a happy ending.
6. Final suspense, "Keep untangling," works out details of the resolution.
7. Conclusion, "Wrap it up," brings the story to some sort of decent—or indecent—end.

The segmentation of the narrative text into stage, peak, and pre- and post-peak episodes is based on surface structure (SS) features of various kinds, for example, boundary markers, expressions of continuity or discontinuity in time, place, event, and agent (participant reference span), etc. Surface structure slots thus identified are correlated with notional structure (NS) schema slots.

4.2 Macrosegmentation of a text

A surface slot like an episode usually encodes one schema slot notionally. We may identify, for example, the first episode as inciting moment when it is demarcated by boundary features and has a unity of grammar, meaning, and theme. That is, if an episode is identified as a unit, then one corresponding NS slot is sought, not two or more, so that the prepeak episode is simply labeled *inciting moment*, rather than being chopped into two slots of inciting moment and developing conflict just because an initial "Get something going" includes further conflict ("Keep the heat on"). This is illustrated below in our analysis of the sample story, where there is only one episode before the peak and that episode is notionally an inciting moment, which is followed by the climax, the highest point of tension.

The surface and notional slots may correlate with each other with the climax surfacing as the peak episode, or may be skewed to have the climax as the prepeak episode and the denouement as the peak. It is possible for a text to display peak-like features in two separate episodes. Then a profile with two peaks results, either a double peak profile with two action peak episodes or one with a main peak and a final, thematic, peak (Longacre 1981). Also possible is a text that has no discernible peak episode with unusual surface features. In such a case, the episodes may simply be numbered as episode 1, 2, 3,... and the resulting profile would not have a curve but rather be flat. Peak-like features may sometimes be found marking the inciting moment (Hwang 1987: chapter 3).

The Mark Twain passage charted above is much too brief to allow us to do macrosegmentation. It is also not a whole text with unity of its own but a portion taken out of a long novel. We may note, however, that in the passage, two items in the (S-initial) introducer column correspond to major breaks. *In a minute* in S1 relates this passage temporally to, and at the same time sets it apart from, the previous text material, and *But* in S12 divides the passage into two halves as a thesis and an antithesis in a contrast paragraph. *Lord* in S16 is a vocative in quasi-quoted material (the inner speech or thought of the narrator), expressing an intense feeling, and does not serve as a boundary marker.

For our analysis of a whole text into macrosegments, we have chosen an English short story of thirty-two sentences. The story of "Hans" (Gee 1955:106–107) is printed in eight orthographic paragraphs (¶) in the book, as shown in (14).[5]

(14)

¶1   1 The winter afternoon was dark and grey over old Strasbourg. 2 Little flurries of snow came whirling down between the chimneys and a biting wind blew in the narrow streets. 3 Above the roofs, rising high into the clouds, stood the great cathedral, its stones dim in the gathering gloom, its windows catching the lights within.
¶2   4 Fine people were hurrying up the broad steps—ladies with furs, gentlemen in splendid attire, many of them coming in their carriages. 5 Little Hans watched them. 6 Perished with cold, ragged, an unwanted bit of humanity, he snuggled between

---

[5] Reprinted by permission of the Epworth Press.

two buttresses—a retreat from the wind—and wished *he* dare go into the cathedral where all was warm and bright, and where (as he could dimly hear) the organ was pealing loudly.

¶3 7 Suddenly a little girl left her mother as she came up the steps, ran towards him (all loveliness as she smiled) and thrust a big rosy apple into his hands. 8 "That's for you, little boy," she said.

¶4 9 Then she and her mother went in at the great west door, and Hans stared at the apple. 10 He thought at first he would eat it there and then, but he wanted to keep it for a time, so he held it in his hands, and went timidly to the door of the cathedral. 11 Most of the folk were in, and the service had begun. 12 No one turned him away. 13 He plucked up courage and crept inside, slinking into a pew at the back.

¶5 14 Only vaguely could he understand the service, but it was wonderful. 15 He loved the singing, the colour, the warmth. 16 Then something terrible happened. 17 Before he realized it, dignified men coming down the aisles were taking up the collection, and Hans—poor Hans—had nothing to give. 18 He would have run out had he not been too frightened to move. 19 What was he to do? 20 Others were giving money—he could hear it. 21 He had nothing . . . nothing to give God except his apple, and he could not give *that*. 22 He dare not. 23 What would all the people say? 24 What would the man in the fine clothes say—the one standing on the steps amid all the bright candles at the far end? 25 And wouldn't God be angry, too?

¶6 26 It seemed to Hans as if all eyes were fixed on him when, in an agony of fear, he timidly placed the red apple on the plate. 27 He held his breath, but no one spoke, and the man who took the apple did not frown. 28 He allowed it to remain on the plate with the silver coins. 29 Slowly he walked along the aisle and up the steps to the choir, where he handed the plate to the priest, who blessed the gifts and then reverently placed them on the altar.

¶7 30 And behold, as little Hans watched, the apple changed. 31 It became shining gold—the most precious of all gifts, and well-pleasing in the sight of God.

¶8 32 His joy was boundless.

We summarize the content of each paragraph in our text as follows.

¶1 (S1–3)		Cold winter afternoon in old Strasbourg with the great cathedral
¶2 (S4–6)		Cold and ragged Hans watching people and wishing to go inside the warm cathedral
¶3 (S7–8)		A girl giving an apple to Hans
¶4 (S9–13)		Hans going to the door of the cathedral and creeping inside
¶5 (S14–25)		Hans in agony at the collection time, having nothing but the apple
¶6 (S26–29)		Hans giving the apple and the priest blessing the gifts
¶7 (S30–31)		The apple becoming shining gold, as Hans watched
¶8 (S32)		Hans' joy

The appendix at the end of the chapter displays this story in chart form following our charting method discussed in section 4.1. We propose the macrosegmentation of the text as in table 4.2 and the profile diagram as in figure 4.1.

Table 4.2. Macrosegmentation of "Hans"

SS Slot	NS Schema Slot	Sentences	Content
Stage	Exposition	S1–6	Coldness & Hans outside cathedral
Prepeak Ep	Inciting Incident	S7–13	Girl giving apple to Hans
Peak Ep	Climax	S14–25	Hans in agony at collection time
Postpeak Ep	Denouement	S26–29	Apple given & taken to altar
Closure	Conclusion	S30–32	Apple turning into gold

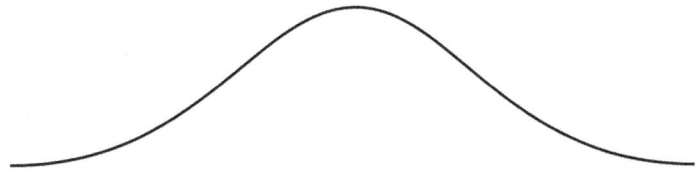

Stage   Prepeak Ep   Peak Ep   Postpeak Ep Closure

Figure 4.1. Profile diagram of "Hans"

Notice the importance of the sentence-initial introducers, which mark the onset of a new discourse-level slot: *Suddenly* in S7 starting the prepeak episode, *Only vaguely* in S14 the peak episode, and *And behold* in S30 the closure. Other introducers may mark the beginning of a subunit within an episode (as in *Above the roofs* in S3, *Then* in S9 and 16, and *Slowly* in S29). In the peak, the question word *What* is fronted three times as required by English grammar rules, and the unusual sentence-initial conjunction *And* in S25 serves a cohesive function of tying this last RHETORICAL QUESTION (not seeking information, unlike normal questions) to the previous three questions with *What*. The fronted position of the question word is nothing unusual for English, but the occurrence of questions—rhetorical questions here—in the stream of narration is a marked feature.

The first two (orthographic) paragraphs in the story set the stage for the story, introducing the city, the cathedral, people going to church, and little Hans watching them and wishing to go inside. While the first one introduces the larger setting with inanimate objects related to the city and the cathedral, the second introduces the participants: fine people dressed up in warm clothes and then Hans in sharp contrast with these people. S6 describes his initial state—*perished with cold, ragged, an unwanted bit of humanity*—along with his wish. Although there are two paragraphs orthographically, they function as one unit at the level of discourse.

The punctiliar adverb *Suddenly* in S7 marks the onset of the eventline beginning the prepeak episode. The little girl gives an apple to Hans in S8 with a short speech, which is the only direct quotation in this text. This portion of the story is given entirely from the girl's perspective.

After the girl and her mother go in (S9a), Sentences 9–13 describe Hans' gradual movement toward the cathedral following them, ending with his creeping inside and slinking into a pew. It seems that ¶3 and ¶4 may group together as the first episode. A continuous sequence of events occur: the girl's action of giving the apple, her going in the door (with her mother), Hans' thinking and creeping inside. This episode depicts the inciting incident in the schematic notional structure.

There are several simple past tense forms in the stage, but they are either stative verbs with inanimate subjects (*came whirling down, blew, stood*) or have a durative sense (*watched, snuggled, wished*). In the prepeak episode, however, we find ten verbs reporting eventline information (*left, ran, thrust, said, went in, thought, wanted, went, plucked up, crept*). There are several more verbs in simple past (such as *came up* in an *as*-clause and the durative verb *stared*), but they are not on the eventline. Perhaps *He plucked up his courage* in S13 is metaphorical for a process meaning 'became courageous', but *crept inside* and *slinking* tell us the little boy's actions.

A preposed adverbial expression *Only vaguely* in S14 marks the beginning of a new episode. S14–15 together present the setting of this episode in which *something terrible* occurs. We hear how he loved the service—his internal feelings of satisfaction. Then the episode continues promisingly as if we will have action sequences with S16 *Then something terrible happened*, which is a FORESHADOWING referring cataphorically to what is to follow. Yet, in the entire episode we find not a single eventline verb. There is also a progressive change in VANTAGE POINT from a third-person perspective (clearly shown by the unique form of reference *Hans—poor Hans*), to *he* with reflective mode (e.g., S19 *What was he to do?*), and to his direct thoughts without any reference to him at all in S23-25 (e.g., S23 *What would all the people say?*). Notice also the shift in tense from past to present and future, and more use of modals: S18 *He would have run out had he not been too frightened to move* and S22 *He dare not* to S23 *What would all the people say?* The last three sentences are sort of PSEUDO-DIALOGUE (talking to oneself). Negatives are also featured in this episode with seven occurrences: *nothing* (3 times), *had he not, could not, he dare not, wouldn't God*. There are only two other negatives in the entire text: *no one* in S12 and S27. Two progressives occur in this episode also (with another one in the stage), perhaps adding the sense of immediacy to the reader—as if it is happening right in front of your eyes. This is not easily achieved with the use of past tense or perfective aspect.

All these features add up to mark this episode as the peak corresponding to notional climax, the highest tension point of the story. The eventline is suspended to describe the inner thoughts of Hans in agony.

In addition, sentences in this section are relatively short and choppy—some with dashes, giving a sense of discontinuity and reflecting a series of agonizing thoughts as they pass through the mind of Hans. While five sentences are combinations of clauses (S17, 18, 20, 21, 24), seven are single-clause sentences (S15, 16, 19, 22, 23, 24, 25), which is a higher ratio of simple structures than in any other section of the story. It is rather an off-norm feature to have a series of simple sentences in narrative discourse. It helps to mark the episode as peak by a shift in sentence length in the episode.[6] These short crisp sentences heighten the boy's dilemma at the offering time. Also note the shortest sentence in the text: S22 *He dare not*.

The postpeak episode shows a dramatic shift in sentence length and complexity. Now the sentences become longer and more complex. The eventline is resumed after the nonevents in the peak episode. The postposed *when*-clause encodes the first event (*placed the red apple on the plate*) after the eventline has been suspended at peak. Then a sequence of events occurs with the usher handing the plate to the priest who blesses the gifts.

The closure (NS conclusion) starts with *And behold* (both words are eye-catching). S31 may be an example of juxtaposition in which *it was* is elided in the second clause: *It became shining gold—[it was] the most precious of all gifts, and well-pleasing in the sight of God*. S32 finishes the text with a short sentence. We have grouped together these three sentences of two short orthographic paragraphs as one discourse unit of closure. Alternatively, however, one could analyze them as two separate units: second postpeak episode (NS final suspense) and closure. Something dramatic happens in S30–31—the apple changed to gold—which might be more than what one would normally consider a closure to a story.

The overall profile structure displays a CHIASTIC structure, shown in figure 4.2 with the content viewed from Hans' perspective. It is noteworthy that the two structures, discourse profile and CHIASMUS, coincide with each other here.[7] The first two sections (stage and prepeak episode) contrast in content with the last two (postpeak and closure) in mirror image. The structure clearly shows the contrasting states of Hans: Cold and ragged at the initial state and joyous at the final state.

---

[6] Only four other simple sentences occur in the story.
[7] In many other cases scholars have shown that the chiastic nature of the content has its own structure apart from the grammatical structure of a passage (Longacre 1992b).

```
Stage          S1–6        Hans cold outside the cathedral
    Prepeak Ep  S7–13       Hans receives an apple and goes inside the
                            service
        Peak Ep     S14–25      Hans in agony in collection time
    Postpeak Ep S26–29      Hans gives the apple which is placed on the
                            altar
Closure         S30–32      Hans joyous when the apple became gold
```

Figure 4.2. Chiastic structure of "Hans"

The chiastic structure could simply be shown as:

```
Hans unhappy
    Hans receives the apple
        Hans in agony
    Hans gives the apple
Hans happy
```

Figure 4.3. Simplified chiastic structure of "Hans"

A note is added about the relation between a discourse-level slot and its filler (see Longacre 1996: chapter 9; Hwang 1989). An episode may be filled by one or more paragraphs. When two or more paragraphs are considered to have a close unity with each other as opposed to surrounding units, they may form an embedded discourse. For example, two sequences of events at one location, in a travelogue covering several places, may be two grammatical paragraphs, each functioning as an episode in the embedded discourse, but may be analyzed best as one episode in the overall text. Conversely, there are one-paragraph texts which, while they are relatively short, may be divided into macrosegments at the discourse level. The stage in a short narrative may simply be filled by one sentence, rather than a paragraph, as may also be the case with the closure at the end.[8]

4.3 Comparative charting as a translation check

One very helpful form of charting is comparative charting of a spontaneous native text against a translation. The important specification here is that the two texts be similar in subject matter. For example, a native text about a hero of the culture (not an animal story) can be compared with a translation of the Joseph narrative of Genesis 29ff. Let both texts be charted and then laid side by side for comparison. The translator who has performed such comparative charting usually is able to detect any tell-tale differences between the two.

---

[8] Thus, discourse-level units may be filled not only by a paragraph (called *primary exponence*) but also by a sentence (level-skipping) and a discourse (recursion), showing a variety of exponence possibilities as the units in other levels of grammatical hierarchy. See Longacre (1996: chapter 9) and Hwang (1989) for further discussions.

Take the case, for example, of the translator who is working in a language characterized by medium to long sentences with marking of same or different subjects from clause to clause indicated in the verb morphology. The translator may immediately perceive that, contrary to the structure of the native text, his translation is characterized by rather short and choppy sentences with frequent introduction of pronouns to track participants. In brief, he may say "My sentences are too short and I've used too many pronouns." Emendation of the translation in the direction of capturing the grammar and discourse style of the target language is then possible.

4.4 Conclusion

In this chapter we have presented a text-charting method based on the constituent structure of grammar, using a two-paragraph passage from a book by Mark Twain. We have discussed macrosegmentation, or chunking analysis, using a short story as retold by H. L. Gee. We have also suggested a method of comparative charting as a translation check.

4.5 Exercises

(1) In analyzing a narrative text in the target language, how would you set up a chart to assist in the analysis? Give the layout of your chart and enter a sentence or two on it.

(2) Try to do a rough macrosegmentation of a target language text. Do you notice any of the episodes marked to be the peak? What are some of the peak marking features that are found?

Appendix 4. Constituent chart of "Hans"[9]

Sample	Meaning
Text	moved (e.g., fronted) text
[Note]	analyst's note
<text>	complement clause
{text}	relative clause
«text»	direct quotation

---

[9] This particular chart was done by Lars Huttar, and the first part of this chart appears in Huttar (2003:79).

S#	Notes	Introducers		Preposed Dependent Clauses				Independent Clauses			Postposed Dependent Clauses			
		S-I	S-M	conj.	S	V	O, etc.	S	V	O, Comp, Others	conj.	S	V	O, etc.
1	stage							The winter afternoon	was	dark and grey over Old Strasbourg.				
2a			and					Little flurries of snow	came whirling down	between the chimneys				
b								a biting wind	blew	in the narrow streets.				
3a	VS order	Above the roofs,			Ø	rising	high into the clouds,	[in O]	stood	the great cathedral,		its stones	Ø	dim in the gathering gloom,
b												its windows	catching	the lights within.
4a								Fine people	were hurrying	up the broad steps				
b										—ladies with furs, gentlemen in splendid attire,		many of them	coming	in their carriages.
5								Little Hans	watched	them.				
6a					Ø	Ø	Perished with cold,							
b					Ø	Ø	ragged,							

Appendix 4. Constituent chart of "Hans"

S#	Notes	Introducers		Preposed Dependent Clauses				Independent Clauses			Postposed Dependent Clauses			
		S-I	S-M	conj.	S	V	O, etc.	S	V	O, Comp, Others	conj.	S	V	O, etc.
c	durative				Ø	Ø		he	snuggled	between two buttresses—a retreat from the wind—				
d			and					Ø	wished					
e								< he	dare go	into the cathedral {where all was warm and bright, and where (as he could dimly hear) the organ was pealing loudly.} >				
7a	punctiliar	Suddenly						a little girl	left	her mother	as	she	came	up the steps,
b			Ø					Ø	ran	towards him (all loveliness as she smiled)				

S#	Notes	S-I	S-M	conj.	S	V	O, etc.	S	V	O, Comp, Others	conj.	S	V	O, etc.
c			and					Ø	thrust	a big rosy apple into his hands.				
8a								«That	's	for you, little boy.»				
b								she	said.					
9a		Then						she and her mother	went in	at the great west door,				
b			and					Hans	stared	at the apple.				
10a								He	thought	at first				
b								<he	would eat	it there and then,>				
c			but					he	wanted					
d			so					<Ø	to keep	it for a time,>				
e								he	held	it in his hands,				
f			and					Ø	went	timidly to the door of the cathedral.				
11a								Most of the folk	were in,					
b			and					the service	had begun.					

Appendix 4. Constituent chart of "Hans"

S#	Notes	Introducers			Preposed Dependent Clauses				Independent Clauses				Postposed Dependent Clauses			
		S-I	S-M	conj.	Before	S	V	O, etc.	S	V	O, Comp, Others	conj.	S	V	O, etc.
12									No one	turned **him** away.	[in V]				
13a									He	plucked up	courage			slinking	into a pew at the back.
b			and						Ø	crept inside,			Ø		
14a	VS order after adv	Only vaguely							[in V]	could **he** understand	the service,				
b			but						it	was	wonderful.				
15									He	loved	the singing, the colour, the warmth.				
16		Then							something terrible	happened.					
17a				Before	he	realized	it,	dignified men {coming down the aisles}	were taking up	the collection,				
b			and						Hans— poor Hans—	had	nothing to give.				
18a	Contra-factual								He	would have run out					
b									[in V]	had **he** not been	too frightened to move.				

S#	Notes	Introducers		Preposed Dependent Clauses				Independent Clauses			Postposed Dependent Clauses			
		S-I	S-M	conj.	S	V	O, etc.	S	V	O, Comp, Others	conj.	S	V	O, etc.
19	Rh.Q	What						[in V]	was **he** to do?					
20a								Others	were giving	money				
b								—he	could hear	it.				
21a								He	had	nothing ... nothing to give God except his apple,				
b			and					he	could not give	that.				
22								He	dare not.					
23	Rh.Q	What						[in V]	would **all the people** say?					
24	Rh.Q	What						[in V]	would **the man in the fine clothes** say	—the one {standing on the steps amid all the bright candles at the far end} ?				
25		And						[in V]	wouldn't **God** be	angry, too?				

Appendix 4. Constituent chart of "Hans"

S#	Notes	Introducers S-I	Introducers S-M	Preposed Dependent Clauses conj.	Preposed Dependent Clauses S	Preposed Dependent Clauses V	Preposed Dependent Clauses O, etc.	Independent Clauses S	Independent Clauses V	Independent Clauses O, Comp, Others	Postposed Dependent Clauses conj.	Postposed Dependent Clauses S	Postposed Dependent Clauses V	Postposed Dependent Clauses O, etc.
26a								It	seemed	to Hans				
b	Adv phr occurs between subord conj and S		<as if					all eyes	were fixed	on him>	when, in an agony of fear,	he	timidly placed	the red apple on the plate.
27a								He	held	his breath,				
b			but					no one	spoke,					
c			and					the man {who took the apple}	did not frown.					
28a								He	allowed					
b								<it	to remain	on the plate with the silver coins.>				
29a		Slowly						he	walked	along the aisle and up the steps to the choir,				
b										{where he handed the plate to the priest,				

S#	Notes	Introducers		Preposed Dependent Clauses				Independent Clauses			Postposed Dependent Clauses			
		S-I	S-M	conj.	S	V	O, etc.	S	V	O, Comp, Others	conj.	S	V	O, etc.
c										{who blessed the gifts and then Ø reverently placed them on the altar.}}				
30		And behold,		as	little Hans	watched,		the apple	changed.					
31								It	became	shining gold— the most precious of all gifts, and well-pleasing in the sight of God.				
32								His joy	was	boundless.				

Chapter 5

How the Listener/Reader Follows a Story

In following a story the listener/reader needs to have some clue or clues that enable him to follow the story. Various explanations, paraphrases, and comments occur in the course of a story, but how are the actual happenings of the story tagged so that they can be recognized for what they are? Commonly, around the world, verbs in clauses that report happenings are identified in some way. Verbs that report happenings may be marked with a simple past tense, a perfective aspect, or a special sequential form. Another option is that these verbs are not marked at all, and that lack of marking which would normally indicate some other explicit discourse function actually indicates happenings that advance the story.

For a language with inflected verbs, some form that is aspectually perfective or temporally presented as completed is selected (Comrie 1976:5; Hopper 1979:215). For a language in which information regarding the tense-aspect-modality of the verb is scattered throughout the clause (as in some African languages), verbs with the appropriate attendant markings are chosen. For some languages, the least marked verb or totally unmarked verb is considered to implicitly carry this function. In a language such as Thai, where there is no system of verbal inflection, a process of elimination identifies clauses that encode such happenings (Burusphat 1991). But, however marked, openly or by default, clauses that refer to happenings that advance the story are distinguished. Paul Ricoeur (1985), building on the work of Harald Weinrich (1964), suggests that marking certain verb forms for the "followability" of a story (and also marking mainlines in other discourse types) is perhaps the primal function of tense/aspect systems in language.

5.1 Salience scheme for English

A chain of clauses that refer to story-advancing happenings can be simply called the *storyline*. The storyline, however identified, may be considered to have a position of privilege in a story. It encodes information of primary importance. Because it exists, the reader/listener can follow the successive happenings of the story. Note the following story for an illustration (Longacre 2006:345–346).

> 1 I *made* my usual trip to the supermarket this past Tuesday. 2 I *parked* the car, *entered* the store, *grabbed* a shopping cart, and *made* my usual passes up and down the various aisles. 3 While meditating on the higher prices of some staple items and picking up a few bargains in the process, I *mounded* the cart high with my purchases. 4 Coming to the checkout counter I was fourth in line with other people having similar orders. 5 Finally, when I got up to the cashier, everything *was tallied* and I *was presented* with the bill. 6 I *reached* into my purse for my wallet—and it wasn't there! 7a My first thought was theft; there must have been a pickpocket in the crowd, 7b but then I soon *realized* that the simple truth was that I had left my wallet on the dresser at home. 8 So there I was, without cash, checkbook or even a credit card. 9 With much chagrin I *confessed* my predicament to the cashier, then *asked* him to keep the shopping cart and its bundled and sacked purchases right there while I went up to see the manager at Customer Service. 10 They were able to put my shopping cart and its purchases aside for me while I went home to get my wallet. 11 I *came back*, *paid* my bill, and finally *got* my stuff out to the car. 12 I never have felt so humiliated and stupid for a long time!

Note first of all that this paragraph qualifies for being a story in that it tells us not simply of an ordinary routine of supermarket shopping but of how the routine was shattered by the narrator's discovery that she had no means to pay for all the groceries and household goods that she had just checked out. At this highpoint of the story the narrator, instead of saying, "I *discovered* that I didn't have my wallet," simply says, *"it wasn't there."* We note in passing that this is one of the ways of marking such a highpoint, namely, by omitting the storyline verb that is implied and reporting baldly what she discovered in that instant. It is similar to a quotation in which the quotation formula is elided.

Sentences prior to this moment-of-discovery sentence report the customary moves of a shopper as storyline (with storyline verbs italicized). Sentence 7 is ANTITHETICAL. Clearly, the second part of the sentence, 7b, is on the storyline by virtue of the simple past tense verb *realized*. But what about 7a? Implicitly, the two parts of S7 are not only in contrast but are marked as constituting a sequence, which could be paraphrased: *First I thought X, then I realized Y*. But, instead of a simple past tense verb *I thought* we find a nominalized form of the verb, *(my first) thought*. Again, the irregular expression of the cognitive event (sudden realization) may be attributed to its being portrayed as climax. So both 7a and 7b can be construed as storyline distorted by climax. S8 is, however, clearly summary and depictive rather than storyline. The reason for assigning this sentence to such summary status has to do with

5.1 Salience scheme for English

the functions of the verb 'be' in most languages, that is, such stative verbs do not report events but are commonly expository or descriptive. In S9 the storyline resumes with the verbs *confessed* and *asked*. In the same sentence, however, a simple past tense occurs in a subordinate temporal clause: *while I went up to see the manager at Customer Service*. Here what could have been a storyline verb *(went up)* is grammatically DEMOTED by its occurrence in an adverbial clause. S10 simply reports as the resulting situation *They were able to*.... It also contains a subordinated clause which demotes what could have been a storyline verb *I went home*.... S11 contains three storyline verbs: *came back, paid,* and *got*. S12 is commentary rather then storyline.

All the above illustrates the clues whereby a reader picks his way through a narrative with recognition of the storyline versus background material. At the same time it illustrates how storyline verbs may be demoted by grammatical subordination, and elided and metamorphosed at a high moment of the story without the hearer/reader losing track of what is going on. The hearer/reader is alerted to the importance of that moment in the story by the omission of a storyline verb or some such device.

The storyline, however, is not the only sort of information conveyed in the story; it is accompanied by other lines of information.

A story may also report background activities or prolonged occurrences that are simultaneous with one or more happenings on the storyline. In English, such concomitant activities are regularly indicated by the progressive *–ing* verbs: *His wife was hanging out the family wash as he left*. A special conjunction such as *meanwhile* can make such simultaneity explicit. A cognitive state may be registered as background: *He knew all the time that something was bothering her*. This is distinct from a cognitive event that is likely to be storyline: *He suddenly realized that something was bothering her*.

One further line of additional information is the flashback. A flashback refers to a happening which is recounted out of chronological order. Thus, a sentence consisting of two storyline clauses may say: *Bill jumped into his car and went downtown*. But this sentence may be followed by *He had already gone downtown twice that morning*. Or the following sentence may be *It had snowed during the night*. While such a flashback may be as brief as those illustrated here, it may be quite lengthy, maybe even amounting to a story embedded in the main story.

A further type of information is descriptive or expository setting information. Here the verb 'be' in English is prominent, and in many languages verbless copulative clauses occur. *John was a Lance Corporal in the Marines. The weather was bitterly cold. Summit County is the highest point in northern Ohio.* Of occasional relevance here are active intransitive verb clauses with inanimate subjects: *The property line extends back 3000 feet. The road gleamed white in the moonlight.* Clearly, all such constructions are the stuff out of which expository discourse is made. While a sentence or two of this nature may be interspersed with other types of information in a story, a passage of greater length can be considered to be an embedded expository paragraph or even an embedded expository discourse.

Three other types of information are found in stories. Sometimes a storyteller goes out of the way to mention what didn't happen. Thus we find sentences such as: *He could have done something to relieve her embarrassment, but he didn't.* Or a sentence *He wanted to help her but couldn't figure out anything to do in the circumstances.* Here all such elements as *didn't, should have, might have,* and the like can be relegated to a category which we can term *irrealis.* Such elements are usually quite marginal to a story, but occasionally may rise to importance, for example, in a disaster story where anticipated help never arrives.

A further type of information can be summarized as evaluation or author COMMENTS. Clearly, such elements as the following can be considered to stand outside the story: *I recall that place on the trail as slippery and treacherous* or *Casey was always making jokes of this sort.*

Still another element that is certainly not part of the basic story-telling function is the use of adverbial clauses, participles, and noun phrases in backreference—which is used as a kind of cohesion or mortar in the text. Thus, we may have a sentence *John took off promptly at 6:00 P. M. in his Piper Cub. Shortly after he took off, he noticed a noise in the engine.* Here the clause *after he took off* contributes no new information to the discourse but serves to relate the following clause to the preceding. Instead of a full clause in backreference, we may have a participial clause, *After taking off* or even a noun phrase *After the takeoff.*

In figure 5.1, these types of information are ranked together in a salience scheme that is relevant to English narrative (see Longacre 1989, 1996).

> Band 1. Storyline: verbs with simple past tense
> > Band 2. Background activities: past progressive -*ing* verbs
> > > Band 3. Flashbacks: *had* verbs
> > > > Band 4. Setting (expository/descriptive): *be* clauses; active verbs with inanimate subjects
> > > > > Band 5. Irrealis: negatives and modals
> > > > > > Band 6. Evaluation or author comments/intrusions
> > > > > > > Band 7. Cohesion: adverbial clauses/participial clauses/noun phrases in back-referential function

Figure 5.1. Salience scheme for English

Typically, a story has a laminated structure, as implied in figure 5.1. While Band 1, the storyline, is the principal and, in fact, the one indispensable element, it is reinforced by other lines of information: Band 2, backgrounded simultaneous activities or ongoing situations; Band 3, flashbacks; and Band 4, bits of exposition and description. Still further removed from the storyline are Band 5, negative and irrealis elements; and Band 6, evaluation or author comments. Finally, there also occur sentence-initial elements in back-referential function in Band 7.

5.1 Salience scheme for English

Languages can employ techniques to change or move information to or from the storyline through promotion or demotion. All elements below Band 1 are normally off the storyline unless PROMOTED to it. Such promotion, for example, can be effected by employing a punctiliar adverb such as *suddenly* with a clause from Bands 2–5. Thus, we encounter such sentences as *Suddenly, he was eating that banana as if his life depended on it* or *Suddenly, he had realized his life-long ambition*. In the former an element of Band 2 is promoted to Band 1, while in the second case an element of Band 3 is promoted to Band 1. Even a clause from Band 4 can be so promoted (*Suddenly, he was in control of the situation again*), and even an element from Band 5 (*Suddenly, he didn't know what to do*).

Furthermore, grammatical subordination may demote from the storyline even clauses with verbs that would normally qualify for that function: *When he arrived home, he sized up the situation.* Here the routine and rather predictable event of arriving at home is grammatically subordinated and removed from the storyline. But languages differ in the use of demotion. While English freely puts many reported events into subordinated adverbial clauses, Biblical Hebrew is likely to retain many of these on the storyline, for example, in the Hebrew equivalent of 'He got up, he went home, he arrived there, he saw the situation.'—where even the quite predictable action of getting up before one goes anywhere is given storyline status. It would be more natural in English to say here something on the order of: 'He decided to go home. When he arrived there, he saw the situation.' In this example, Hebrew has four storyline verbs, whereas English has two storyline verbs and one demoted by grammatical subordination.

But the scheme in figure 5.1 that is valid for English gives little idea of the elaborations that a given language may present. For example, some otherwise routine storyline events may be highlighted as crucial by special morphosyntactic marking in a language. Or primary and secondary storylines may be distinguished with the latter more routine and predictable. For Halbi, Woods (1980) posits three storylines—primary, secondary, and tertiary—all clearly distinguished in the morphology of the verbs. TERTIARY STORYLINES resemble bits of procedural discourse embedded in the ongoing story. Spanish has two past tenses, the preterite and the imperfect. While the imperfect absorbs some of the functions of the past progressive in English, it is the more general backgrounding tense used, for example, in the setting of a story to picture an ongoing situation prior to the first happening which is signaled by the advent of a simple past tense verb. French has the *imparfait* serving a function quite similar to the Spanish imperfect. French has, however, two additional past tenses, the *passé simple* and the *passé composé* distinguished as to formal and literary versus informal style rather than by storyline distinctions.

5.2 Salience scheme in chaining languages

All the above discussion has not taken into account languages of a chaining variety (see chapter 7). Such languages can be of two types: (1) languages which link an indefinite number of medial verbs to a final verb, and (2) languages which link a special initial verb form to an indefinite number of consecutive verb forms. Here, the analyst must proceed carefully in evaluating the various grammatical and lexical factors and possible occurrence of discourse particles. Thus, in MEDIAL-FINAL languages, the question of the relative dominance of the medial versus the final verb inevitably occurs. Is the final verb on the storyline and are all medial verbs off the line? In languages with long narrative chains, it is rather improbable that only the final verb will be on the line. It is much more probable that all the medial verbs, except possibly the first which can be back referential, are on the storyline together with the final verb. In Aguaruna of Peru, a particle *ka* marks some medials as more important than others (Larson 1978). In some languages, however, the final verb may itself be semantically vacuous: 'He did A, did B, did C, did D, and **was there**.' Here the final verb is in process of being grammaticalized to an auxiliary, and may be disregarded as far as reporting a storyline happening.

Likewise, in an INITIAL-CONSECUTIVE structure of the sort found in a number of African languages, we expect the initial verb to be on the storyline whatever the status of the consecutive verbs that follow, and the latter are indeed most plausibly on the line as well (Longacre 1990). But we may encounter a situation where the formally distinct and apparently dominant initial verb is being grammaticalized to an auxiliary. Here, both in respect to medial-final chaining and initial-consecutive chaining, the verb which is most fully inflected and which we would expect to be grammatically dominant may in fact be grammatically an auxiliary verb.

Nevertheless, even in chaining languages storyline schemes can be posited. After all, the listener/reader must be given a clue(s) as to what are the primary sequential happenings of the stories and what material in the text is more marginal. In constructing a salience ranking scheme we are simply trying to make explicit those clues and demonstrate the integrity of the story. Notice the diagram in figure 5.2 by Imanuel Christian (1987:97) for Gujarati, an Indic language with medial-final chaining:

5.2 Salience scheme in chaining languages

1. Primary event line. Punctiliar aspect and compound verbs (-i+y-)
   2. Secondary event line. Punctiliar aspect & non-compound verbs (-y-)
      3. Suppressed event line. Medial verbs with -i
         4. Minor events. Medial verbs with -i+ne
            5. Primary background. Non-punctiliar aspect & compound verb
               6. Secondary background. Progressive and perfective aspects (-t- and -t- + -y-)
                  7. Minor background information (-i and -i+ne)

Figure 5.2. Salience scheme for Gujarati (Indic)

Christian ties the discourse structure of Gujarati narrative closely into its morphosyntactic structure. We present his summary from pp. 97–98:

> It has been shown...that various features of the language, when seen in the light of discourse structure, manifest heightened significance, in that Gujarati narrative discourse utilizes these features to indicate various levels of information in discourse.
>
> The primary event line, or the most pivotal events, in narrative are presented by punctiliar compound verbs. The compound verbs, used as independent final verbs in a sentence, mark suddenness, unexpectedness, and intensity of an event. They present fast progress in the event line; this is where the action takes place and the event line takes off and picks up speed.
>
> The secondary event line in narrative is presented by the uncompounded verbs with completive aspect. The secondary event line slows down the action and adds more detail which builds up the tension in the narrative—a tension that is finally resolved by the fast movement of the narrative when the compound forms appear.
>
> The two different forms of medial verbs present two different levels of information. The medial verbs with the suffix -i present the third level of information, suppressed event line material. Events presented on this level add further detail to the narrative by providing information about what has happened before an event on the primary or secondary event line takes place. The medial verbs with the suffixes -i+ne, on the other hand, present minor events which are very close to being background material, but are not really a part of the background.
>
> Similarly, the background information in the narrative can also be divided into different levels according to the importance of the information in the discourse, and on the basis of the different verb structures. Compound verbs which are not part of the primary event line because they carry durative or stative aspect, present the primary background information. Verbs with progressive and perfective aspects present the secondary background information. Past progressive is used exclusively for background material. It is used in the introduction of participants, in setting the stage for a narrative, and also for supportive material in the main body of a narrative. In some narratives, present progressive also serves a function similar to that of the past progressive. The background information presented by past perfect provides information about the situation previous to the time of the narrative and actions that are out of chronological order. Minor background information is presented by medial verbs. Medial verbs, whose final verb is off the

event line, present background information that is subordinated to the information presented by their final verb.

In table 5.1, we reproduce a salience scheme for Sabaot, a Southern Nilotic language of initial-consecutive chaining structure.

Table 5.1. Salience scheme for Sabaot (Larsen, in Longacre 1990:68)

Bands	Verb/clause forms
1. Peak	Frequent use of indefinite verb forms (passives) Imperfect aspect used on consecutive verb forms
2a. Primary storyline	Consecutive verbs in coordinated clauses
2b. Secondary storyline	Past tense in coordinated clauses Initial subordinated clause ('when') with non-descriptive verb
3. Background activities/states	Imperfect aspect in any clause type Initial subordinated clause ('when') with descriptive verb Non-initial subordinated clause ('as/because') in explanatory function
4. Flashback	Distant Pluperfect (often emphatic) Middle Pluperfect (usually emphatic) Recent Pluperfect (emphatic)
5a. Major setting	Verbless clause (equative) Past tense in coordinated/relative clause with "staging" verbs such as 'be' (existential), 'have', 'be named', locational, or temporal
5b Minor setting	Preposed locational or temporal expressions (word, phrase, or clause)
6. Author comment	+/- exclamation +/- evaluation word/phrase/clause + evaluation content (which may be a proverb in the present tense)
7. Cohesion	Any clause type with back-reference and/or 'like that'

In this table, Larsen nicely summarizes the uses of Sabaot tense/aspect forms in narrative. The primary storyline has verbs which are marked for person but not for tense. The secondary storyline, however, is marked for past tense as well as for person. Larsen characterizes the secondary storyline as events that are either SCRIPT PREDICTABLE or at least not crucial to the main story. Verb forms in the imperfect aspect are found marking backgrounded activities/states. There are three PLUPERFECT verb forms marking flashback to distant, medial, or recent times. A few other niceties round out the summary of narrative structure: (1) The imperfect can occur on consecutive verbs at the peak of a story. (2) The past tense occurs on such verbs as 'be', 'have', 'be named' when they occur in setting. (3) Verbless (equative) clauses also occur in setting. Finally, (4) an author comment, when in the form of a proverb, has a present tense verb.

Note that the peak can be marked by consecutive verbs in imperfect aspect, while regular storyline is marked simply with consecutive verbs, and secondary storyline by both coordinated verbs with the past tense and subordinated verbs. Lower bands are much like English.

5.3 Conclusion

Whether the narrative under study is in English, Gujarati, or Sabaot, the verb morphology of the language is put to work to contribute to the progress of the story, that is, to mark the storyline and attendant bands. The verb morphology does more than orient the reader/hearer temporally and to signal qualitative differences in happenings and activities; it ultimately exists to expedite that very special form of discourse, the narrative. Of course, it also is put to work in other discourse types, but that can be considered to be an adaptation of its function.

The storyline scheme may be helpful in drawing trees of local spans in a given language. Unless some unusual factor intervenes, clauses will dominate in the tree structure according to their placement in such a scheme. Here we can speak of dominant versus ancillary function, and this distinction will help determine tree structure. See chapter 8 for a more detailed discussion of these concerns in drafting such trees.

5.4 Exercises

(1) In a native text in the target language, what clues are found to help the reader/listener follow the storyline of a narrative? Make a quick guess or two to be checked out later.

(2) Can you posit a preliminary salience scheme based on different forms of verb tense and aspect and different types of information?

Chapter 6

Participant Reference: Discourse Operations and Ranking

Participant reference contributes crucially to the cohesion and coherence of a text. A text of any type is about one or more discourse topics. A story may be about a participant involved in events and actions, while an expository text may be about a topic, such as forgiving, love, election, or health. The same entity or concept is not referred to by the same linguistic expression throughout the text. Variable forms are used at different points in the text, for example, a noun phrase with a relative clause, a pronoun, and ellipsis (zero anaphora), although they all refer to the same entity.

Much research has been done on variables in participant reference based on INFORMATION FLOW, some using quantitative methods. Following Staley (2007) and Huang (2000), we may group them into three models. First, the topic continuity or recency model is used by Givón and others with good statistical results showing the iconicity principle: "The more disruptive, surprising, discontinuous or hard to process a topic is, the more coding material must be assigned to it" (Givón 1983:18). Second is the hierarchy or episode model, which finds evidence for heavier coding material across structural boundaries (Hinds and Hinds 1979, Fox 1987, and Tomlin 1987b). Third, the cognitive or memorial-activation model is concerned with cognitive factors such as memory and attention (Prince 1981, Tomlin 1987b, Chafe 1994, and Gundel, Hedberg, and Zacharski 1993). The first two models have to do with the nature of discourse structure, which is both linear and hierarchical. They are closely related to the more fundamental issue of cognition. These three models are not discrete entities but are based on the primary focus of the researchers. In addition, Dooley and Levinsohn (2001) present a model combining two interacting strategies, sequential and VIP (very important participant) strategies, so as to account for default and marked forms of reference. Their method in eight steps is quite practical in cross-linguistic application, making the important distinction between subject and non-subject.

While these methods are insightful to explain overall variable forms, they do not fully consider discourse operations interacting with discourse structure and ranking among participants in discourse. Longacre (1995b) presents discourse operations as one of three variable factors to describe participant references. In this chapter we discuss a variety of discourse operations influencing the choice of referring expressions (see also Hwang 2007). To illustrate them we use naturally occurring textual data found in two short stories in English. Three factors influencing the referential choice—participant reference resources, ranking, and discourse operations—are first discussed in section 6.1, following Longacre (1995b). They are given in a general and universal way, which is to be applied to individual languages. Sections 6.2 and 6.3 present the application of the method to the sample texts. There are issues involving constructions beyond the NP, for example, word order shift in the clause and construction types such as focus-presupposition, topic-comment, and PRESENTATIONAL CONSTRUCTIONS, which are mentioned as applicable to the particular texts.

6.1 Three variable factors

6.1.1 Participant reference resources

Each language has its own inventory of resources to refer to participants. English uses a noun phrase (NP) with varying degrees of qualifying adjectives or relative clauses, a noun, a pronoun, or a zero or null reference. Participant reference resources vary across languages, but we can list the following six general forms, from full NPs to zero/null reference (adapted from Longacre 1995b):

1. Nouns, including proper names, accompanied by qualifiers ranging from (in)definite articles, adjectives, and relative clauses, within the NP or going beyond to separate sentences
2. Nouns without qualifiers (except as a required element, e.g., the definite article in English)
3. SURROGATE NOUNS, such as terms of kinship, social role, and occupation
4. Pronouns and deictics
5. Bound elements (affixes and clitics, e.g., verb agreements for subject and object, possessor affixes on nouns, and switch reference markers on verbs)
6. Zero or null reference

These resources form a scale similar to the topicality scale in Givón (1983), from those for the most discontinuous to those for the most continuous and accessible. The top three points are separated here instead of being just one NP category. Different discourse operations greatly affect the kind and the length of NP employed at a given point in discourse. A language may use resources from different points along this scale. The usage of indefinite versus definite articles versus a bare singular NP presents a problem for insightful explanation in languages like English. In Korean and Japanese the usage of topic versus subject particle is also a difficult choice to make. The functions of these particles overlap with those in the article usage but only to a certain extent.

Pronouns and deictics notoriously vary in their functions in different languages. It is difficult to imagine an English story without pronouns, but it is not uncommon to run into a story in Korean or Japanese with no pronouns (Honda 1989). In these languages, the functional equivalent to pronouns can be either a minimal head noun or zero anaphora.

Bound elements of affixes and clitics apply only to those languages that have agreement or indexing patterns. In English, verb agreement occurs only in third person singular present tense, which is infrequent in stories, since they are typically in past tense. In Greek and Spanish, verb agreement is required whether the subject is explicit or not. Possessor affixes may occur in head-marking languages, for example, 'hat-3sg John' where 'his.hat' is the head of the possession phrase. Switch reference languages mark cataphorically whether the following clause in the chain of the sentence has the same or different subject, usually as suffixes to the verb. Zero anaphora is less common in verb agreement languages, but is frequently found in Korean, Japanese, and Chinese (Pu 1997).

6.1.2 Ranking

Participants may display different patterns of reference depending on their ranking in the story, from major (central and non-central) and minor (restricted or limited role) to props (human or non-human).

6.1.3 Discourse operations affecting participant reference

Ten types of discourse operations that have been found to influence a reference form in languages are listed in figure 6.1 with mnemonic indexing letters. A text or a given language might not use all ten, or more may be added.

F	First mention within a story
I	Integration into the story as central
T	Tracking routinely
R	Restaging or reinstatement
B	Boundary marking episode or sub-episode
C	Confrontation and/or role change
L	Locally contrastive/thematic status
E	Evaluation or comment by the narrator
A	Addressee in dialogue
X	Exit

Figure 6.1. Discourse operations that influence reference form in languages

When a participant is first mentioned (F), the most explicit form of NP tends to be used, with descriptive adjectives or relative clauses. The indefinite article may be used in English, or the expression *a certain* to signal new information. Operation F may call for an NP in subject role in a presentational construction (with a VS order), especially in the case of major participants, or the NP may simply appear in object or other roles for minor participants and props.

In some texts, a participant is integrated (I) as central by repeating the form used for F or using more information than is needed for identification. Right after F, a succeeding sentence may refer to the referent with a full NP with a demonstrative, for example, *this hat seller*.

TRACKING ROUTINELY (T) is an operation that does not call for any special marking, such as continuous, subsequent references to a referent already introduced inside the discourse unit boundary. T is expected to use the form least explicit, such as zero anaphora, an affix, or an unstressed pronoun. When a pronoun is not enough for disambiguation, however, as in the case of the subject switch in English involving same-gender participants, a proper noun or some other stronger form typically used in restaging may occur. The form for T would be commonly used in reporting eventline information.

Restaging (R) and boundary marking (B) may co-occur, since frequently a participant may be restaged in a new episode, but they need not coincide, so we set them up as two types of operations. Confrontation (C) and local contrast (L) may also occur at the same time, or even evaluation (E). At the point of confrontation or climax, often the eventline is suspended and some evaluative comment may occur. In a language like Koine Greek, when countering the previous speaker's point, the addressee (A) in a dialogue exchange may take a special form—an articular pronoun—as subject in the following sentence, instead of only a verb affix (Levinsohn 2000). An exit (X) from the story may be specially marked in some stories, for example, when a noun or NP used at the beginning of the story or episode is repeated at the end.

6.2 "Hans"

We will start with the short story of "Hans" (see chapter 4 for the text). Hans, the central participant of the story, is the only one who is given a name and occurs in all the episodes. He is first mentioned (F) as *Little Hans*, a proper noun with an adjective in S5. Then he is mostly kept track of (T) by a pronoun or zero. Zero anaphora occurs in a non-initial clause of a sentence or in a clause with a NON-FINITE verb such as a participial clause with *-ing*. When he is refocused after the girl gives him an apple, the proper noun *Hans* with no adjective is used in S9. This use is like restaging (R) although he is never offstage. The name *Hans* occurs in S26 after a series of sentences giving his inner thoughts, and it helps mark the episode boundary (B). At the point of highest tension, when Hans has no money at the offering time, he is appropriately referred to as *Hans—poor Hans*. This can be attributed to confrontation (C) and/or author evaluation (E). The PREDICATE NOMINAL in S6 (*an unwanted bit of humanity*) along with other descriptions of him (*perished with cold, ragged*) may be considered E as well.

The focus shifts away from Hans again after he places the apple on the offering plate, and the actions of the usher and priest are reported. Then the closing section starts with *And behold* in S30, and *little Hans* is used again (almost like X), forming an INCLUSIO with the identical F. The last sentence has a pronominal reference in *His joy*.

Table 6.1 shows reference forms used for some of the participants and props in *Hans* in relation to discourse operations.

Table 6.1. Matrix of discourse operations and participants for "Hans"

Discourse Operation	Hans	Girl	People	Apple	Cathedral	Priest
First mention (F)	Little Hans	a little girl	Fine people... ladies with furs, gentlemen in splendid attire	a big rosy apple	the great cathedral	the man in the fine clothes...; the one standing
Tracking (T)	he/his/him; Ø (in non-initial clause or with non-finite verb)	she/her; Ø	them	it	its; Ø	
Restaging (R)	Hans; little Hans		(most of) the folk	the apple	the cathedral	the priest
Boundary (B)	Hans; little Hans					
Confrontation/ Local contrast (C/L)	Hans–poor Hans		all the people; others	his apple; *that*; the red apple		
Evaluation (E)	Hans–poor Hans; an unwanted bit of humanity			shining gold–the most precious of all gifts, and well-pleasing in the sight of God		

The girl is first mentioned (F) in the subject role with an indefinite article and adjective, *a little girl,* and the apple similarly but in the object role, *a big rosy apple*. Tracking (T) for both is accomplished through pronouns (*she, it*) along with zero reference, following the same rule used for Hans. The girl exits (X) from the story after her brief role as the agent who gives the apple, but the apple, although an inanimate prop, is significant throughout the plot structure. It is referred to at confrontation (C) as: *his apple* and *that* (the latter printed in italics). For local contrast (L), it is *the red apple* with a color term, apparently in contrast to silver coins on the plate and even to the gold color that it becomes. Typical for props, it occurs in the object role until it restages (R) as *the apple* in S30 as subject. It retains its subject role with the pronoun *it* in the next sentence, with a long evaluative description (E) of what it turns into: *It became shining gold—the most precious of all gifts, and well-pleasing in the sight of God.*

The people are first mentioned as *Fine people...ladies with furs, gentlemen in splendid attire,* and further referred to as a pronoun: *(many of) them* and *their*. They are restaged as *(most of) the folk* and contrasted with Hans locally as *others* and *all the people*, which may be considered confrontation (C) occurring at climax.

The ushers are first mentioned as *dignified men coming down the aisles*, and the particular usher who took the apple as *the man who took the apple*, an NP with a relative clause. Further tracking of him is by the pronoun *he* three times as subject. The priest is introduced (F) with a definite article as one who is accessible in the framework of the service in a cathedral: *the man in the fine clothes...the one standing on the steps amid all the bright candles at the far end*. Later he is restaged as *the priest*. Not being a continuous topic, he is never referred to by a pronoun but as *the priest* with a long relative clause.

The cathedral is introduced as *the great cathedral* with a definite article, the most imposing church in the city of Strasbourg. This first mention occurs in a sentence very unusual in its syntactic structure. The adverb phrase *Above the roofs* in S3 is fronted, and then the preposed participial clause occurs with zero reference (Ø *rising high into the clouds*). The main clause is in a VS word order (*stood the great cathedral*), and is followed by two postposed clauses providing further description (*its stones dim in the gathering gloom, its windows catching the lights within*). The inverted order is not unusual after a sentence-initial adverb phrase, as is also seen in S14. But we should still ask the question why the adverb is fronted triggering the VS order, that is, why not *The great cathedral stood rising high into the clouds above the roofs...*? The sentence that introduces the cathedral links the descriptions of the city and its bleak circumstances (S1–2) and the people going to church (S4). Fronting the phrase *Above the roofs* ties the sentence more closely with S2, which describes the city with *the chimneys* and *the narrow streets*. This sentence is a presentational construction without being the typical *there was* type, but still in a VS order. Tracking of the cathedral within the immediate context is done by the usual pronominal reference (*its*), as shown in the two postposed clauses in the same sentence. Further reference in non-continuous sentences is made as a noun with only the definite article *the cathedral*.

6.3 "The Three Little Pigs"

The story[1] starts with *Once upon a time there was a mother pig who had three little pigs*, a very common formulaic aperture in stories of this kind. The mother is introduced first with an indefinite article and then the main participants are introduced in a relative clause. The mother pig exits from the story in the next sentence when she (*their mother*) warns of the wolf. The three little pigs act as a group at first, then gradually each little pig is in focus. Reference form variation is similar for the first and second little pigs, who exit from the story midway by being eaten by the wolf.[2]

In the first part of the story about house building, the pattern of reference is similar for all three. A full NP reference as the first/second/third little pig occurs after an episode boundary. The same full NP may be repeated across a sub episode unit (operation B), as in S26 after closing the quotation in S25.

(15) S25 "I shall build a stronger house than yours," said **the third little pig**.
S26 **The third little pig** walked on, along the road by himself.
S27 Soon **he** met a man who was carrying some bricks.

In S26 the third little pig continues on in the subject role (after S25 with a VS order in the quote formula), but still takes a full reference because it occurs at the discourse boundary. Once in the same unit, a pronoun reference is used for tracking (T) when there is no subject switch. When there is a switch within an episode, each of the little pigs is referred to as *the little pig*, without the number designation, since there is no ambiguity.

Once the third little pig is left alone, *the little pig* is used in the last three sub episodes for B as well. Three times, inside an episode, in (16), the phrase is used without the article, treating it more like a name. Earlier, the wolf uses it like a name when he calls out to each little pig in that form, "*Little pig, little pig, let me come in*" in rhythmic repetition.

(16) S100 As **little pig** was going home, **he** saw the wolf coming up the hill.
S101 **Little pig** was very frightened, so **he** jumped inside his butter churn.
S102 The butter churn began to roll over and over, down the hill.
S103 It rolled faster and faster.
S104 It knocked the wolf down.
S105 The wolf did not know what had knocked him down.
S106 He was so frightened that he ran away as quickly as he could.
S107 **Little pig** jumped out of his butter churn and Ø carried it home.

---

[1] Extracts taken from "The Three Little Pigs" by Vera Southgate. Published by Ladybird Books. 1965. Used by kind permission of Ladybird Books.

[2] Due to space limitation, the text and a matrix of discourse operations and participants are not given for this story.

6.3 "The Three Little Pigs"

The occurrence of this phrase without an article where a pronoun might have been sufficient in S101 is particularly intriguing, since the same subject chain continues from the previous sentence. This excessively strong form might be attributed to operation C at peak. This is where the third little pig comes in closest contact with the wolf—a physical contact with the wolf while inside the butter churn—away from his safe brick house.

There are thus variable forms in reference among full NP forms shifting from the beginning of the story to the end, such as those used for the third little pig, which form a chiasmus.

The third little pig	(first individual reference)
The little pig	(inside an episode; when left alone)
Little pig	(C/L at peak)
The little pig	(final sub episode)
The third little pig	(E in last sentence)

Figure 6.2. Variable NP forms in reference create chiasmus in "The Three Little Pigs"

After the form without the article occurs, *the little pig* is used four times, then the last sentence of the story ends with the fullest form: S123 *The third little pig was too clever for him*. This full reference is used for two reasons: for operation E and for closing the story about the three little pigs even though the first two die earlier. One other E occurs earlier in the story (in S68) with the ordinal number, again even after the death of the two. Such global level E calls for the perspective of the whole story.

(17) S67 "Very well," said **the little pig**.
 S68 But **the third little pig** was <u>a clever little pig</u>.
 S69 **He** knew that the wolf just wanted to eat **him**.

A same subject chain within the same sentence uses zero anaphora in non-initial clauses, as in (18), with the exceptions to be discussed below.

(18) S37 The wolf knocked on the door <u>and</u> Ø said, "Little pig, little pig,..."
 S90 He ran all the way home <u>and</u> Ø shut his door quickly.
 S107 Little pig jumped out of his butter churn <u>and</u> Ø carried it home.

The first exception is when there is a shift in the semantic nature of the verbs in the second clause. In the following examples, the first verb describes an internal feeling while the second verb describes an outward behavior or action. Slight local discontinuity is also shown by the kind of conjunction (*but* and *so*, as opposed to *and* above) and the use of a comma marking the two clauses off.

(19) S62/77 The wolf was very angry, <u>but</u> **he** pretended not to be.
     S84   The little pig was very frightened, <u>but</u> **he** pretended not to be.
     S101   Little pig was very frightened, <u>so</u> **he** jumped inside his butter churn.

The second exception occurs in huffing and puffing, both within the quote and narration. This excessive reference of *he* to the wolf in repetition seems to be for a rhythmic pattern. Note also the repetition of *and*, which adds to the rhythm.

(20) S41   "Then I'll huff <u>and</u> I'll puff <u>and</u> I'll blow your house in," said **the wolf**.
     S42   So **he** huffed <u>and</u> **he** puffed <u>and</u> **he** huffed <u>and</u> **he** puffed.
     S43   The house of straw fell down <u>and</u> **the wolf** ate up the first little pig.

The third exception occurs when the word order of the first clause is inverted to VS following a direct quotation, where S identifies the speaker. The unusual order of the subject after the verb apparently creates slight discontinuity in topicality, so a pronoun is used. Notice that *and*, which is a conjunction of continuity, is used, but with a comma signaling minor discontinuity: *"Yes," said the man, <u>and</u> he gave the third little pig some bricks* (S30).

In discussing Mandarin Chinese, Pu (1997) similarly notes local incoherence or minor thematic discontinuity when a pronoun is used over zero anaphora, such as local topic change, after a time or locative phrase, intervening materials, and storyline interruption. In addition, both in English and Mandarin, a pronoun instead of zero anaphora may occur for referential emphasis.

6.4 Summary for English participant reference

We formulate general rules of the English participant reference system based on the patterns found in the two stories. The rules are sensitive to different discourse operations, for example, F and T, and to the ranks of the participants.

<u>First mention</u>: Nouns (including proper names) plus qualifiers, such as the article, adjective, relative clause, and descriptive sentences.

1. Central participant: Adjective + proper name; full NP (with adjective or number)
   Little Hans; the third little pig

2. Major participant: Full NP (with number and adjective)
   the first/second little pig; the wolf

3. Minor participant or prop (singular): Indef. article + adjective/relative clause + generic noun
   a little girl; a big rosy apple; a man who was carrying some straw/ sticks/bricks

4. Prop or location accessible to the reader: Def. article + (adj.) + noun
   the great cathedral

5. Minor participants (plural) in background: Adj./prep phrase/ relative clause + generic noun
   Fine people...ladies with furs, gentlemen in splendid attire...; dignified men coming down the aisles

6. Minor participant (singular) in foregrounded frame who is identifiable in context: Def. article + generic noun + prep phrase/relative clause
   the man in the fine clothes...the one standing on the steps amid all the bright candles at the far end; the man who took the apple

7. Minor participant related to major participant: Genitive pronoun + kin term
   her mother; their mother

Tracking routinely: Pronouns or zero reference
1. Pronouns: within the same discourse unit/episode
2. Zero reference: in non-initial clauses in the sentence (with same subjects and semantically similar verbs) or in participial clauses with *-ing*

Restaging or Boundary marking: Proper name, or noun with a definite article (without qualifiers except for disambiguation)
   Hans, the apple, the folk, the cathedral, the priest, the plate; the first/second/third little pig; the little pig

Confrontation at climax, overlapping in function with Local contrast: Noun with appropriate qualifier (a crucial quality relevant to plot, which is often different from the one used in F), or noun or NP with no article
   Hans—poor Hans; his apple, that, the red apple; all the people, others; little pig

Evaluation: Full NP or clause with evaluative adjective
   Hans—poor Hans; the most precious of all gifts and well-pleasing in the sight of God;
   The third little pig was a clever little pig; the third little pig was too clever for him

In English narrative, different forms of participant reference—zero, pronoun, or NPs of varying lengths and qualities—are well motivated based on discourse operations and the rank of the participant. Ranking of the participant or prop affects most crucially the forms used in first mention: central, major, minor, or prop. Ranking is less important to other operations like restaging and tracking, and general rules for each operation may be set up for all participants. All discourse operations, except tracking, call for the use of the NP in the sample texts. Since the choice among variable NP forms is dependent on the type of operation, it is crucial to include discourse operations in the study of participant reference.

6.5 Conclusion

This chapter has shown that discourse operations and ranking are important considerations governing the use of variable forms in referencing the participants in narrative. A central participant may be introduced by a long NP in the subject role with descriptive information, whereas a minor participant may be introduced in an object role. A minimal or full NP, rather than a pronoun or zero, may be used after a discourse structure boundary even when there is little or no referential distance, as when *the third little pig* was repeated across the sentence boundary, with no subject switch. A referent is restaged by a minimal NP, usually a noun plus the definite article, rather than by a pronoun or a zero. In addition to the methods developed for the study of reference in terms of cognition and discourse structure over the last few decades, it is hoped that the application of discourse operations and ranking can shed further insight, especially in understanding the marked and exceptional cases and the variable NP forms.

6.6 Exercises

(1) In a native text in the target language, how do references to the central and major participants differ from references to non-major participants? Take a quick guess or two to be checked out later.

(2) Do you notice any discourse operations that impact the participant reference forms in the text?

Chapter 7

Clause Combining in Discourse

The clause is the basic grammatical unit of communication, in which NPs and VPs are combined to form propositions, whereas the words and phrases in themselves could only point to entities and concepts. When clauses are combined to form a sentence or a paragraph of two or more sentences, we can express the relationships that are possible at the inter-propositional level, such as temporal succession or OVERLAP, contrast or COUNTER-EXPECTATION.

Such semantic and notional structure relations between propositions are dealt with more in depth in Longacre (1996: chapter 3), and a summary is given in appendix 7A with examples from English. The inter-propositional relations are described in three broad groups: basic, elaborated, and frustration relations. See appendix 7A for a complete list of inter-propositional relations and their examples.

These notional relations are important in the logical and temporal development of discourse, and in a given language some relations may be expressed on the surface structure as a sentence and others as a paragraph, or all may be expressed as either a sentence or a paragraph. When there is a choice between a sentence and a paragraph in a language, we expect discourse conditioning. A variation in surface structure is not without a reason, but for a purpose. It is usually conditioned by discourse context, along with cognitive and socio-cultural contexts. This chapter focuses on the surface structure devices of combining clauses in the sentence and the functions of different devices in discourse, illustrating with textual data from English, Migabac, and Korean. Sentence combining in the paragraph is dealt with in chapter 8.

7.1 Co-ranking and chaining structures

Clauses may be combined in the sentence primarily in two ways in languages: by co-ranking or chaining.[1] Co-ranking structures, such as those in English and many Indo-European languages, combine clauses into a sentence with its NUCLEUS and MARGINS. The nucleus is the most characteristic part and independent of the margin, while the margin may go with a variety of nuclei (Longacre 2007a:373). Both the nucleus and margin may be internally complex with more than one clause (as in *He was sick for a while but he recovered quickly after the doctor made a correct diagnosis and prescribed appropriate medicine.*). The clauses in the nucleus of the sentence are of equal rank in terms of their verb inflections. That is, the verbs of the BASES, which are functional subparts of the nucleus, are fully inflected for tense, aspect, and modality (TAM), hence the term co-ranking. The nucleus may be supported by margins of adverbial clauses (Thompson, Longacre, and Hwang 2007), such as prior time margin (marked in English by *when* or *after*), cause margin (*because*), and conditional margin (*if*). These margins may be marked by subordinating conjunctions, a non-finite form of the verb, or word order. The co-ranking structure of English sentences is described by Longacre (1970, 2007a), and we present summaries of that system in appendices with illustrative examples. Appendix 7B displays the nucleus types, which include a simple sentence with one base, and other types with two or more bases such as coordinate, antithetical, alternative, reason, and result sentences. Appendix 7C shows the margins, for example, prior/concurrent/subsequent time margin, cause or purpose margin, and concessive margin.

Chaining structures, on the other hand, do not normally have verbs of equal rank within a potentially unbounded chain of clauses. In the more common, head-final chaining structures found in verb-final languages of many parts of the world, for example, Papua New Guinea, South America, Korea, Japan, Kazakhstan (Keyes 2001), and India (Dravidian languages), the final clause of the chain has a privileged status of carrying the dominant verb with full inflection. Other verbs of the chain, commonly called the *medial verbs* (or *gerunds, participles,* or *stems*), have deficient marking for one or more grammatical categories of tense, aspect, and modality. These verbs depend on the final verb for TAM. The principle of economy in language is at work here in that the same tense as that of the final verb is assumed in a chain of clauses. Furthermore, many chaining languages make use of SWITCH REFERENCE SYSTEMS, in which an affix of the verb indicates whether the following (or final) clause has the same or different subject as its own. A same subject chain is often indicated by a null affix, again reflecting the principle of economy; there is no marking when the same subject continues and marking only when there is a switch of subject. Longacre (2007a) names such head-final chaining as *medial-final chaining,* and the less common HEAD-INITIAL CHAINING (mostly found in verb-initial languages in Africa) as *initial-consecutive chaining.* (See also Haiman and Munro 1983,

---

[1] The two structures may occur within the same language, or one structure may exclusively characterize the sentence structure of a given language.

Longacre 1983b, and monograph treatments of individual languages in Farr 1999 and Roberts 1987).

7.2 Clause combining devices

In both written and oral texts, clauses may stand alone as a single-clause simple sentence, or combine together to form a two- or multi-clause sentence. We express ourselves by putting together temporally and logically related propositions. There may be several modes of combination available in languages, not just coordination and subordination (see Givón 2001, chapter 18; articles in Haiman and Thompson 1988 and Bybee and Noonan 2002).

We present the following clause combining devices[2] as on a continuum of increasing integration between clauses and describe how they function in discourse (Hwang 2006).

1. Juxtaposition (clauses intonationally joined but with no conjunctions)
2. Coordination (conjoined by conjunctions like *and, but, or, so*)
3. Chaining (functionally coordinate but syntactically dependent in inflections like tense)
4. Subordination (adverbial clauses with conjunctions like *when, if, before*, etc.)
5. Embedding (relative clauses and complement clauses)

Juxtaposition (*He's courageous; he's not fearful*) may group together with coordination; it just lacks an overt conjunction. English uses several clause combining devices within the sentence: coordinate conjunctions (*and, but, or, so*), subordinate conjunctions (*as, because, when*), and detached participial clauses (with the verb in *-ing*). From a cross-linguistic perspective, participial clauses are similar to medial clauses in chaining structures, in that their verbs are not fully inflected for TAM.[3] They seem to have both subordinate and coordinate qualities.[4] They are syntactically dependent, but functionally they are clauses of almost equal rank with the final clause and with loose or vague semantic connection to the independent clause, having no explicit temporal or logical connector (Genetti 2005; Haiman and Thompson 1984 and 1988; Thompson 1987).

Adverbial clauses (**When he came home**, he checked the mailbox), as Matthiessen and Thompson (1988) argue, should not be considered an embedded adverbial adjunct within a main clause. The adverbial clause

---

[2] The expression *clause linkage* is also used to refer to "the range of linguistic devices used to connect clauses" (Mushin 2005:1).
[3] See Genetti (2005) for a discussion of the term *converb* as related to the participial clause and the medial clause in a chaining language. See also Haspelmath (1995) on converb.
[4] Hence the term *cosubordination* in "A Synopsis of Role and Reference Grammar" (Van Valin 1993).

plus the main clause is a clause combination (see also Thompson, Longacre, and Hwang 2007). Complement and relative clauses, however, represent an embedding relationship among clauses. A complement clause (***That Jack missed the plane** is incredible*) is a clause functioning as an argument of another clause, and a relative clause (*...the man **who came from Nebraska***) is a clause within a noun phrase. Thus, prototypical relative and complement clauses are treated differently from adverbial subordination. There are exceptional cases, however, such as nonrestrictive relative clauses, and complement clauses of parenthetical epistemic expressions like *I think*, that are not considered embedding (Bybee 2002, Thompson 2002). While all five devices may be used in English, chaining of clauses with a non-finite, participial form of the verb is limited in frequency (*Walking to the car, thinking about the issue, he realized his mistake*).

We might say that English prefers coordination and subordination, but Oto-Manguean languages of Mesoamerica prefer juxtaposition (Longacre 2007a). A language like Korean, however, may make little use of juxtaposition and coordination, while chaining and subordination are quite common. Other languages like Korafe may use not only chaining structures but also coordination and serialization[5] more commonly than subordination (Farr 1999). Thus, given the task of expressing all the notional structure relations between propositions, each language may have its own preferred devices.

Each discourse may also have different ways of combining clauses on the surface structure. Why are two propositions sometimes presented as two separate sentences, as one coordinate sentence with two main clauses, as a subordinate clause plus the main clause, or as one clause embedded in a complex clause structure? We seek to answer the question from discourse context using an English text in the next section; namely, how discourse conditioning explains selective means of clause combining in the story. Certain sections of discourse may display different patterns of clause combining. Main clauses generally correlate with mainline or foreground information, while adverbial and embedded clauses (4–5 above) correlate with supportive or background information (Labov 1972; Tomlin 1985, 1987a and b). But, as discussed below, an adverbial clause may report foreground information and create a special effect.

7.3 Distribution and functions of clause combining devices in English

We examine the Hans story discussed in chapter 4 to show the distribution of clause combining devices in English across discourse-level units, such as the stage and episodes, and present an analysis of the sentence structures.[6] The stage of the story presents the great cathedral and the central participant,

---

[5] *Serialization* or *serial verb construction* refers to a series of two or more verbs that are highly integrated to function as a unit or which share an argument with no conjunction to separate the verbs (Farr 1999:153; Scancarelli 1992:268).

[6] The text appears in full in chapter 4.2 and its constituent chart is given in appendix 4A.

7.3 Distribution and functions of clause combining devices in English

Hans. The stage is the exposition in the notional structure schema. The prepeak episode reports the notional structure of inciting incident of a little girl giving an apple to Hans and his going into the warm cathedral. The notional climax of tension occurs at the peak episode, where poor Hans has nothing to give at the collection time. Denouement, the untying of the knot, the tension, follows in the postpeak episode, where Hans offers the only thing he has, the apple. The story ends with the closure, the notional conclusion, where the apple turns into shining gold on the offering plate, making Hans joyous. We repeat the discourse structure of the text in table 7.1, with discourse-level slots in surface and notional structures with summary contents.

Table 7.1. Discourse structure of "Hans" with discourse level slots in surface and notional structures with summary contents

SS Slot	NS Slot	Sentences	Content
Stage	Exposition	S1–6	Coldness & Hans outside cathedral
Prepeak Ep	Inciting Incident	S7–13	Girl giving apple to Hans
Peak Ep	Climax	S14–25	Hans agonizing at collection time
Postpeak Ep	Denouement	S26–29	Apple given & taken to altar
Closure	Conclusion	S30–32	Apple turning into gold

The units of discourse may be described on the basis of their unique features of clause combining. Two slots, the prepeak and postpeak, are packed with actions and have longer sentences in coordination. Their sentences encode foreground information for events occurring in sequence, as is expected of narrative material.

But the stage and peak do not include eventline information, and are structured to contrast poor Hans with well-dressed people going to or offering money at church. The stage includes seven participial clauses (in angle brackets) and two nonrestrictive relative clauses (NRRC, in square brackets), which describe the cathedral, the people, and Hans.

(21) S3   Above the roofs, <rising high into the clouds>, stood the great cathedral, <its stones dim in the gathering gloom>, <its windows catching the lights within>.

S4   Fine people were hurrying up the broad steps—ladies with furs, gentlemen in splendid attire, <many of them coming in their carriages>.
S5   Little Hans watched them.
S6   <Perished with cold>, <ragged>, <an unwanted bit of humanity>, he snuggled between two buttresses—a retreat from the wind—and wished he dare go into the cathedral [where all was warm and bright], and [where (as he could dimly hear) the organ was pealing loudly].

In S3, after the sentence-initial adverbial phrase, a preposed participial clause (shown in angle brackets with boldfaced *-ing*) occurs before the main clause in VS order, similar to a presentational construction used in introducing a major participant with *there*. Then two participial clauses follow, with explicit subjects referring to parts of the cathedral, *its stones* and *its windows*. The first one describing the stones is viewed as a participial clause, with the copula *being* omitted before *dim*. The copula in English, being semantically bleached, is frequently omitted when it is not the main verb. This can be seen in the three preposed participial clauses in S6 as well, where *being* does not appear in any of the clauses.

S6 gives a physical description of the boy (in three participial clauses and the first main clause) along with his thoughts in the second main clause in a coordinate structure. The complement clause of the second clause has two nonrestrictive relative clauses, which provide further descriptions of the cathedral as he perceives it.

At peak, after a longer sentence in S21, there is an extremely short sentence (*He dare not*), followed by three more single-clause rhetorical questions in parallel structure. The gradual progression to short, choppy sentences, reflects the climax of tension at the moment. The peak episode is marked to show turbulence in the flow of the narrative by the change in style from clause combining to single-clause sentences. Here seven sentences out of twelve are short single-clause sentences, with the ratio of clause per sentence at 1.5.[7]

The closure includes the significant event of the apple changing into gold. That event takes place without any action on the part of a participant. The three sentences here include only four clauses, giving a very low ratio of clause per sentence of 1.3. Thus, the peak and closure display a low ratio, but the other units—the stage, prepeak, and postpeak—show the ratio of 3.0, 2.7, and 2.25 respectively. The differing patterns of clause combining may be shown for the discourse level units as follows:

---

[7] The number of clauses is not always proportional to the length of the sentence although the two are related.

Table 7.2. Differing patterns of clause combining for discourse level units

Stage	(S1–6)	7 participial clauses, 2 sentences (5 coordinated clauses), 2 NRRC
Prepeak	(S7–13)	6 long sentences (16 coordinated clauses)
Peak	(S14–25)	7 short single-clause sentences
Postpeak	(S26–29)	Back to long sentences, 2 NRRC
Closure	(S30–32)	Shorter sentences with simpler structure

We present functions of the five general devices of clause combining in English, largely based on the Hans story. These devices will serve similar functions in narratives in other languages that use primarily co-ranking structures. A single-clause sentence, although not combining clauses, needs to be discussed in contrast to other devices as to their discourse function. It is a marked form in narration and functions to draw our focus carefully and deliberately on the information that is significant or emotionally involved, for example, *Little Hans watched them* (S5), *Then something terrible happened* (S16), *He dare not* (S22), and a series of rhetorical questions at the climax. The sort of deliberateness can be seen in the famous speech attributed to Julius Caesar, too: *I came. I saw. I conquered.* The more common reporting of events would be to conjoin them in a single sentence.

7.3.1 Juxtaposition

Only one example occurs in our text: *Others were giving money—he could hear it* (S20) after the first rhetorical question showing the inner thought of Hans (*What was he to do?*). The juxtaposed sentence enables giving the content of his thinking first. It is as if the narrator does not want to take time to start with the identification of the person thinking, which would be the usual English order *(He could hear that others were giving money)*. It reflects the exigency of the tension point. Often this type of linkage is used for paraphrases (*He is courageous; he is not afraid*), but it could result from the deletion of a coordinating conjunction. An example from another short story,[8] *We were not afraid; we did not want revenge*, could have *and* instead of a semicolon. Some sentence types, such as those expressing proportions, have two clauses juxtaposed, as in *The longer we prayed, the calmer the children became*, taken from the same text.

7.3.2 Coordination

Coordinated clauses in a sentence are the main workhorse of narrative, reporting eventline information in temporal sequence. More than half of

---

[8] The story is called "When Violence Hits Home," written by Jean Elster and included in "Mixed Messages" (1997), *Cornerstone* 26.111:24–25.

all the clauses in our text (53%) belong to this category. In the prepeak episode, consisting of seven sentences, sixteen of nineteen clauses are of this type, with a series of events occurring in succession. Some examples follow, where braces mark adverbial clauses, and the parentheses are from the text as written.

(22) S7 Suddenly a little girl left her mother {as she came up the steps}, ran towards him (all loveliness as she smiled) **and** thrust a big rosy apple into his hands.
    S9 Then she and her mother went in at the great west door, **and** Hans stared at the apple.
    S10 He thought at first he would eat it there and then, **but** he wanted to keep it for a time, **so** he held it in his hands, **and** went timidly to the door of the cathedral.

Coordinated clauses may be in temporal or logical sequence, or may be a simple listing of propositions. Two related propositions, which are not events, may be coupled together with *and*, or contrasted with *but*, or marked by other specific conjunctions. In S27 in the postpeak episode, three clauses in coordination state what happens—or rather, what does not happen—immediately after Hans puts the apple on the offering plate. Here the conjunction *but* expresses counter-expectation, and the conjunction *and* expresses coupling, as expected.

(23) S27 He held his breath, **but** no one spoke, **and** the man who took the apple did not frown.

The peak episode has three occurrences of *and*, none of which encodes temporal succession. The two occurrences of the sentence-medial *and* (S17 and S21) encode counter-expectation. Thus there is a skewing in having *and* here instead of the usual conjunction *but* to express counter-expectation.

7.3.3 Chaining or participial clauses

Participial clauses[9] do not occur frequently in English and may have a bookish ring as Myhill and Hibiya (1988:363) point out with an example: *Sitting down, taking out a pencil, he began to write.* They commonly share the same subject as the main clause, whether preposed or postposed. When they do not, an explicit subject occurs, as in S3–4 (shown in (21)) where the subject of each of the participial clauses is in a part-whole relationship with the subject of the main clause, namely, the cathedral and *its stones* and *its windows*, and *fine people* and *many of them*. In "Hans," they embellish the main clause

---

[9] Koine Greek in the New Testament at times resorts to strings of participial clauses as a stylistic recourse to make all verbs dependent on one main clause verb. See Healey and Healey (1990) and Longacre (1999a). See also Longacre (1996:44–45) on a long pile-up of participles at the beginning of Matthew 14:19 as a marker of peak.

descriptions of the cathedral and Hans in the stage of the narrative. One other occurrence of postposed participial clause reports an action of Hans in S13.

(24) S13   He plucked up courage and crept inside, <slink**ing** into a pew at the back>.

Participial clauses may have a functional distribution between the preposed and postposed, similar to adverbial clauses. But, unlike adverbial clauses, they do not normally carry overt conjunctions to mark the semantic and rhetorical relations between propositions. Since they leave such relations unmarked and open, they are able to involve the hearer/reader more to infer the appropriate relation. Being closer to the main clause, without the overt subject or verbal inflections, they reflect a closer integration across clauses than adverbial or coordinated clauses.

7.3.4 Adverbial clauses

While adverbial clauses generally report background information, their functions vary depending on their position with respect to the independent clause, whether preposed or postposed, or initial or final (Thompson 1985, Ford 1993, Thompson et al. 2007). Hwang (1994:693–694) compares the functions of adverbial clauses by position as follows: Preposed clauses serve thematic, orienting, and cohesive functions marking the boundary at the discourse level, as well as a back-referencing function within the paragraph, closely tying sentences together. Postposed clauses serve a semantic function, similar to coordination, but giving a greater integration with the main clause at the sentence level.[10] They may also function to create dramatic effect for an unexpected turn of events significant at the discourse level.

There are only four examples in our sample text, too few to make a generalization. The *as*-clause in S7 (*as she came up the steps*) is used to link the girl to Hans, who watches the people going up the steps of the cathedral. The two preposed clauses in S17 and S30 serve a cohesive function of narrating script-predictable information at the given situation. The *as*-clause in S30 (*as little Hans watched*) may help to mark the boundary for the closure, along with the sentence-initial *And behold*. But S26 illustrates the case of dramatic effect.

(25) S26   It seemed to Hans as if all eyes were fixed on him {**when**, in an agony of fear, he timidly placed the red apple on the plate}.

The main clause continues with the thought of Hans following his agonizing series of rhetorical questions.

---

[10] Dooley (personal communication) points out that this functional distinction between preposed and postposed clauses may be expressed in terms of focus in information structure: orientation vs. assertion.

(26) S19 What was he to do?
    S23 What would all the people say?
    S24 What would the man in the fine clothes say—the one standing on the steps amid all the bright candles at the far end?
    S25 And wouldn't God be angry, too?

The main clause in S26 continues the reflective mode used earlier, but then a remarkable postposed adverbial clause with *when* reports perhaps the single most prominent action of the story. Hans puts the apple on the offering plate! This example does not conform to the general observation that adverbial clauses encode background information and main clauses encode foreground information, which has been noted from Labov (1972) to Tomlin (1985, 1987b) and Givón (1987). It illustrates that postposed clauses sometimes have an unusual function of dramatically marking unexpected and surprising foreground information, which tightly integrate with the preceding main clause. The normal coding pattern of foreground information in main clause and background information in subordinate clause is not followed here. Rather, the initial main clause is durative in orientation for setting or background information, and the postposed adverbial clause reports an event.[11] A skewing from the normal coding is always for some effect, here reporting an unexpected turn of event.

Clearly, adverbial clauses have different functions in discourse from other clause combining constructions. In a language like English, where both preposed and postposed clauses occur, a functional distribution may be observed by position in both adverbial and participial clauses.

7.3.5 Relative clauses

Restrictive relative clauses, which help identify the head noun, are cases of embedding of a clause within a noun phrase. They are not clause combining, which involves "clauses whose function can be stated in relation to other clauses" (Matthiessen and Thompson 1988:279). Nonrestrictive relative clauses, providing additional information, however, may represent clause combining in English. The two examples in S6 state background information about the cathedral. Those in S29 report temporally sequential events to that in the main clause, which is possible in languages with postnominal relativization.

(27) S29 Slowly he walked along the aisle and up the steps to the choir, [where he handed the plate to the priest, [who blessed the gifts and then reverently placed them on the altar]].

---

[11] This type of sentence is often found at the beginning of a discourse or episode, as in *The last drops of the thundershower had hardly ceased falling when the Pedestrian stuffed his map into his pocket, settled his pack...* (Lewis 1984:1), and *Day had broken cold and gray, exceedingly cold and gray, when the man turned aside from the main Yukon trail and climbed the high earth bank, where a dim and little-traveled trail led eastward through the fat spruce timberland* (London 1945:9).

They report script-predictable information as to what happens at the offering time at service. In this sentence, they denote events that are routine and less salient than they would have been in a coordinate structure.[12] The events in S29, due to its grammatical subordination of relative clauses, are bundled together in a highly integrated manner. Hwang (1990b, 1994, and 1996) discusses distinct discourse functions of relative clauses in postnominal and prenominal (Korean) systems, for example, the introduction of participants and props in postnominal systems, and abstract themes or teaching in prenominal systems. Cohesive functions and marking minor or displaced events are found to be common in both types.

7.3.6 Complement clauses

Complement clauses that are clause combining occur mostly in conversational data, frequently with *I think* or *I know* (Thompson 2002). Those that occur in our text are the cases of embedding. An exception to this is the case of quotation, both direct and indirect. That is, a sentence with a quote formula and a quote is viewed to consist of two clauses in combination: *"That's for you, little boy," she said* in S8 and *He thought at first he would eat it there and then* in S10. Rather than the quote being embedded as a complement clause, it is best to see them as having two main parts (see Longacre 1996:86–89 and 2007:388 for discussions).[13]

7.4 Distribution and functions of clause combining devices in chaining structures

7.4.1 Migabac chaining

Migabac is a switch reference language from Papua New Guinea. The sentences can be a long chain of clauses that resemble a paragraph structure. McEvoy (2008) describes a short text of ten sentences, of which the last two are long chains. The text in literal translation in (28) below shows one clause per line, and (29) displays the transcribed text with gloss and free translation (McEvoy 2008:80–82). The words in parentheses are added for implicit references to make the English readable. Only the first sentence is a single-clause structure, and the rest range from two to ten clauses per sentence. The longest chain, S9, has nine medial clauses and a final clause.

---

[12] In Koine Greek, continuative relative clauses are a type of nonrestrictive relative clause, which are also used in linking events in chronological sequence in narrative (Levinsohn 2000).
[13] Mattiessen and Thompson (1988:318) also note: "Clauses of reported speech combined with clauses of 'saying' are not treated as embedded clauses by Halliday."

(28) The Cassowary Story in literal translation into English

1. One man, a woman, all his boys, they existed at a jungle house.
2. While they continued to exist,
    another day their father went to the jungle
    & put a vine (trap).[14]
3. He put (it) on a cassowary trail
    & came.
4. While he came & continued to exist[15]
    it became three days
    & their father said like this,
    "Who must go see the vine I put in the jungle?"
5. Their mother said,
    "I go see."
6. After she said (that),
    she went.
7. She went & saw (that)
    a cassowary came & continued to exist on the trail
    & a vine held on its leg.
8. After it (vine) held,
    it (cassowary) cut the vine
    & went down to the base of a very big tree
    & stood.
9. Their mother went & saw (that)
    it stood
    & she threw a knife
    & cut the cassowary on its neck
    & the cassowary threw (its) leg
    & missed their mother
    & broke the very middle of one tree
    & their mother was startled
    & her leg hands shook
    & she stood.
10. After she stood,
    the cassowary died
    & went down rolling & laid in a ditch
    & their mother went
    & said (what happened) to their father
    & they (mother & father) came & carried (the cassowary)
    & went to the house.

---

[14] In this literal translation, '&' is used to separate serial verbs and clauses chained within a sentence. When '&' occurs within a line, it marks a serial verb, and when it occurs on a new line, it marks a clause chain. Tail-head linkage across sentences is indicated by *after* for sequential and *while* or *when* for simultaneous verbal suffixes.

[15] McEvoy analyzes the two verbs *come* and *exist* as forming a serial verb construction within a single clause. Serial verb constructions in Migabac have a shared subject among its verbs and often involve motion or existential verbs. Only the final verb in a serial verb construction receives a switch-reference or tense suffix. They are also found in S7, 9, and 10 in this story.

7.4 Distribution and functions of clause combining devices in chaining structures

(29) The Cassowary Story (*Kesowa siduc*) in Migabac[16]

1. *Ngic monic ngigac madec-foc=ine yenge*
   man one   woman boy-all=his   they

   kate   mac=ka   ga-ibong.
   jungle house=to exist-3P.REM.PAST

   'One man, a woman, all his boys, they existed at a jungle house.'

   FT: A man, his wife, and all his boys were living at their jungle house.

2. *Gac-gu-ebong   wenac monic=ka mamac=ngineng=ti*
   exist-DUR-3P.SIM.DS day   one=at   father=their=SUB

   kate=wa   hike-lu   muc lo-wec.
   jungle=to go-SEQ.SS vine put-3S.REM.PAST

   'While they continued to exist, another day their father went to the jungle & put a vine (trap).'

3. *Kesowa   yefe=ina   lo-lu   kwesi-wec.*
   cassowary trail=on.its   put-SEQ.SS   come-3S.REM.PAST

   'He put (it) on a cassowary trail & came.'

   FT: One day while they lived there, their father went into the jungle in order to set a vine trap. He set it on a cassowary trail and returned to their house.

4. *Kwesi ga-cgu-eme=wa   wenac habackang ai-me*
   come exist-DUR-3S.SIM.DS=at   day   three   become-3S.SEQ.DS

   mamac=ngineng=ti yanguc   mi-wec,
   father=their=SUB like.this say-3S.REM.PAST

   "Ma=di   hike kate=wa   muc   lo-bac   ngani-na?"
   who=SUB   go   jungle=to vine put-1S.NEAR.PAST see-3S.IMP

   'While he came & continued to exist, it became three days & their father said like this, "Who must go see the vine I put in the jungle?"'

5. *Nenggac=ngineng=ti mi-wec   nga, "nani hike ngani-be"*
   mother=their=SUB   say-3S.REM.PAST   and   I.SUB go   see-1S.SEQ.DS

   'Their mother said, "I go see."'

6. *Mi-lu   hike-wec.*
   say-SEQ.SS go-3S.REM.PAST

   'After she said (that), she went.'

---

[16] McEvoy uses a hyphen (-) for affix boundary and = for clitic boundary. Abbreviations used here for the data are listed in the abbreviation list.

FT: After three days passed, their father asked, "Who will go check on the trap that I placed in the jungle?" Their mother replied, "I will go check on it." Then she left.

7. Hike ngani-me   kesowa   yefe=ina   kwesi   ga-cgu-eme
   go   see-3S.SEQ.DS cassowary trail=on.its come   exist-DUR-3S.SIM.DS

   muc=ti   hige=ina   ba-wec.
   vine=SUB   leg=on.its   hold-3S.REM.PAST

   'She went & saw (that) a cassowary came & continued to exist on the trail & a vine held on its leg.'

8. Ba-me   muc   welo-cke-lu
   hold-3S.SEQ.DS   vine cut-3S.O-SEQ.SS

   yoc=towa   sugucne   debang=ina   hau-lu   doma-wec.
   tree=great   big   base=on.its   go.down-SEQ.SS   stand-3S.REM.PAST

   'After it (vine) held, it (cassowary) cut the vine & went down to the base of a very big tree & stood.'

9. Nenggac=ngineng   hike   ngani-me   doma-me
   mother=their   go   see-3S.SEQ.DS   stand-3S.SEQ.DS

   fitec   wicke-lu   kesowa   ube=ina   welo-cke-me
   knife   throw-SEQ.SS   cassowary   neck=on.its   cut-3S.O-3S.SEQ.DS

   kesowa=di   hige   wicke-lu   nenggac=ngineng   lilo-lu
   cassowary=SUB   leg   throw-SEQ.SS   mother=their   miss-SEQ.SS

   yoc   monic   hewac.hewac   kpodu-me   nenggac=ngineng
   tree   one   middle   break-3S.SEQ.DS   mother=their

   kwatacke-lu   hige   mole=ine   teng.teng   kwe-me
   be.startled-SEQ.SS   leg   hand=her   carrying   stab-3S.SEQ.DS

   doma-wec.
   stand-3S.REM.PAST

   'Their mother went & saw (that) it stood & she threw a knife & cut the cassowary on the neck & the cassowary threw (its) leg & missed their mother & broke the very middle of one tree & their mother was-startled & her leg hands shook & she stood.'

FT: She went and saw that a cassowary had come along the trail and got caught in the trap. Then the cassowary had cut the vine and now stood by a large tree. Their mother threw a knife at the cassowary and cut its neck. Then the cassowary kicked at their mother but missed her and broke a tree right in the middle. Their mother jumped and she stood trembling.

10. Doma-me   kesowa   homa-lu   loding.loding   hau
    stand-3S.SEQ.DS cassowary die-SEQ.SS rolling   go.down

    kpie=wa   fa-me   nenggac=ngineng   hike-lu
    ditch=in lie-3S.SEQ.DS   mother=their   go-SEQ.SS

    mamac=ngineng   mi-cno-me   kwesi tengke-lu
    father=their   say-3S.BEN.O-3S.SEQ.DS come   carry-SEQ.SS

    mac=ka   hike-iboc.
    house=to   go-3D.REM.PAST

'After she stood, the cassowary died & went down rolling & laid in a ditch & their mother went & said (what happened) to their father & they (mother & father) came & carried (the cassowary) & went to the house.'

FT: As she stood there, the cassowary died and rolled down and lay in a ditch, so their mother went and told their father what happened. They came and carried the cassowary to their house.

The initial clauses in S2, 4, 6, 8, and 10 provide temporal setting and refer back to the previous sentence in tail-head linkage. Such back-referencing function is commonly assumed by sentence-initial adverbial clauses in a language like English. But in this story from Migabac these initial clauses contain no subordinating conjunction; there is only the verb. The usual switch reference suffix on the verb denotes same (SS) or different subject (DS) and simultaneous (translated as 'while') or sequence (as 'after') relative to the following clause. For example, -me indicates 3S.SEQ.DS, and -lu SEQ.SS. While there are distinct forms for a DS chain according to the person and number of the current, marked clause, the form for an SS chain indicates only the temporal relationship (-lu for sequence and -la for simultaneous). The final clause verb has tense marking, which applies to the previous clauses in the chain, for example, the remote past in -wec for 3S.REM.PAST.

The last two sentences of the story consist of ten and seven clauses respectively, marking a contrast with the earlier sentences, which have one to four clauses. McEvoy attributes this feature of a long chain, as in S9-10, to be one of the peak-marking features, noting that greater detail is used to slow the eventline in longer sentences. He describes other features of peak, such as expressions of emotions or feelings, and repetitions and paraphrases.

7.4.2 Korean chaining

The final clause in the Korean sentence has more grammatical markings for tense, aspect, and modality than the medial clauses, and the language primarily uses a chaining structure in combining clauses. There are many connectives that are suffixed to the medial verbs with a variety of meanings; however there is no switch reference marker, either by itself or in combination with temporal relations, such as sequence and simultaneity, as in many languages in Papua New Guinea (Longacre 2007a). Any correlation between same/different subject and sequence/simultaneity is at best decided on a statistical basis (see H. Kim 1992, Y.-S. Kim 2000).

Here we will simply look at a Korean short story called "The Beauty and the Monk" for variations in the sentence length and clause combining (Hwang 1987 and 1989). Example (30) presents a literal translation in English to reflect the Korean structure. The final clause verbs are in boldface, and the medial clause verbs, translated in English with -*ing* forms, are underlined. The words in parentheses are supplied to make the English rendering readable. The square brackets mark relative clauses, and the angle brackets, complement clauses. The full text in transcription with gloss and free translation appears in (31).

(30) "The Beauty and the Monk" in literal translation into English.

1. Behind the Tonghak Temple in Chungchong Namto Province loftily **stands** the Brother-and-Sister Pagoda now.
2. About this pagoda (there) **is** a legend [bearing romance and horror].
3. A monk <u>keeping</u> the temple alone, **was** earnestly **conducting** the Buddhist masses.
4. One day in the middle of the night, a tiger's roaring sound **was heard** from outside.
5. Since (he was) <u>crying</u> so plaintively and sadly, (the monk) <u>holding</u> a torch, **went out** to see.
6. Sure enough, a big tiger <u>opening</u> his big mouth, <u>roaring</u> as before, **looked** imploringly.
7. The monk <u>knowing</u> <that (he was) not <u>going</u> to harm him>, <u>going</u> close, **looked into** the mouth with the torch.
8. Something long **was stuck** in the throat.
9. <u>Perceiving</u> <that (the tiger was) doing so because of this>, the monk <u>putting</u> his hand into (the throat), **pulled out** the object.
10. The tiger finally <u>stopping</u> crying, <u>wagging</u> the tail as if (he was) thankful, **disappeared**.
11. The thing [pulled out of the throat] **was** a silver hair rod.
12. The monk **thought** <that (it) must have stuck (there) while (he was) catching and eating a woman>.
13. (It) **was** dawn several days after this event took place.
14. From outside, a tiger's roar **was heard** again.
15. The monk <u>wondering</u> <what happened>, **went out** to see.

7.4 Distribution and functions of clause combining devices in chaining structures

16. A big tiger <u>carrying</u> a woman, <u>coming</u>, <u>being crying</u>, and as soon as <u>seeing</u> <the monk coming out>, <u>putting</u> the woman on the ground, **disappeared** slowly.
17. The monk <u>having looked</u> at the woman quickly, but (she) **had already fainted.**
18. <u>Pouring</u> cold water (on the woman), <u>massaging</u> (her), (he) **awakened** the woman again.
19. (She) **was** a beautiful young girl.
20. (She) **was** a precious daughter of a nobleman [who lived in Seoul].
21. The monk **advised** the woman <to go to Seoul immediately>.
22. (It) **is** because (people) at home would be worried <that (she) must have died, being captured and taken by a tiger>.
23. However, the girl **refused** it (= to do so).
24. The fact **is** that (she) wants to spend (her) life together with the monk [who saved her life].
25. The monk **was embarrassed**.
26. (It) **is** because (he) cannot marry (her) as a person [who is practicing asceticism].
27. Therefore, (the monk) <u>taking</u> the girl as a sister, <u>cutting</u> (her) hair, **devoted** to Buddhism together (with her).
28. In order to commemorate this miracle-like meeting of the brother and the sister and their commendable sincerity, people later <u>erecting</u> a pagoda, **called** (it) the Brother-and-Sister Pagoda.

(31) "The Beauty and the Monk" in transcription with glosses[17]

    Minye-wa   *sunim*
    beautiful.woman-and monk

1 *Chwungcheng* *nam-to*   *tonghak-sa*   *twi-ey*
   Chungchong   south-province Tonghak-temple behind-at

   o.nwui   *thap-i*   *cikum-to* *wuttwuk* *se-iss-ta.*
   brother.sister pagoda-NOM now-also   loftily   stand-RESULT-DECL

'Behind the Tonghak Temple in Chungchong Namto Province loftily stands the Brother-and-Sister Pagoda now.'

2 *I*   *thap-ey-nun*   *nangman-kwa* *kongpho-ka* *sely-e.iss-nun*
   this pagoda-at-TOP   romance-and   horror-NOM   bear-RESULT-PR.M

   censel-i   *iss-ta.*
   legend-NOM exist-DECL

'About this pagoda (there) is a legend bearing romance and horror.'

---

[17] A modified Yale-romanization is used for transcription of the Korean data.

3 *Etten   sunim-i   honcase   cel-ul   cikhi-mye*
   certain   monk-NOM   alone   temple-ACC   keep-while

   yelsimhi   pulkong-ul   tuli-ko.iss-ess-ta.
   earnestly Buddhist.mass-ACC   hold-PROG-PAST-DECL

   'A monk keeping the temple alone, was earnestly conducting the Buddhist masses.'

4 *Enu   nal   kiphun   pam   pack-eyse   holangi   wulpucic-nun*
   certain   day   deep   night   outside-at   tiger   roar-PR.M

   soli-ka   tul-ly-ess-ta.
   sound-NOM   hear-PASS-PAST-DECL

   'One day in the middle of the night, a tiger's roaring sound was heard from outside.'

5 *Hato   kwusengci-ko   sulphu-key   wul-kiey*
   very   plaintive-and sad-ly   cry-because

   hwaytpul-ul   tul-ko   naka-po-ass-ta.
   torch-ACC   hold-and   go.out-see-PAST-DECL

   'Since (he was) crying so plaintively and sadly, (the monk) holding a torch, went out to see.'

6 *Kwayen   khun   holangi-ka   ku   khun akali-lul   pelli-ko*
   as.expected big   tiger-NOM   the   big   mouth-ACC   open-and

   yecenhi   wulpucicu-mye   muesinka-lul   aywen.ha-nun   tut   hay-ss-ta.
   as.before   roar-while   something-ACC   implore-PR.M   as.if   do-PAST-DECL

   'Sure enough, a big tiger opening his big mouth, roaring as before, looked imploringly.'

7 *Sunim-un   caki-lul   haychi-ci.an-ulye-nun-cwul   al-ko   kakkai   ka-se*
   monk-TOP   self-ACC   harm-NEG-intend-PR.M-NOMZ   know-and   closely go-and

   hwaytpul-lo   ku   ip-an-ul   tulyeta.po-ass-ta.
   torch-with   the   mouth-inside-ACC   look.into-PAST-DECL

   'The monk knowing that (he was) not going to harm him, going close, looked into the mouth with the torch.'

8 *Mok-ey   muesinka   kitalan   kes-i   kel-ly-e.iss-ess-ta.*
   throat-at   something   long   thing-NOM   stick-PASS-RESULT-PAST-DECL

   'Something long was stuck in the throat.'

7.4 Distribution and functions of clause combining devices in chaining structures

9 *I   kes   ttaymun.ey kule-nun   kes-ilako   cikkam.ha-ko*
   this   thing because   do.so-PR.M fact-QUOT perceive-and

   sunim-un   son-ul   nee-se   ku   kes-ul   ppop-a.cwu-ess-ta.
   monk-TOP   hand-ACC put.into-and   the   thing-ACC pull.out-BENEF-PAST-DECL

   'Perceiving that (the tiger was) doing so because of this, the monk putting his hand into (the throat), pulled out the object.'

10 *Holangi-nun   pilose   wulum-ul   memchwu-ko   kamsa.ha-ta-nun   tusi*
   tiger-TOP   finally   cry-ACC   stop-and   thankful-DECL-PR.M   as.if

   kkoli-lul   hwiceu-mye   salacy-e.pely-ess-ta.
   tail-ACC   wag-while   disappear-COMPLETIVE-PAST-DECL

   'The tiger finally stopping crying, wagging the tail as if (he were) thankful, disappeared.'

11 *Mok-eyse   ppaynay-n   kes-un   un   pinye   y-ess-ta.*
   throat-from pull.out-P.M thing-TOP   silver hair.rod   be-PAST-DECL

   'The thing pulled out of the throat was a silver hair rod.'

12 *Etten   yein-ul   capa-mek-taka   kel-li-n   kes-ilako*
   certain   woman-ACC   catch-eat-while   stick-PASS-P.M   fact-QUOT

   sunim-un   sayngkak.hay-ss-ta.
   monk-TOP   think-PAST-DECL

   'The monk thought that (it) must have stuck (there) while (he) catching and eating a woman.'

13 *I   il-i   iss-un-ci   myechil   hwu-uy   saypyek*
   this   event-NOM   exist-P.M-after   several.days   after-POSS   dawn

   i-ess-ta.
   be-PAST-DECL

   '(It) was dawn several days after this event took place.'

14 *Pakk-eyse   tto   holangi-uy   phohyo-ka   tul-ly-et-ta.*
   outside-from   again   tiger-POSS   roar-NOM   hear-PASS-PAST-DECL

   'From outside, a tiger's roar was heard again.'

15 *Sunim-un   tto   musun   il-i   iss-na-hay-se*
   monk-TOP   again   what   event-NOM   exist-Q-think-so

   naka-po-ass-ta.
   go.out-see-PAST-DECL

   'The monk wondering what happened, went out to see.'

16. *Khun holangi-ka etten yein-ul ep-ko wa-se*
    big tiger-NOM certain woman-ACC carry-and come-and

    wul-ko.iss-taka sunim-i nao-nun kes-ul po-ca ku
    cry-PROG-while monk-NOM come.out-PR.M fact-ACC see-as.soon.as the

    yein-ul ttang-ey naylye.noh-ko-nun esulleng.esulleng
    woman-ACC ground-at put.down-and-TOP (manner of slow walk)

    salacy-e.pely-ess-ta.
    disappear-COMPLETIVE-PAST-DECL

    'A big tiger carrying a woman, coming, being crying, and as soon as seeing the monk coming out, putting the woman on the ground, disappeared slowly.'

17. *Sunim-un kuphi yein-ul po-ass-una imi*
    monk-TOP quickly woman-ACC see-PAST-but already

    kicel.hay-iss-ess-ta.
    faint-RESULT-PAST-DECL

    'The monk having looked at the woman quickly, but (she) had already fainted.'

18. *Chan mul-ul phe.put-ko muncilu-ko hay-se kyewu*
    cold water-ACC pour.down-and rub-and do-so barely

    ku yein-ul tasi kkayena-ke.hay-ss-ta.
    the woman-ACC again wake.up-CAUS-PAST-DECL

    'Pouring cold water (on the woman), massaging (her), (he) awakened the woman again.'

19. *Myolyeng-uy alumtawun chenye y-ess-ta.*
    young.age-POSS beautiful girl be-PAST-DECL

    '(She) was a beautiful young girl.'

20. *Sewul sa-nun mo taykam tayk-uy kwiyewun*
    Seoul live-PR.M certain nobleman house-POSS precious

    ttanim i-ess-ta.
    daughter be-PAST-DECL

    '(She) was a precious daughter of a nobleman who lived in Seoul.'

7.4 Distribution and functions of clause combining devices in chaining structures

21 *Sunim-un yein-eykey kot sangkyeng.ha-tolok*
monk-TOP woman-to immediately go.to.Seoul-to

kwenko.hay-ss-ta.
advise-PAST-DECL

'The monk advised the woman to go to Seoul immediately.'

22 *Cip-eyse-nun holangi-eykey cap-hye-ka-se cwuk-ess-ulila-ko*
home-at-TOP tiger-by catch-PASS-go-so die-PAST-PRESUM-QUOT

kekceng.ha-ko.iss-kess-ki ttaymun i-ta.
worry-PROG-PRESUM-NOMZ reason be-DECL

'(It) is because (people) at home would be worried that (she) must have died, being captured and taken by a tiger.'

23 *Kulena i chenye-nun i-lul kecel.hay-ss-ta.*
but this girl-TOP this-ACC refuse-PAST-DECL

'However, the girl refused it (=to do so).'

24 *Caki-uy sayngmyeng-ul kwuhay-cwu-si-n sunim-kwa*
self-POSS life-ACC save-BENEF-HONOR-P.M monk-with

phyengsayng-ul hamkkey cinay-ya-kess-ta-nun
lifetime-ACC together spend-OBLIGATORY-VOLITIONAL-DECL-PR.M

kes i-ta.
fact be-DECL

'The fact is that (she) wants to spend (her) life together with the monk who saved her life.'

25 *Sunim-un tanghwang.hay-ss-ta.*
monk-TOP be.embarrassed-PAST-DECL

'The monk was embarrassed.'

26 *Swuto.ha-nun mom-ulo kyelhon.hal.sswu-ka*
practice.aeceticism-PR.M body-as way.to.marry-NOM

ep-ki ttaymun i-ta.
not.exist-NOMZ reason be-DECL

'(It) is because (he) cannot marry (her) as a person who is practicing asceticism.'

27 Kulihaye ku   chenye-lul nwui-lo   sam-ko   meli-lul
    therefore the   girl-ACC   sister-as set.up-and   hair-ACC

    kkakk-a.cwu-ko   hamkkey   pulto-ey   cengcin.ha-yess-ta.
    cut-BENEF-and   together Buddhism-to   devote-PAST-DECL

'Therefore, (the monk) taking the girl as a sister, cutting (her) hair, devoted to Buddhism together (with her).'

28 Twis   salam-tul-i   i   kicek-kwa.kathun   o.nwui-uy
    later   person-PL-NOM   this   miracle-like   brother.sister-POSS

    sangpong-kwa   ku   kyaluk.han   cengseng-ul   kinyem.ha-ki.wihayse
    meeting-and   the   commendable   sincerity-ACC   commemorate-to

    thap-ul   seyw-e   ilum-ul   o.nwui   thap-ilako
    pagoda-ACC   erect-and   name-ACC   brother.sister   pagoda-QUOT

    hay-ss-ta.
    do-PAST-DECL

'In order to commemorate this miracle-like meeting of the brother and the sister and their commendable sincerity, people later erecting a pagoda, called (it) the Brother-and-Sister Pagoda.'

There is a variation in sentence length in the story: longer sentences in S6-7, S9–10, S16, and S27, and shorter sentences in S23 and S25. The number of clauses per sentence ranges from one to six (or seven in S16 if we count the embedded clause as well). Thus the longest chain is found in S16 with five medial clauses and the final clause. The peak episode occurs in S21–27, where every sentence is a single-clause structure except S27. This sentence has a double function: it serves as the result thesis within the paragraph and also marks the closure of the whole story. There is also an alternation of tense between the past reporting events in S21, 23, and 25 and the present in S22, 24, and 26, providing the reason for each event (see Hwang 1987 and 1989 for details). Nowhere else do we see such a pattern in the story. In contrast to the Migabac story, where the peak episode displays longer sentences in a chain, in this Korean story we find shorter, single-clause sentences at the peak (as in the Hans story in English).

We may assume that the speaker or text producer generally bundles related ideas and events together in the sentence. However, it is the speaker's choice to determine the length of the sentence and to group a certain number of clauses together, even though the choice may be semi-automatic. Such a choice seems to depend on the favored structure of the language, co-ranking or chaining, and the discourse unit like the peak.

Related to the issue of sentence length in chaining constructions is the question about which actions are selected for the heavily inflected final clause. The final clause may carry the main event or closure event in an event sequence (Dooley, personal communication). In examining chaining languages in East and West Africa, Longacre (1990:173–174) observes that, in medial-final chaining, there are three possibilities. In some languages, as in Koorete, the final clauses outweigh the medial in terms of storyline dominance of main events. In other languages, as in Afar, the medial clauses have a higher storyline rank, and the final clauses may be in the process of grammaticalization of becoming auxiliary verbs. More commonly, however, as in most Ethiopian languages, both medial and final clauses are of equal storyline status. This last possibility is likely the case in Migabac and Korean also.[18]

7.5 Conclusions

This chapter has shown how discourse conditioning can explain selective means of clause combining. A language may be characterized as primarily using a co-ranking or chaining structure, and the frequency of clause combining devices may vary greatly. English favors a co-ranking structure and uses coordination and subordination extensively with more limited use of juxtaposition and chaining. Languages that favor chaining structures will resort to chaining as the most frequent clause combining construction, and the verb in the head clause (final or initial, depending on the type) is often the only one that is fully inflected for tense and modality.

In the English story of "Hans," sentences are choppy at the peak episode, reflecting the climax of tension, and several of the sentences are made up of single clauses. The episodes before and after the peak have long sentences with clauses in coordination. The stage contains long sentences as well, but these are due more to participial clauses than to coordinated sentences. The sentences in the closure are shorter and simpler. Each story seems to have a unique pattern—especially at different discourse level slots such as the peak—involving such features as a shift to longer or shorter sentences, or a distinct means of clause combining, or the grounding of information from foreground events to background and setting.

While single-clause sentences reflect a deliberate focus on the proposition, coordinated sentences bundle closely-related propositions together. Participial and adverbial clauses function to mark off subsidiary and cohesive concerns from the main and nuclear propositions. However, such normal coding can be skewed to achieve a dramatic effect of surprise, as in the case of the postposed *when*-clause reporting a significant event. Skillful placement of participial and adverbial clauses is responsive to the flow of information in discourse, showing a functional distribution between preposed and postposed clauses. Nonrestrictive relative clauses may encode temporally and logically subsequent information in languages in which the relative clause normally follows the noun it modifies. Such grammatical subordination may show a demoted status of information, as in script predictable sequences of events.

---

[18] For further discussions of the functions of clause chaining, see Myhill and Hibiya (1988), Mushin (2005), and Genetti (2005).

Languages with chaining structures likewise display discourse conditioning in variations of sentence length and clause combining devices. The peak episode, in particular, shows a shift to longer or shorter sentences from the normal flow of discourse, and a shift from shorter chain to multi-clause chain or from chaining to single-clause sentences.

7.6 Exercises

For all these questions, give appropriate beginning answers to get you thinking.

(1) State in your own words how clauses combine in the target language. Specifically, does the target language display co-ranking or chaining structures or both?

(2) For co-ranking structures, do adverbial clauses precede or follow main clauses? Do some precede and some follow? What kinds of information are in each?

(3) For chaining structures, is the chaining medial-final (head-final) or initial-consecutive (head-initial)?

(4) Is there any switch reference system reflected in the verb morphology?

Appendix 7A. Notional structure combinations of propositions[19]
(Summary from Longacre 1996: chapter 3)

BASIC RELATIONS

1. CONJOINING

1.1. Coupling (NS nontemporal *and* relations)
  Coupling with the same first term
   He's short and he's fat.
  Coupling with different first terms and without reciprocity
   He paints and his wife collects postage stamps.
  Coupling with different first terms and with reciprocity
   She lectures to him, and he listens to her.
  Parallel coupling
   I spit on your coat; I spit on your hat; I spit on your dress.
   The men, women and children talk English.

1.2. Contrast (NS *but* relations; at least two opposed pairs)
  Contrast by negation
   I went downtown but she didn't.
  Contrast by antonyms
   I went downtown but she stayed home.
   I belong to the Establishment during the week but to the Counter-Culture over the weekend.
  Contrast by exception
   Everybody went to sleep except Grandfather.
   Nobody fell asleep except Grandfather.

1.3. Comparison (degree conjoining)
   Bill is bigger than John.
   John loves Mary as much as he loves Sue.
   John loves Mary less than Bill loves Jane.
   Bill is the biggest.

2. ALTERNATION (NS *or* relations)

2.1. Two possible alternatives
  Alternation by negation
   Either he did it or he didn't.

---

[19] Longacre used the term *predications*, which is here changed to *propositions,* following the more common practice in linguistics. While all examples are combinations of propositions at the notional structure, some are single-clause structure on the surface, as shown in the parallel coupling and contrast by exception.

Alternation by antonyms
Is he alive or dead?
Either the man is working or his wife is working.
Are you going to your village by canoe or by plane?

2.2. More than two alternatives
Either John will come, or Mary will come, or Sue will come.
Let's beg, borrow, or steal a watch.
He'll come today, tomorrow, or sometime next week.

3. TEMPORAL

3.1. Temporal Overlap (NS *meanwhile* and *at the same time* relations)
Span-Span
As he walked along he prayed.
Event-Span (and vice versa)
He glanced back as he walked on.
While he was walking, he stumbled.
Event-Event
As I brought my head up, she tossed the knife.

3.2. Temporal Succession (NS *and then* relations)
Span-Span
They played tennis for an hour, then swam for another hour.
Event-Span (and vice versa)
He put the wood on the stove and then sat there for an hour.
It rained all morning but cleared up about noon.
Event-Event
He sat down, took the book, and opened it.
He gave her some water, and she drank it.

4. IMPLICATION (*if...then* logical relations)

4.1. Conditionality
Hypotheticality (unweighted NS *if* relations)
If he comes, I'll go.
If she doesn't go, I won't go either.
Conditionality with universal quantifier
Wherever you go, I'll be thinking of you.
Whomever we sent got lost.
Everyone who goes there gets lost.
Contingency (NS *if* plus temporal reference)
You have to pay before you can occupy the room.
Then I will marry, when I have some money. (Ibaloi)
Proportion (correlative statements)
The bigger they are, the harder they fall.
The harder I work, the less I seem to earn.

4.2. Causation
Efficient cause (NS *because* relations)
You came because your wife made you come.
Final cause (NS *in order to* relations)
You came in order to get a free meal.
Circumstance (NS *in the circumstance that...* relations)
Since he's doing his best, let's leave him alone.

4.3. Contrafactuality
Had he come, I would have gone.
If he hadn't gone, I would have come.

4.4. Warning
We shouldn't let our torches go out, because if we let our torches go out we won't find our way home.

ELABORATED RELATIONS

5. PARAPHRASE

5.1. Equivalence paraphrase
He capitulated immediately; he surrendered on the spot.
I went home; I went to the house.
Shouldn't we call in the law, or notify the police, or get some sort of protection?

5.2. Paraphrase employing negation
Negated antonym paraphrase
It's not black; it's white.
It's white, not black.
Negated higher gradient paraphrase
It's not hot, but it's warm.
He's a good man, but he's no paragon of virtue.
Negated extremes paraphrase
It's neither hot nor cold; it's just warm.

5.3. Generic-specific paraphrase
He cooked it, he fried it in vegetable oil.

5.4. Amplification paraphrase
He sang; he sang two songs.

5.5. Specific-generic paraphrase
They dug up Assyrian ruins; they did some excavation.

5.6. Contraction paraphrase
I won't go to see him; I just won't go.
We'll bury the fish in the ashes, we'll hide (it). (Wik-Munkan, Australia)

5.7. Summary paraphrase
John works at the sawmill; Jim at the repair shop; and Al at the printshop—that's what they're all doing.

6. ILLUSTRATION

6.1. Simile (requires at least one point of similarity)
She is like a rose.
She acts like a baby.

6.2. Exemplification
Choose a good name, e.g., Michael.
Any color will do: either red, white, green, or blue.

7. DEIXIS (any sort of identificational-contrastive pointing)

7.1. Introduction
There was a young man named Amkidit, he lived on the mountain.

7.2. Identification
The Spanish picked him up on their way, and he was the one who showed the way up here. (Ibaloi)
Kimboy went back and got a hammer, and that was what they used. (Ibaloi)

7.3. Other Deixis
There was a man called Peter; he was an electrician.
Peter was an electrician; he worked for Thomas Smothers.

8. ATTRIBUTION

8.1. Speech attribution (quotations) (speaker-spoken relation)
"Yesterday," he said, "I saw her at the fair."
He says that he saw her at the fair yesterday.
He thought, "I've seen her somewhere before."

8.2. Awareness attribution (knowledge) (knower-known relation)
I know that he's coming.
I saw that he was in a bad mood.

Appendix 7A. Notional structure combinations of propositions 121

FRUSTRATION RELATIONS

9. FRUSTRATION (involves a normal expectation as a presupposition and four possible elements: a proposition, blocking circumstance, reverse of the expectation, and a surrogate that occurs instead)

9.1. Frustrated coupling (frame)
> *She's fat but she's not sloppy.*

9.2. Frustrated succession (script)
> *They started out for Paris, but someone slipped a time bomb into their car and/so they never arrived.*

9.3. Frustrated overlap
> *He drives down crowded streets, but doesn't look out for pedestrians.*
> *He drives down crowded streets, but doesn't look out for pedestrians, so he struck a child the other day.*

9.4. Frustrated hypothesis
> *Even if she comes, I'm not going to go with her.*

9.5. Frustrated contingency
> *Even when I have the Money, I'm not going to get married.*

9.6. Frustrated efficient cause
> *He was poisoned but didn't die.*

9.7. Frustrated final cause
> *He came, but didn't get a free meal.*

9.8. Frustrated attribution
> *He SAYS that she is intelligent.*
> *He says that she is intelligent, but she really isn't.*
> *I thought that you were quite wrong, but you weren't.*

9.9. Frustrated Modality (frustrated inertial guidance systems)
Frustrated intent
> *I intended to go, but some friends dropped in, so I didn't.*
Frustrated obligation
> *I should have gone, but I didn't.*
Frustrated facility (ability)
> *I could have promoted him, but I didn't.*

Appendix 7B. English sentence types by nuclei

Except for the simple sentence, Longacre (1970:795) has the following fifteen sentence types in five groups, three in each group in a matrix: juxtaposition, concatenation, explanation, implication, and quotation.

0. Simple S(=Sentence) One clause in nucleus (± margins)

JUXTAPOSITION

1. Paraphrase S
   It's the most beautiful place on the island; it's a veritable paradise.

2. Recapitulation S (with repetition of the verb)
   I went home; I went home to see what was really going on.

3. Echo Question S[20] (with repetition of subject and auxiliary verb)
   You won't go downtown alone, will you?
   You'll go right now, won't you?

CONCATENATION

4. Coordinate S *...and...* (indefinite number of bases)
   I went over to Gaul, saw the situation there, and conquered it for Rome.
   I came, I saw, I conquered.

5. Antithetical S *but/yet/only...* (two bases: thesis and antithesis)
   My horse is black, but yours is white.
   He spoke to her but she didn't reply.

6. Alternative S *(either)...or... / (neither)...nor...* (two or more bases)
   Is he coming or not?
   We must try to better our lot in life, raise our standard of living, or do something to improve ourselves.

EXPLANATION

7. Reason S *..., for...*
   I gave in, for what else could I do?
   What could I do, for there was simply no place to go.

8. Result S *so/ so...that... / too...to (Verb)/ because...therefore*
   The soup was very hot, so we couldn't eat it.
   The soup was too hot to eat.

---

[20] This sentence type is now widely referred to as *tag* questions.

9. **Equational S** *be* (and others)
   The reason he can't go is because he's getting married.
   His main purpose in coming is so that he can confuse the issue.

IMPLICATION

10. **Concessive S**   even if...still... / though...yet... / although...nevertheless...
    Even though things are bad, nevertheless they could get worse.

11. **Contrafactual S**   (contrary-to-fact condition) *if* + past perfect...*(then)*...
    Had he arrived, all would have been well.
    If he had seen the animal on the road, then he would have avoided it.

12. **Correlative S**   as...so... / as many as...so many...
    As Maine goes, so goes the nation.
    The more I run, the healthier I feel.

QUOTATION

13. **Direct Quotation S**
    He said, "I'm going downtown."

14. **Indirect Quotation S** (with adaptation of the Quoted to speaker's viewpoint)
    He said that he would come here today.
    I thought that he would come here today.

15. **Indirect Question S**
    He asked if you were interested.

Appendix 7C. English sentence margins
(from Longacre 1970)

The first five types tend to occur preposed to the nuclei and the last four types postposed.

PREPOSED SENTENCE MARGINS

1. Sentence Topic *as for / even...*
   As for John, his horse died.
   Even my father, he was disturbed by what they were doing in the name of law and order.
   Risk, that is what adds spice to life and makes it worthwhile.

2. Prior Time Margin *when / after...*
   After/when Ed came downstairs, Mary slipped out the front door, went around the house, and came in the back door.

3. Conditional Margin *if...*
   If Ed slept five minutes overtime, his father got cross with him and made things generally unpleasant.

4. Concessive Margin *although / even if...*
   Although Ed never slept more than five minutes overtime, his father got cross with him and made things generally unpleasant.

5. Circumstantial Margin *since / in that...*
   Since (In that) she knew that it would be tolerated, she got very angry; she threw a temper tantrum worthy of a three-year-old child.

POSTPOSED SENTENCE MARGINS

6. Concurrent Time Margin *as / while...*
   Bill went out the back door, as John came in the front door.
   I'll watch while you sleep.
   While Ed was coming downstairs, Mary slipped out the front door, went around the house, and came in the back door.

7. Subsequent Time Margin *until / before / till...*
   Mary stayed until Ed came downstairs.
   Mary left there before Ed came downstairs.

8. Cause Margin *because...*

Because Ed occasionally slept five minutes overtime, his father got cross with him and made things generally unpleasant.

She got very angry; she threw a temper tantrum worthy of a three-year-old child, because she knew that it would be tolerated and might even result in her getting her way again, as in past years.

9. Purpose Margin *(in order) to / in order that / so that...*

In order to keep Ed from sleeping overtime, his father got cross with him and made things generally unpleasant.

She got very angry; she threw a temper tantrum worthy of a three-year-old child, so that she might get her way again, as she had done in past years to the detriment of the whole family.

Chapter 8

Drafting Trees for Discourses and Paragraphs

The purpose of a tree diagram is to graphically display relationships between sections, paragraphs, and sentences within larger discourse wholes. What form shall a tree take? Traditionally, in lower level grammar, trees have been branching diagrams. In this tradition, notice the following diagram of Proverbs 4:10–12, a fragment of hortatory discourse.

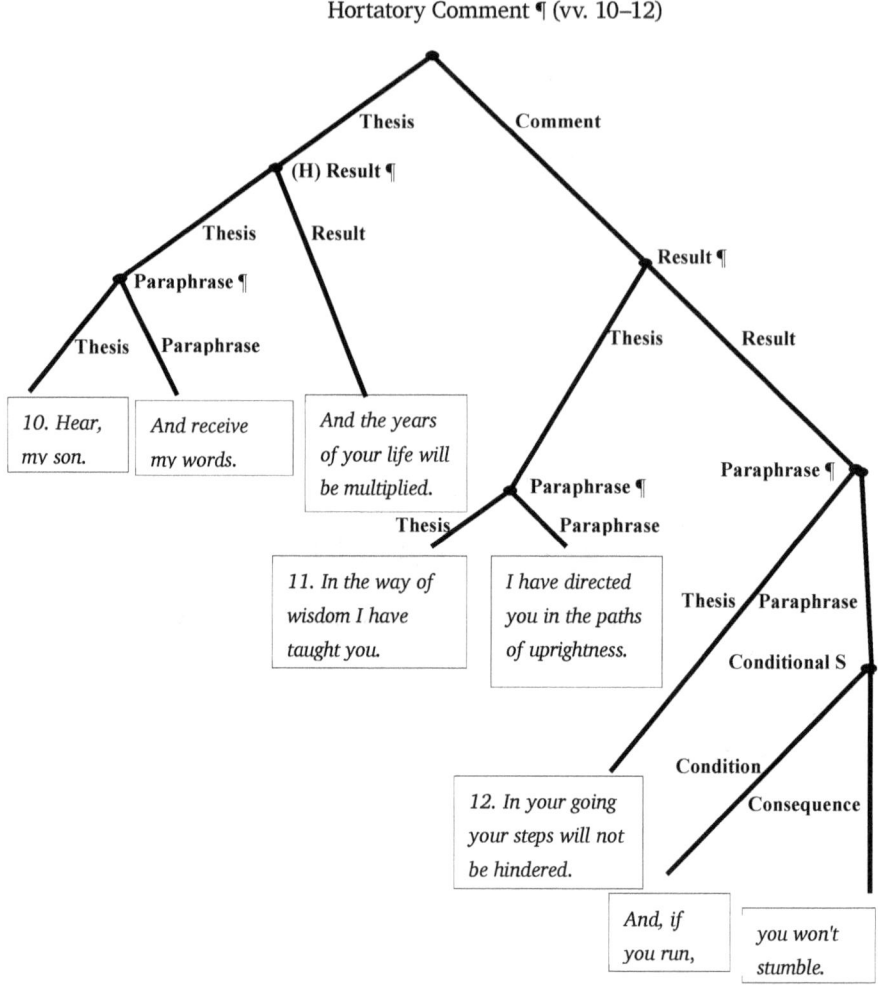

Figure 8.1. Branching tree of Proverbs 4:10–12

Such diagrams are effective as graphic representations but are hard to reproduce in print. It is simpler to rotate the tree ninety degrees toward the right, so now the top of the tree is on the right (see Longacre 1989, Hwang 1989).

Drafting Trees for Discourses and Paragraphs 129

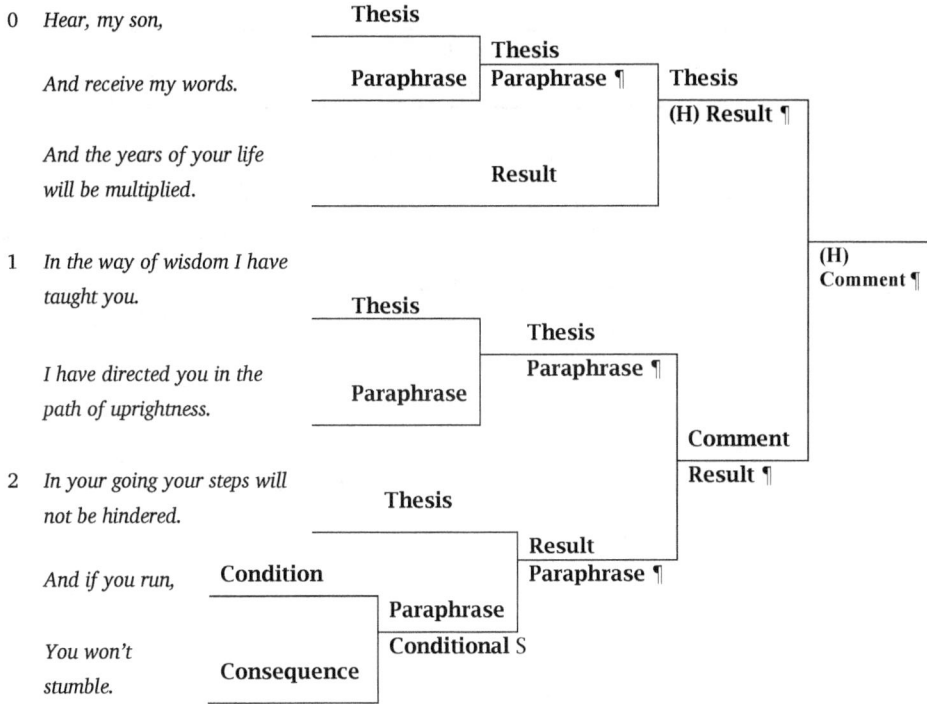

Figure 8.2. Horizontal tree turned to the right

A further type of tree structure using the computer is proposed by Gerald Harkins (2005). This type of diagram is used in Rhetorical Structure Theory (RST) and is adapted by Harkins in figure 8.3 for the same text, Proverbs 4:10–12. This type of tree has the advantage of clearly showing the nuclear element, the thesis, by a straight line, and the supportive elements by arrows.

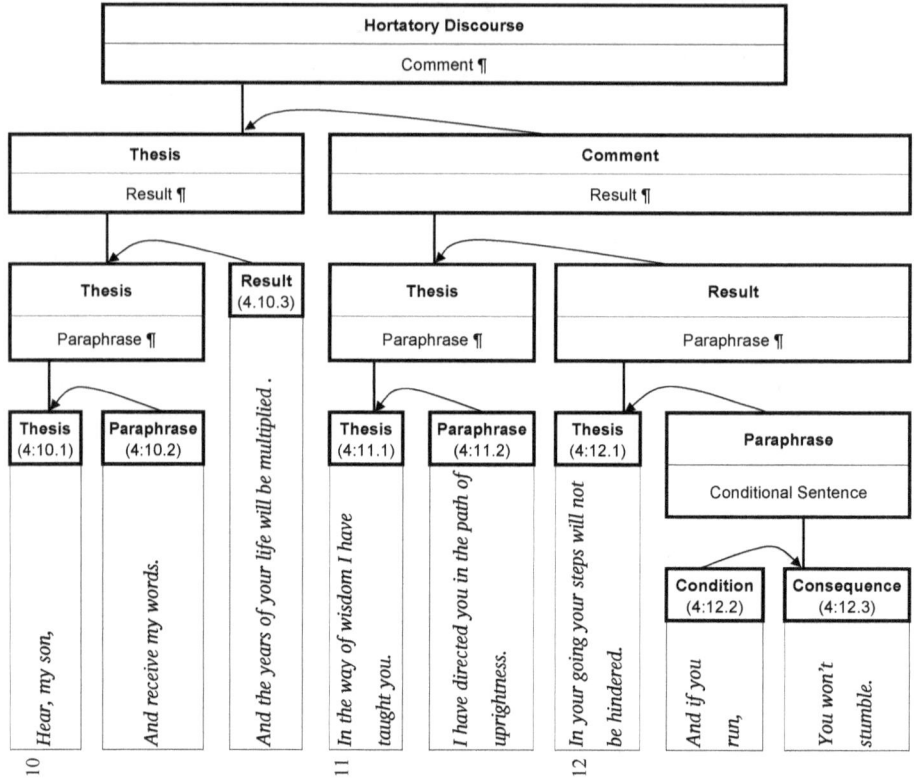

Figure 8.3. Tree with straight lines for theses and arrows for supportive elements

Or we can make the tree into an indentation diagram (figure 8.4), which is even easier to reproduce in print. The top of the tree is now on the left hand margin. Branches are expressed as progressive indentations. Notice in this form the comparative spaciousness of the diagram in which we now include the Hebrew text itself and not simply the English gloss.

(H) Comment ¶
    Thesis: (H) Result ¶
        Thesis: Paraphrase ¶
            Thesis: שְׁמַ֣ע בְּ֭נִי 10
                Hear, my son,
            Paraphrase: וְקַ֣ח אֲמָרָ֑י
                And receive my words.
        Result: וְיִרְבּ֥וּ לְ֝ךָ֗ שְׁנ֣וֹת חַיִּֽים
            And the years of your life will be multiplied.
    Comment: Result ¶
        Thesis: Paraphrase ¶
            Thesis: 11 בְּדֶ֣רֶךְ חָ֭כְמָה הֹרֵיתִ֑יךָ
                In the way of wisdom I have taught you.
            Paraphrase: הִ֝דְרַכְתִּ֗יךָ בְּמַעְגְּלֵי־יֹֽשֶׁר
                I have directed you in the paths of uprightness.
        Result: Paraphrase ¶
            Thesis: 12 בְּ֭לֶכְתְּךָ לֹא־יֵצַ֣ר צַעֲדֶ֑ךָ
                In your going your steps will not be hindered.
            Paraphrase: [Cond. S]
                Condition: וְאִם־תָּ֝ר֗וּץ
                    And, if you run,
                Consequence: לֹ֣א תִכָּשֵֽׁל
                    You won't stumble.

Figure 8.4. Tree as indentation diagram

    The indentation levels apply to the apparatus of the tree. The original language data and its gloss can be given almost anywhere, which proves convenient. But a typographical distinction between the data or gloss and the other elements is often helpful. The main node, which is closest to the left, is labeled *(Hortatory) Comment Paragraph*.[1] In the first indentation we find *Thesis* and *Comment*, which are the two main parts of the passage. But the structure of the thesis is that of a result paragraph, with a further indentation to the right occurring with *Thesis* and *Result*. *Thesis* and *Paraphrase* follow at the third level of indentation corresponding to *Thesis: Paraphrase Paragraph* above. While *Comment: Result Paragraph* is at the first level of indentation, each half (*Thesis* and *Result*) has the structure of a paraphrase paragraph symbolized as *Thesis* and *Paraphrase* at the third level of indentation. Finally,

---

[1] The initial letter of the discourse type in which the paragraph is found is put in parentheses, e.g., (N) for narrative, (P) for procedural, (H) for hortatory, and (E) for expository.

under the last *Paraphrase*, two further units at a fourth level indentation indicate the condition and consequence of the conditional sentence.[2]

The different types of tree diagrams and the indentation diagram introduced here are notational variants of the same analytical result, each with pros and cons depending on the purpose at hand.

A list of possible paragraph types is in appendix 8A, but see Longacre (1996: chapter 4) for discussion with illustrations. In our analysis, we use the label *thesis* for the dominant, nuclear element, which is on the mainline of the discourse type (see also chapter 5 of this book). Supportive elements are labeled according to their relationship to the thesis, reflecting the paragraph type, for example, *reason*, *comment*, and *paraphrase*. Appendix 8B includes dialogue paragraph types (from Longacre 1996: chapter 5), some of which are illustrated in section 8.2.

8.1 Representations of extensive sections including whole discourses

At this point, we need to distinguish discourse elements from elements of the paragraph, and to recognize that trees of whole discourses or extensive portions of such discourses are feasible. Two rather ambitious excerpts of analysis are available as models: the final chapter in *Joseph: A Story of Divine Providence* (second edition), and Longacre's analysis of chapter 3 of Arthur Hailey's novel *The Final Diagnosis*. The former is available both as a printed volume (Longacre 2003a) and electronically. The latter is also available as an article (Longacre 2004) and electronically (Longacre 2003b). We discuss the chapter from Hailey's novel here because it is a complete embedded narrative functioning within the broader framework of the whole novel; it therefore illustrates the approach to analysis of units larger than the paragraph.[3]

Elements proper to analysis on the discourse level include what we might call several discourse schemas or templates. Narratives that are stories, as opposed to simple reports, have a narrative schema: stages, episodes, closure, and finis. Climax and denouement are privileged episodes that correspond to maximum tension and a decisive event that makes resolution of the plot possible. In French, this is put nicely as *nouement* and *denouement*. In hortatory discourse a schema that consists of four elements seems to be adequate: authority (of exhorter), situation, exhortation, and motivation.

The indentation tree in figure 8.5 indicates the main divisions of chapter 3 of *The Final Diagnosis*. This chapter contains the story of Dr. Pearson performing an autopsy. For the most part, in this summary diagram, analysis is not presented below the second level of embedding. The stage of the whole chapter is an embedded narrative discourse, which consists of its own stage

---

[2] In this type of paragraph analysis, we don't normally analyze the sentence-internal structure, but here two parts of the conditional sentence are included to show a further level of indentation.

[3] This extensive citation and quotation from the Hailey novel is by permission of the author and copyright holder, as follows: *The Final Diagnosis* (chapter 3) © 1959 Arthur Hailey. Used by permission.

8.1 Representations of extensive sections including whole discourses 133

and its own six episodes. Dr. Pearson, the central participant, is off-stage in this part of the chapter, but preparations are being made for the autopsy and his coming is foreshadowed.

Episode 1 of the chapter has the structure of a long narrative sequence paragraph that consists of a setting and four sequential theses; it has to do with the entrance of Pearson. Episode 2 is a long compound dialogue paragraph, which records the doctor's preliminary remarks, some of which are directed at the nurses who have come to view the autopsy and some of which are directed at the two resident doctors who are assisting. Episode 3 is an embedded narrative discourse with its own inciting incident and peak; it records the initial incisions of the autopsy. Episode 4 is a narrative comment paragraph. Although its thesis is narrative, its comment contains an embedded expository discourse—down several layers of embedding. This section of the chapter recounts further progress on the autopsy and Dr. Seddons' evaluation of the pathology as he watches the work proceed. The last episode (episode 5) is an embedded narrative discourse. It has two peculiarities: (1) Its first two episodes are simultaneous. (2) Its last episode is the peak episode and recounts the main discovery made in the autopsy.

Stage: Embedded Narrative Discourse (Central participant, Pearson, is off stage but his coming is anticipated)
    Stage: (E) Coordinate ¶
    Episode 1: Embedded Narrrative Discourse (Weidman and the janitor)
    Episode 2: (N) Comment ¶ (Rinne and Weidman)
    Episode 3: Compound Dialogue ¶ (McNeil and Nurse Penfield)
    Episode 4: Resolved Simple Dialogue ¶ (Rinne and McNeil)
    Episode 5: Compound Dialogue ¶ (Seddons and McNeil)
    Episode 6: Embedded Narrative Discourse

Episode 1: (N) Sequence ¶ (Entrance of Pearson)
    Setting: (N) Simple ¶
    Seq. Thesis 1: Quote ¶
    Seq. Thesis 2: Sequence ¶
    Seq. Thesis 3: Sentence
    Seq. Thesis 4: (N) Sequence ¶

Episode 2: Compound Dialogue ¶ (Greetings and preliminary remarks of Pearson)
    Exchange 1: Resolved Simple Dialogue ¶ (with the nurses)
    Exchange 2: Unresolved Stepped Dialogue ¶ (with the nurses; aside to Seddons)
    Exchange 3: Resolved Simple Dialogue ¶ (mainly at Seddons and McNeil)
    Exchange 4: Unresolved Simple Dialogue ¶ (sales pitch to the nurses)

Episode 3: Narrative Discourse (Initial incisions)
    Episode 1 (Inciting incident): Comment ¶
    Episode 2 (Peak): (N) Simultaneous ¶

Episode 4: (N) Comment ¶ (Further progress on the autopsy; Seddons evaluates)
    Thesis: (N) Sequence ¶
    Comment: Cyclic Rhetorical Q-A (N) Comment ¶ (Thesis: (N) Comment ¶, which embeds an Expository Discourse in its Comment)

Episode 5: Narrative Discourse (Pearson finds something unexpected)
    Episode 1: Compound Execution ¶ [or: (N) Sequence ¶]
    Episode 2: (E) Cyclic Reason ¶ (Vivian's reaction—simultaneous with Episode 1)
    Episode 3: Compound Dialogue ¶ (Student nurses ask questions)
    Episode 4 (Peak): Compound Dialogue ¶ (The discovery)

Closure: Narrative Discourse
    Stage: Sentence
    Episode: Compound Dialogue ¶

Finis: Sentence (Pearson leaves in a cloud of cigar smoke)

Figure 8.5. Discourse structure of chapter 3 of *The Final Diagnosis*

Such a tree is typically rather irregular in structure. While the stage, five episodes, closure, and finis are the main units, they are not composed of the same depth of complexities. The stage, episode 3, episode 5, and closure are composed of narrative discourses. Episode 1, episode 2, and episode 4 are composed of paragraph structures. Finis is composed simply of a sentence.

Episode 1, which is considered to be composed of a narrative sequence paragraph with a setting and four sequential theses, could alternatively be analyzed as an embedded narrative discourse with its own stage and four episodes. Although paragraph structures are well established as distinct on a level between discourse and sentence, there is considerable parallelism of structure between discourse and paragraph. As a discourse tree branches, it may branch out into embedded narrative discourses or paragraphs but the former will eventually branch out into paragraphs.

Episode 2, which is a compound dialogue paragraph, is composed of a number of exchanges, which, again, is roughly similar to a narrative discourse where the exchanges of the former resemble the episodes of the latter.

Episode 4 is a narrative comment paragraph which includes, after several layers of embedding, an embedded expository discourse. Dr. Seddons, watching the progress of the autopsy, explains to himself why pathology is not for him. Finally, finis at the end is formed by a single sentence. But the preceding closure is an embedded narrative discourse whose stage is also made up of a single sentence.

What is basic is the branching that finds its way from discourse to paragraph to sentence, whatever recursion may occur here and there. The tree, of course, could be carried out into further details than we have done here. Finer branching would take us into the structure of component clauses and phrases—comparable to the twigs and leaves on a tree. Most of what we need for discourse analysis can be obtained without extending our analysis that far. Clause and phrase level analysis is the typical use of trees in the internal analysis of sentences and is part of a time-honored tradition in grammar. However, sometimes at a high point of a discourse the structure of even clauses and phrases is affected. Here we are reminded that the tree of a discourse is a structured whole from its main trunk or trunks out to its last twig and leaf!

8.2 Representations of paragraph structures

The relations that we find on the paragraph and sentence levels have been well described by various writers with varied nomenclature (e.g., Mann and Thompson 1988 and 1992 for Rhetorical Structure Theory; Callow and Callow 1992 for Semantic Structure Analysis). In this chapter we follow the inventory of such relations as given in Longacre 1996 in chapters 3–5.

(32) (E) Coordinate Paragraphs

Stage: (E) Coordinate ¶
  Introduction: (E) Coordinate ¶
    Thesis 1: In contrast with the heat and activity of the floors above in the white-tiled corridor of the hospital's basement, it was quiet and cool.
    Thesis 2: Nor was the quietness disturbed by a small procession—Nurse Penfield and along side her a stretcher gliding silently on ball bearing casters and propelled by a male orderly wearing rubber-soled shoes below his hospital whites.
  Thesis 1: Rhetorical Q & A (E) Amplification ¶
    Thesis: How many times had she made this journey, Nurse Penfield speculated, glancing down at the shrouded figure on the stretcher.
  Amplification: (E) Amplification ¶
    Thesis: Probably fifty times in the past eleven years.
    Amplification: Perhaps more because it was not something you kept score of—this final journey between the ward and the hospital's morgue, between the territory of the living and the dead.

Thesis 2: (E) Coordinate ¶
    Thesis 1:   A tradition [was] this last walk with a patient who had died, discreetly timed and routed through back corridors of the hospital, then downward in the freight elevator so that the living should take no darkness or depression from death so close at hand.
    Thesis 2:   It was the last service from nurse to her charge an acknowledgement that, though medicine had failed, it would not dismiss the patient summarily; the motions of care, service, healing, would continue for at least a token time beyond the end.

Example (32) illustrates coordination on several levels. In the introduction to the paragraph, Nurse Penfield is presented along with the recently deceased as they make their way to the autopsy lab. In the body of the paragraph, two further theses are coordinated. Both theses are developed as embedded paragraphs. While the first thesis is developed as an amplification paragraph, it is given a rhetorical question-and-answer surface overlay. As the nurse tries to answer her own question, she somewhat deprecates her own answer on the grounds that this activity wasn't something that you kept score of. The second main coordinated thesis of the paragraph itself is a coordinate paragraph that presents this final walk as a tradition. As illustrated here and elsewhere, coordination is basically a default relation. In the absence of a more specific relation, such as temporal relations of sequence or simultaneity, or logical relations such as causality, antithesis, or paraphrase, coordination can be posited as a default structure.

(33) Contrast Paragraphs

    Step Down: (E) Contrast ¶
        Introduction: Elaine Penfield followed the attendant out.
        Thesis: (E) Amplification ¶
            Thesis: Her journey was done, tradition honored, the extra unasked service given.
            Amplification: She had gone the second mile: now her duty lay with the sick, the living.
        Antithesis: (E) Contrast ¶
            Thesis: She had a feeling, though, that Dr. McNeil had come close to suggesting something.
            Antithesis: But there would be another time.

In this example, once we get past the introduction, there is a double antithesis: Nurse Penfield had done her duty but she felt, as she left the room, that Dr. McNeil was on the verge of suggesting something to her (the context tells us that he had a date in mind). But the antithesis itself is a contrast paragraph; nothing had developed but there would be another time.

(34) Alternative Paragraph with an Embedded Example Paragraph

Amplification: (P) Alternative ¶
    Alt. Thesis 1: "Sometimes that permission is unrestricted, as in this case, and then we can examine the entire head and torso."
    Alt. Thesis 2: (P) Exemplification ¶
        Thesis: "At other times we may get only limited permission."
        Example: (P) Reason ¶
            Reason: "For example a family may ask specifically that the cranial contents be undisturbed."
            Thesis: "When that happens in this hospital we respect their wishes."

This example illustrates a relation—and a paragraph type—in which theses are neither coordinated nor contrasted but are presented as logical alternatives. It is part of a speech by Dr. Pearson in which he presents options available to the pathologist: he can have unrestricted permission to conduct an autopsy or restricted permission. The latter alternative is developed with an example paragraph.

(35) (N) Sequence Paragraphs

Episode 1: (N) Sequence ¶ (Entrance of Pearson)
    Setting: (N) Simple ¶
        Setting: There were footsteps coming down the corridor.
        Thesis: Seddons touched her arm and whispered, "We'll talk again—soon."
    Seq. Thesis 1: (N) Quote ¶
        LI/QF: Then the door was flung open and the student nurses moved back respectfully as Dr. Pearson strode inside.
        Quote: He greeted them with a crisp "Good morning."
    Seq. Thesis 2: (N) Sequence ¶
        Seq. Thesis 1: Then, without waiting for the murmured acknowledgments, he strode to a locker, slipped off his white coat and thrust his arms into a gown which he had taken from the shelf.
        Seq. Thesis 2: Pearson gestured to Seddons, who stepped over and tied the gown strings at the back.

Seq. Thesis 3: Then, like a well-drilled team, the two moved over to a washbasin where Seddons shook powder from a can over Pearson's hand, afterward holding out a pair of rubber gloves into which the older man thrust his fingers.
Seq. Thesis 4: (N) Sequence ¶
   Setting: All this had been accomplished in silence.
   Seq. Thesis 1: Now Pearson shifted his cigar slightly and murmured a "Thanks."
   Seq. Thesis 2: (N) Comment ¶
     Thesis: (N) Amplification ¶
       Thesis: He crossed to the table and, taking the clipboard which McNeil held out to him, began to read it, apparently oblivious of everything else.
       Amplification: So far Pearson had not even glanced at the body on the table.
     Comment: (N) Comment ¶
       Thesis: Watching the performance covertly, as he, too, moved across, it occurred to Seddons that it was like the entry of a maestro before a symphony.
       Comment: All that was missing was the applause.

This is an example of a narrative sequence paragraph. Notice the signals of chronological sequence: *Then* in sequential thesis 1, sequential thesis 2, and sequential thesis 3. In sequential thesis 4, where an embedded narrative sequence paragraph occurs, the embedded paragraph's own introduction has the summary remark *All this had been accomplished in silence* with a verb in the pluperfect. But the very next sentence begins with *Now*.

No longer are we confronted with theses that are simply coordinated with each other. Rather, in the above example we find sequential theses arranged in a chronological framework. Sequential thesis 1 is an embedded quote paragraph, in which the first sentence functions as both LEAD-IN and quote formula (LI/QF). Amplification and comment paragraphs occur towards the end of this sequence paragraph; they are discussed further on in this chapter.

(36) (N) Simultaneous Paragraphs

Seq. Thesis 1: (N) Simultaneous ¶
   Thesis: Next, using the sharp levered rib cutters, he cut his way into the rib cage, exposing pericardium and lungs.
   Simultaneous: The gloves, instruments, and table were now beginning to be covered with blood.

Seq. Thesis 2: (N) Simultaneous ¶
    Setting: Seddons, gloved also, on his side of the table was cutting back the lower flaps and flesh and opening the abdomen.
    Thesis: He crossed the room for a pail and began to remove the stomach and intestines, which he put into the pail after studying them briefly.
    Simultaneous: The odor was beginning to be noticeable.

This example is from a narrative sequence paragraph. But each of the events reported in sequence is a sequential thesis, which is structured as a simultaneous paragraph. In each sequential thesis the action of the men performing the autopsy is reported as *thesis*, while concomitant circumstances—the spreading blood in sequential thesis 1 and the odor in sequential thesis 2 are reported in *simultaneous*. It is instructive to note the differing verb forms that are used. While simple past tense verbs report the actions in *thesis*, verbs in the past progressive report the concomitant circumstances with the verb *was beginning* in both sentences. This leads us to label these two simultaneous paragraphs *thesis* and *simultaneous*, with the nuclear part, *thesis*, first. It is interesting to note that the setting in the second paragraph also has a verb in the past progressive.

(37) Another (N) Simultaneous Paragraph

Simul. Thesis 1: (N) Simultaneous ¶
  Thesis: (N) Amplification ¶
    Thesis: Using the skill, ease, and speed of long experience, Pearson began the autopsy with a deep "Y" incision.
  Amplification: (N) Sequence ¶
    Seq. Thesis 1: With three strong knife strokes he brought the top two branches of the "Y" from each shoulder of the body to meet near the bottom of the chest.
    Seq. Thesis 2: There from this point he cut downwards, opening the belly all the way from chest to genitals.
  Simultaneous: There was a hissing, almost a tearing sound, as the knife moved and the flesh parted, revealing a layer of yellow fat beneath the surface.

Simul. Thesis 2: (N) Comment ¶
  Thesis: (N) Sequence ¶
    Seq. Thesis 1:   Still watching the student nurses, McNeil saw that two were deathly white, a third had gasped and turned away; the other three were stoically watching.
    Seq. Thesis 2: (N) Contrast ¶
      Thesis: The resident kept his eye on the pale ones; it was not unusual for a nurse to keel over at her first autopsy.
      Antithesis: But these six looked as if they were going to be all right; the color was coming back to the two he had noticed and the other girl had turned back, though with a handkerchief to her mouth.
    Seq. Thesis 3: Simple Dialogue ¶
      IU (Proposal): Quote ¶
        QF: McNeil told them quietly.
      Quote: (H) Reason ¶
        Thesis: "If any of you want to go out for a few minutes, that's all right."
        Reason: "The first time's always a bit hard."
      RU (Response):   They looked at him gratefully, though no one moved.
  Comment: (E) Contrast ¶
    Thesis: McNeil knew that some pathologists would never admit nurses to an autopsy until the first incision has been made.
    Antithesis: (E) Reason ¶
      Thesis: Pearson, though, did not believe in shielding anyone.
      Reason: A nurse had to witness a lot of things that were tough to take—sores, mangled limbs, putrification, surgery; the sooner she learned to accept the sights and smells of medicine, the better for everyone, including herself.

Example (37) differs from (36) in that essentially it presents us with two sequences of actions that are overlapping if not entirely simultaneous; but several layers of paragraph embedding partially obscure the picture. To begin with, simultaneous 1 itself embeds a simultaneous paragraph, whose thesis is an amplification paragraph—and only in the amplification are the actions of Dr. Pearson given in an embedded sequence paragraph. But simultaneous with that series of actions—the initial incisions—some concomitant sensory data are reported, namely, that *there was a hissing, almost a tearing sound* that accompanied the incisions. Then, simultaneous with all the above, the second main half of the paragraph reflects Dr. McNeil's observation of the nurses who are viewing an autopsy for the first time. This in turn embeds contrast paragraphs at two places, develops as dialogue, and ends in a comment, which itself embeds one of the contrast paragraphs. (For the internal structure of the simple dialogue paragraph, see the discussion below for (46) through (48).)

(38) (E) Reason Paragraph

Thesis: From a passage to the right came the hum of machinery.
Reason: Down here were the hospital's mechanical departments—heating plant, hot-water systems, electrical shops, emergency generators.

When the relation expressed in a paragraph is causality, either member of the relationship may emerge as the thesis. If the effect emerges as the thesis, as in the above example, the other member is labeled *reason*. In (38), the intransitive verb *came* in the first sentence is a verb of higher rank than the "be" verb *were* in the second sentence. In keeping with this distribution of verb forms the first sentence is labeled *thesis* and the second is labeled *reason*.

(39) (N) Result Paragraph

Thesis: The family had behaved as well after the death as they had before—solid, emotional but no hysterics.
Result: It had made it easier for Dr. McMahon to ask for permission to autopsy.

Causality is expressed in (39) as well as in (38). But here the first sentence is considered to be of higher rank and labeled *thesis* and the second, *result*.

(40) (Rhetorical Q & A) (E) Amplification Paragraph

Thesis: How many times had she made this journey, Nurse Penfield speculated, glancing down at the shrouded figure on the stretcher.
Amplification: (E) Amplification ¶
   Thesis: Probably fifty times in the past eleven years.
   Amplification: Perhaps more because it was not something you kept score of—this final journey between the ward and the hospital's morgue, between the territory of the living and the dead.

This example is part of what is presented as (32). In it, the amplification paragraph occurs on two levels, that is, recursively as an amplification paragraph within an amplification paragraph. As noted above, this example involves overlay of a rhetorical question-and-answer in the paragraph on the highest level of embedding. Instead of simply stating that she had gone on this journey many times it is turned into a question: *How many times*. The amplification into *probably fifty* takes the shape of an answer. But that in turn is qualified by the further qualification in the last sentence that is in the amplification paragraph on the lower level.

Appendix 7A of this book (Longacre 1996:76–82) presents seven varieties of paraphrase which may be summarized under three heads, in addition to the SUMMARY PARAPHRASE: (1) EQUIVALENCE and NEGATED ANTONYM PARAPHRASE; (2) AMPLIFICATION and GENERIC-SPECIFIC PARAPHRASE; and (3) CONTRACTION and SPECIFIC-GENERIC PARAPHRASE. Under (1) there is no perceptible loss or gain of information between a thesis and its paraphrase; under (2) there is gain of information in the paraphrase relative to the thesis; and under (3) there is loss of information in the paraphrase relative to the thesis. The Hailey corpus, from which we take examples, uses only type (2), which we refer to simply as *amplification paragraphs*. In the study of the Scriptures we find, however, all varieties of paraphrase.[4]

(41) (E) Comment Paragraph

Thesis: Less than an hour ago the body under the shroud had been George Andrew Dunton, living, age fifty-three, civil engineer.
Comment: She remembered the details from the case history on the clip board under her arm.

Comment paragraphs essentially involve a comment on the part of the narrator, or broadly speaking, the composer of the text. It is akin to a footnote incorporated into the body of the text. Such is the range and variety semantically of the comment that we give a few more examples of its use here.

(42) (N) Comment Paragraph with Result Paragraph Embedded in the Comment

Thesis: George Rinne, the pathology department's Negro diener—keeper of the morgue—looked up as the stretcher rolled in.
Comment: (N) Result ¶
    Thesis: He had been swabbing the autopsy table.
    Result: Now it shone spotlessly white.

---

[4] Thus, equivalence paraphrase—or simply paraphrase—is found in such couplets as Proverbs 4:5 "Get wisdom, get understanding," and Prov. 4:8 "Prize her [wisdom] highly and she will exalt you. She will honor you if you embrace her." Negated Antonym Paraphrase is illustrated in Prov. 8:13 "Lay hold of instruction. Do not let go"; and in Prov. 8:15 "Avoid it, don't pass by it;" and in 4:27 "Keep your foot from evil. Don't turn to the right or to the left."

8.2 Representations of paragraph structures 143

(43) (N) Comment Paragraph with a Quote Paragraph Embedded in the Thesis

> **Thesis: Quote ¶**
>   QF: He called after her.
> **Quote: (H) Reason ¶**
>   Thesis: "Keep 'em coming.
>   Reason: We need the practice."
> **Comment:**   Again the timeworn jest, the defensive levity in face of death.

Here, the comment is quite clearly the narrator's comment that explains somewhat the ethos and camaraderie of the autopsy room.

(44) Execution Paragraph

> **Plan: (H) Reason ¶**
>   Reason: "The medical history of this man shows that three years ago he suffered a first coronary attack and then a second attack earlier this week."
>   Thesis: "So first we'll examine the coronary arteries."
> **Execution:**   As the nurses watched intently Pearson delicately opened the heart-muscle arteries.

In this sort of paragraph a speaker declares his intention of doing something, then carries out that intention.

(45) Stimulus-Response Paragraph with an Embedded Induction Paragraph

> **Stimulus: Quote ¶**
>   LI/QF: He had his cigar going now and waved it at the table.
> **Quote: (Argumentative) Induction ¶**
>   Observation 1: "This man has been tuberculous for many months."
>   Observation 2: "It is possible he may have infected others around him, his family, people he worked with, even some in this hospital."
>   Thesis: "If there had been no autopsy, some of these people might have developed tuberculosis, and it could have remained undetected, as it did here until too late."
> **Response:**   Two of the student nurses moved back instinctively from the table.

This example, (45), illustrates two rather rare paragraph types: (1) the STIMULUS-RESPONSE PARAGRAPH in which reaction (often an unexpected or counter strategy) to a situation is reported, and (2) an INDUCTION paragraph in which there is reasoning, beginning with observations and arriving a conclusion. It also illustrates a quote paragraph in which the speaker of the quotation is not explicitly indicated but can be inferred from the lead-in/quote formula (LI/QF), and of course from the previous context.

(46) Simple Dialogue Paragraph (Question-Answer)

> IU **(Question):** "You doing this one?"
> RU **(Answer): Quote ¶**
>   **QF:** The resident shook his head.
>   **Quote:** "Pearson's coming."

This and the remaining examples of this chapter illustrate dialogue paragraphs. This is a simple dialogue paragraph with an INITIATING UTTERANCE (IU) and a RESOLVING UTTERANCE (RU). The former encodes a question and the latter encodes an answer. The whole structure is a question-answer couplet. It is a resolved simple paragraph as shown by the presence of an RU.

(47) Simple Dialogue Paragraph (Remark-Evaluation)

> LI 1: As Weidman, the male orderly, swung the stretcher left, a janitor—either on work break or stolen time—lowered the coke he had been drinking and moved aside.
> LI 2: He wiped his lips on the back of his hand, then gestured to the shroud.
> IU **(Remark): Quote ¶**
>   **Quote:** "Didn't make it, eh?"
>   **QF:** The remark was to Weidman; it was an amiable gambit, a game played many times.
> RU **(Evaluation): Quote ¶**
>   **QF:** Weidman, too had done this before.
>   **Quote:** "I guess they pulled his number, Jack."
> **(Nonverbal)** TU **(Acquiescence):**
>   The janitor nodded, then raised his coke bottle again and drank deeply.

Again, this is a simple dialogue paragraph, but here the IU encodes a REMARK and the RU encodes an EVALUATION of the remark. A few optional features occur: two lead-ins (LI) and a TERMINATING UTTERANCE (TU), which in this case encodes acquiescence. The whole unit is an expansion of a remark-evaluation couplet. Again, the paragraph is resolved by virtue of the occurrence of an RU.

8.2 *Representations of paragraph structures* 145

(48) Cyclic Quoted Simple Dialogue Paragraph (Proposal-Response)

    Introduction: (E) Amplification ¶
        Thesis: How short a time, Nurse Penfield thought, between life and the autopsy room.
    Amplification: (E) Comment ¶
        Thesis: Less than an hour ago the body under the shroud had been George Andrew Dunton, living, age fifty-three, civil engineer.
        Comment: She remembered the details from the case his tory on the clip board under her arm.
LI: (N) Result ¶
        Thesis: The family had behaved as well after the death as they had before—solid, emotional but no hysterics.
        Result: It had made it easier for Dr. McMahon to ask for permission to autopsy.
IU (Proposal): (N) Amplification ¶
        Thesis: "Mrs. Dunton," he had said quietly, "I know it's hard for you to talk and think about this now, but there is something I have to ask. It's about permission for an autopsy on your husband."
        [Note: Paragraph occurs in Quote of Quotation Sentence].
    Amplification: Quoted (N) Contrast ¶
        Thesis: He had gone on, using the routine words, how the hospital sought to safeguard its medical standards for the good of everyone, how a physician's diagnosis could be checked and medical learning advanced, how this was a precaution for the family and others who would use the hospital in time to come.
        Antithesis: But none of this could be done without permission...
RU (Response): The son had stopped him gently and said: "We understand. If you make out whatever is necessary, my mother will sign it."
[Note: Paragraph occurs in Quote].
Terminus: So Nurse Penfield had made out the autopsy form, and here now was George Andrew Dunton, dead, age fifty three, and ready for the pathologist's knife.

This example is basically a simple dialogue paragraph whose IU encodes a PROPOSAL and whose RU encodes a RESPONSE. It is complicated by being

CYCLIC. The introduction and the terminus clearly cross-reference each other by giving the full name of the deceased and his age, labeled as *living* in the introduction and *dead* in the terminus. To further complicate matters, the whole unit is presented as a quotation, that is, as the thoughts of Nurse Penfield. The introduction, the lead-in, and the IU units all contain embedded paragraphs. Nevertheless, the structure is essentially an expansion of a proposal-response couplet, resolved by virtue of the occurrence of an RU (response).

With this example and the two preceding, we have illustrated the basic structure of dialogue in terms of paired utterances, which encode question-answer, remark-evaluation, and proposal-response. These terms are semantically construed broadly as notional structure units to include the universe of discourse at this point—with perhaps the sole exception of outward bracketing pairs, greeting and counter-greeting, leave-taking and counter-leave-taking.

(49) Unresolved Complex Dialogue Paragraph

    LI: (N) Comment ¶
        Thesis: George Rinne, the pathology department's Negro diener—keeper of the morgue—looked up as the stretcher rolled in.
        Comment: (N) Result ¶
            Thesis: He had been swabbing the autopsy table.
            Result: Now it shone spotlessly white.
    IU (Remark): Quote ¶
        QF: Weidman greeted him with the timeworn jest.
        Quote: "Got a patient for you."
    CU (c-Proposal): Quote ¶
        QF: (N) Sequence ¶
            Seq. Thesis 1:   Politely, as if he hadn't heard the line a hundred times before, Rinne bared his teeth in a perfunctory smile.
            Seq. Thesis 2:   He indicated the white enameled table.
        Quote: "Over there."

This example differs from the above examples in two respects. To begin with, instead of one of the regular pairs of semantically corresponding utterances we get a remark not followed by an evaluation but by a proposal. George Rinne is not accepting the dialogue as initiated by Weidman. Instead of speaking to the point (he could have said "Not really a patient" or something on that order), he simply comes out with the proposal to put the "patient" *over there*. If an addressee wants to counter an IU, he can thus come up with a CONTINUING UTTERANCE (CU), which does not offer a resolution but restructures the dialogue along new lines. A CU may encode any token, such as question, proposal, or remark, not paired with an IU as

8.2 Representations of paragraph structures

expected. Secondly, however, Weidman could have accepted the restructured dialogue and given an RU response to the CU *over there*. Weidman could have said "O.K." or something of that sort. This would have been an RU following the CU. But since this RU does not occur, the paragraph remains unresolved.

If a CU occurs in a dialogue paragraph, then it is complex rather than simple. If no RU occurs in a dialogue paragraph, whether it is simple or complex, then it is an unresolved dialogue paragraph.

(50) Compound Dialogue Paragraph [Only four of seven exchanges are given here]

Introduction (LI?): (N) Identification ¶
    Thesis: The autopsy room door swung open and Mike Seddons breezed in.
Identification: (E) Coordinate ¶
    Thesis 1: Mike Seddons was a surgical resident, temporarily assigned to Pathology and he always breezed.
    Thesis 2: His red hair stood up in odd places as though a self-created wind would never leave it static.
    Thesis 3: His boyish, open face seemed creased permanently in an amiable grin.
    Terminus: McNeil considered Seddons an exhibitionist, though in his favor the kid had taken to pathology a lot more readily than some of the other surgical residents McNeil had seen.
Exchange 1: Unresolved Complex Dialogue ¶
    IU (Remark): Quote ¶
        LI/QF: Seddons looked over at the body on the table.
        Quote: "Ah, more business."
    CU (c-Proposal?): McNeil gestured to the case papers and Seddons picked them up.
Exchange 2: Simple Dialogue ¶
    IU (Remark): Rh Q-and-A (N) Sequence ¶
        Seq. Thesis 1 (Q): He asked: "What did he die of?"
        Seq. Thesis 2 (A): Then, as he read on "Coronary, eh?"
    RU (Evaluation): McNeil answered: "That's what it says."
Exchange 3: Simple Dialogue ¶
    IU (Question): "You doing this one?"
    RU (Answer): Quote ¶
        LI/QF: The resident shook his head.
        Quote: "Pearson's coming."
Exchange 4: Simple Dialogue ¶
    IU (Question): Quote ¶
        LI/QF: Seddons looked up quizzically.

Quote:	"The boss man himself? What's special about this case?"
RU **(Answer):**	"Nothing special."

A compound dialogue paragraph is made up of a series of related dialogue paragraphs, whether simple or complex, resolved or unresolved. Each component dialogue paragraph is called an EXCHANGE. A partial example is given here consisting of four out of a series of seven exchanges. Exchange 1 consists of an unresolved COMPLEX DIALOGUE paragraph. We label as a possible proposal the sentence which records an impatient gesture of Dr. McNeil's. It is possibly equivalent to brushing off Seddons' remark in the previous sentence with something on the order of "get down to work." If so, the first exchange consists of an IU (remark), followed by the equivalent of a CU (proposal) but not followed by an RU.

Exchange 2 is a remark-evaluation pairing. But the IU (remark) embeds a rhetorical question plus answer, in which Seddons reads off the answer to his own question. It is thus equivalent to a remark or piece of information, which McNeil evaluates in the RU.

Exchange 3 is a simple dialogue of question-answer structure whose only complication is that the answer includes a gesture of denial in the lead-in plus the verbal answer in the next sentence.

Exchange 4 is a question-answer exchange, and as such structures as a simple dialogue paragraph.

One more feature of this lengthy unit is the structure exemplified in the introduction, namely, the identification paragraph in which a person, in this case Dr. Seddons, is brought on stage and presented.

8.3 Concluding remarks

In this chapter we have shown a number of different discourse and paragraph structures. The presentation of these with trees or indentation diagrams aids in visualizing the levels of embedding. Labels help to display the relationships.

8.4 Exercise

Which sort of tree diagram appeals to you most? Again, initial reactions are called for. You may change your mind later. Meanwhile, try a type of tree structure or indentation diagram on a passage of your choice in the target language text.

Appendix 8A. Paragraph types
(Longacre 1996: chapter 4)

Margins (Setting/Intro or Terminus) may occur with any type

	Paragraph Types	Slot Labels			
	0. Simple ¶	(Setting)†	Thesis	(Terminus)	
Conjoining	1.1 Coordinate ¶	Thesis 1	Thesis 2 . . .		
	1.2 Contrast ¶	Thesis	Antithesis	[or Thesis, Contrast]*	
Alternation	2. Alternative ¶	Alt.Th 1	Alt.Th 2	. . .	
Temporal	3.1 Simultaneous ¶	Sim.Th 1	Sim.Th 2 . . .	[or Thesis, Simul]*	
	3.2 Sequence ¶	Seq.Th 1	Seq.Th 2 . . .		
Implication	4.1 Conditional ¶	Condition	Thesis		
	Contrafactual ¶	Condition	Thesis	Conditionality	
	Universal Quan ¶	Thesis	UQThesis		
	4.2 Reason/Result ¶	Thesis	Reason/Result	Causation	
	Circumstantial ¶	Thesis	Circumstance		
	4.3 Warning ¶	Thesis	Warning		
	4.4 Attestation ¶	Thesis	Evidence 1	Evidence 2 . . .	Inference
	Induction ¶	Observation 1	Observation 2 . . .	Thesis	
Paraphrase	5. Paraphrase ¶	Thesis	Paraphrase		
	Equivalence ¶	ET 1	ET 2 . . .		
	Amplification ¶	Thesis	Ampl 1	Ampl 2 . . .	
	Summary ¶	Thesis	Summary		
Illustration	6. Simile ¶	Thesis	Simile		
	Exemplification ¶	Thesis	Example		
Deixis	7. Identification ¶	Thesis	Identification		
	Comment ¶	Thesis	Comment		
Attribution	8. Quotation ¶	Q(Quote)	QF(Quote Formula)		
	Awareness ¶	Aw(Awareness)	AwF(Awareness Formula)		
Frustration	9. Concession ¶	Concession	Thesis		
	Frustration ¶	Thesis	Counter Thesis	Blocking Thesis	Surrogate Thesis
		[or Thesis, Counter, Blocking, Surrogate]*			

† or Introduction in non-narrative
* [Alternative labels for paragraph slots which are filled by sentences off the mainline.]

Appendix 8B. Dialogue and similar paragraph types
(Longacre 1996: chapter 5)

Paragraph Types	Slot Labels	
	SS	NS
Simple Dialogue ¶	IU	(Q, Pro, Rem)
	RU	(A, Res, Eval)
	TU	(Acq, Rej)
Complex Dialogue ¶ (incl. Abeyance type)	IU	
	CU	(c-Q, c-Pro, c-Rem)
	. . .	or more than 1 unit as in (Res+Pro)
	RU	
Compound Dialogue ¶	Exch 1: Simple or Complex Dialogue ¶	
	Exch 2: Simple or Complex Dialogue ¶	
	. . .	
Execution ¶	Plan	
	Execution (by self or someone else)	
Stimulus-Response ¶ (counter strategy)	Stimulus	
	Response	

Nonverbal/nondialogue margins may occur with any type:

> Setting
> Lead-In   (Band 1 Storyline)
> "Dialogue proper in the Nucleus"
> Correlate   (accompanying nonverbal activity)
> Step-Down (Band 1, concluding a ¶, representing an action taken at its conclusion)
> Terminus

Abbreviations:

SS (Surface Structure)

IU = Initiating Utterance
CU = Continuing Utterance
RU = Resolving Utterance
TU = Terminating Utterance
Exch = Exchange

NS (Notional Structure)

(IU)
Q = Question
Pro = Proposal
Rem = Remark

(CU)
c-Q   = counter-Question
c-Pro = counter-Proposal
c-Rem = counter-Remark

(RU)
A   = Answer
Res = Response
Eval = Evaluation

(TU)
Acq = Acquiescence
Rej = Rejection

Chapter 9

Procedural Discourse

According to our system of classifying discourse, procedural discourse has the plus value of contingent temporal succession (events are in temporal succession with some of them contingent on previous ones), and the minus value of agent orientation (there is no identity of agent reference running through the discourse). The steps of a procedure are ordered and the attention is on what is done or made (topic or patient orientation), rather than on who does it. Also, procedural discourse generally describes actions contemplated or anticipated but not realized—a how-to-do-it discourse, which is plus projection. Procedural discourse can also be used to show how something was done in the past and then it has the value of minus projection. It may be plus/minus tension, depending on the presence or absence of struggle or obstacle. Procedural discourse "varies from the food recipe, to the how-to-do-it book, to the instruction to a particular worker for his activities on a given day" (Longacre 1996:13).

Compared to other types of discourse, not much work has been done on procedural discourse. There are only sporadic papers or book chapters on procedural discourse (e.g., Longacre 1968, Marchese 1987, Ono 1994, Pike 1977). This may be no accident because there seems to be a scale of frequency of use among extended monologue discourse types:

Narrative > Hortatory > Expository > Procedural

This scale might be related to a decrease in universality across cultures from narrative to procedural. While narrative and hortatory are present in every culture and may be highly developed as a specific emic type on the surface structure of the language, extensive explanation of a topic may be less frequent across cultures, with procedural discourse possibly being even less developed. In some cultures, apprenticeship or observation is the way to learn how to do something rather than through explicit verbal instruction (see Paredes and Hepburn 1976). Longacre (1996:13) notes:

> In some nonliterate communities, procedural discourse is almost nonexistent. In such communities, people learn by participating in activities. The verbal components are part of the whole activity complex and never attain the status of a continuous monologue. Nevertheless, even in such communities, the outsider does not find it too hard to elicit from people a discourse telling how to do or how to make something. In such cases, the influence of the outsider results in the speedy evolution of a new discourse type!

Procedural texts from English are analyzed in section 9.1, and section 9.2 discusses a short Korean recipe to show that grammatical features of procedural discourse vary from language to language. Section 9.3 looks at two texts that are less typical of the type and attempts to characterize procedural discourse in comparison with other types of discourse. We note that some instructional texts may not be prototypical procedural discourse.

9.1 Segmentation of English procedural discourse

A procedural schema or template at the discourse level is suggested to have the following slots by Longacre (1992a:111):

1. Problem/Need
2. Preparatory procedures
3. The main efficient procedures
4. Concluding (often utilization) procedures

This type of template, however, does not commonly apply in its full structure to short procedural texts like recipes, which can be analyzed simply at the paragraph level. At the paragraph level, the analysis focuses on the relationship between sentences. Such relationships may be indicated by overt conjunctive expressions, for example, *then* for sequence, *meanwhile* for simultaneity, *but* or *on the contrary* for contrast, or they can be covert and only deducible by the semantic relationships between sentences. The paragraph analysis reveals how the sentences (and embedded paragraphs) within a paragraph are related to each other, and thus reflects the text structure.[1] In order to show the sentences that are on the mainline of the text according to the discourse type, they are labeled *thesis* (or sometimes a specific type such as *sequential thesis*), while other sentences that are not on the mainline are labeled depending on their relation to the thesis sentence: *reason, amplification, comment,* etc. (Longacre 1996: chapter 4).[2]

---

[1] See chapter 8 of this book, Longacre (1989, 1992a, and 1992b), and Hwang (1989) for sample paragraph analyses. See also the papers in Mann and Thompson (1992) for different approaches to segmentation.

[2] Those marked as *thesis* are at the highest level of salience ranking scheme of verb forms for

9.1 Segmentation of English procedural discourse

The first text, "How to make an index," illustrates macrosegmentation at the discourse level. It was written by K. L. Pike (1968) before the computer made many manual tasks unnecessary. The text appears in (51) with some omissions, showing the number of paragraphs within each stage to indicate the extent of deletion. For example, *(10¶ and a sample)* at the end of Stage 1 indicates that for this stage there are ten paragraphs of text and a sample in the original text, which are not fully shown here.

(51) "How to make an index" (Pike 1968)[3]

> How can an author contribute to an index the kind of detailed attention which he alone can give, without costing more direct time and energy than he can afford? <u>If he fails to solve this problem</u>, he will (1) either omit an index completely (which will cut the usefulness of some reference books in half), or settle for a partial index; or (2) have the work done by someone who (a) cannot label a topic..., (b) cannot balance probable reader need... (c) cannot.... For several volumes I have used the following procedure.
>
> Stage 1: The author dictates entries onto a recording machine. (10¶ and a sample)
>
> Stage 2: The typist is <u>then</u> requested to make a running list of the dictated entries, on ordinary paper, with a carbon copy. (5¶)
>
> Stage 3: Proofing for dictated error is <u>now</u> done by comparing numbers in this running typescript, with the page proof. (2¶)
>
> Stage 4: <u>Now</u>, the typist slices all slips with a paper cutter (preserving the carbon copy...). The slips are <u>then</u> sorted and alphabetized. (6¶)
>
> Stage 5: The typist <u>now</u> takes the separate, alphabetized slips, and prepares them for editing. (4¶)
>
> Stage 6: The author <u>now</u> reads the tentative, unedited index, to reach several judgments: (a) Does he think of any topics.... (1¶)
>
> Stage 7: Editing of the paste-on Index can <u>now</u> proceed, <u>to get ready for final typing</u>. For each main entry, the first occurrence is maintained. All succeeding repetitions are crossed out, leaving numbers, and subentries, to be copied by the typist. (3¶ and a sample)

---

procedural discourse, while the others would be lower. For Biblical Hebrew, Longacre proposes that "the *weqatal* form finds its most characteristic use in the mainline structures of predictive, procedural, and instructional discourse" (1994:95). In this chapter we do not present a salience scheme for procedural discourse, but see Longacre (1995a:47) for a scheme for Exodus 25–30 in Biblical Hebrew, and Reeder (1998) for such a scheme in the Pagibete language of Africa.

[3] Underlining of sequence signals and adverbial clauses, and bolding of imperatives have been added to highlight them in the texts. Reprinted from *PMLA* September 1968 by permission of the Modern Language Association of America.

Stage 8: The typist <u>now</u> copies the paste-on index, preparing the final typescript for the publisher. The paste-on sample, shown above, appears in the final manuscript as follows: ... (1¶ and a sample)

Stage 9: Proofing of this typescript is <u>now</u> done against the paste-on sheets. (1¶)

In sum: Author energy is minimized by involving him in the running dictation of entries as well as in initial judgment of the value of entries and the later assessment of coverage. Otherwise, the mechanical details can be handled efficiently by his assistants. A book of some 250 manuscript pages with many bibliographical references may go through these stages in about a week, with author and one typist alternatively involved.

The text consists of nine stages (each ranging from one to ten paragraphs), bracketed by a clear introduction at the beginning (for the need) and a conclusion at the end. Thus, we may propose the following macrosegmentation on the basis of content, with the stages in the middle functioning as procedures:

1. Problem/Need
2. Procedures (Preparatory, Main, and Final or Target)
3. Conclusion

In each of the stages except the first, the very first sentence carries a sequence signal: *then* in Stage 2 and *now* in the rest. The divisions for preparatory, main, and final or target procedures are not explicit. This text uses present indicative tense forms of the verb, which seem to function as mitigated commands in the body of procedures (i.e., Stages 1–9). These verbs may be in the active voice (e.g., *The author dictates entries onto a recording machine*) or passive (e.g., *Proofing for dictated error is now done by comparing numbers in this running typescript...*). The text makes use of various forms of modality, such as *should, can, may,* in place of imperatives but with an added shade of deontic meaning ranging from necessity/obligation to possibility/permission ('must'> 'will' > 'can' > 'may') (Chung and Timberlake 1985:246). There are forty-nine occurrences of modals (30 percent) out of a total of 163 clauses with finite forms of verbs.

Passives and adverbial clauses also occur frequently, in 38 percent and 14 percent, respectively, of the total 163 finite-verb clauses. Passives, especially agentless passives, enable the clauses to focus on the patients and tasks at hand, rather than on the agents. That is, passives achieve an analogous function to imperatives, namely, patient focus, and irrelevant, insignificant, or generic agent.

Among the adverbial clauses, those with *until* and *since* occur only postposed to main clauses, while conditional (*if*) and temporal (*when*) clauses occur both preposed and postposed. Preposed conditional clauses—along with temporal clauses—are often used to mark the topic (Haiman 1978). Marchese

9.1 Segmentation of English procedural discourse

(1987) notes how the use of conditional clauses is a very distinct, typical feature of Godié procedural discourse. Conditional clauses comprise 80 percent of all initial subordinate clauses in her study. They trace a main route correlating with steps that outline the procedure and often co-occur with a paragraph marker and subject discontinuity.

Stage 4 of the Pike text is presented below as (52), followed by its paragraph analysis in figure 9.1. It is a sequence paragraph consisting of two sequential theses, in which sequential thesis 2 displays five layers of embedding.

(52) Stage 4 of "How to make an index"

1. <u>Now</u>, the typist slices all slips with a paper cutter...
2. The slips are <u>then</u> sorted and alphabetized.
3. I prefer to have the typist do this <u>in several stages</u>.
4. She is asked to begin by sorting all main entries into five piles (more piles may slow the work greatly...).
5. Five cards are placed on a table, one vowel-plus-consonant-before-next-vowel...
6. Slips are tossed onto the piles.
7. <u>Then</u> the piles are subdivided according to the initial letter.
8. A <u>third</u> sort calls, again, on the five-vowel-set cards just mentioned, to begin to subdivide the main entries according to the second letter of the word; a <u>fourth</u> sort finishes alphabetizing the second letter of the entries.
9. <u>Fifth</u> (gross) and <u>sixth</u> (refined) sortings alphabetize the entries according to their third letters.
10. <u>Further</u> sortings, gross and refined, alphabetize the entries according to any remaining letters.
11. <u>When only a few entries are left in a group</u>, <u>as the sorting of some bit of the index nears completion</u>, the gross versus refining steps can be omitted and the alphabetizing can be done directly and quickly.
12. <u>If no subentry is indicated on the slips of an entry set, but several page numbers are involved</u>, the slips are sorted according to the sequence of numbers.
13. <u>When a main-entry set has, also, various slips with subentries indicated</u>, the sorting routine above is applied to the subentries, <u>until they too are in appropriate subsets</u>.
14. <u>If the subsets have sub-subentries</u>, the sorting routine is <u>then</u> applied to them.

```
Seq. Thesis 1:  S1
Seq. Thesis 2: Amplification ¶
    Thesis:     S2
    Amplification: Comment ¶
        Introduction:  S3
        Thesis: Sequence ¶
            Seq. Thesis 1: Amplification ¶
                Thesis:         S4
                Amplification: Sequence ¶
                    Seq. Thesis 1: S5
                    Seq. Thesis 2: S6
            Seq. Thesis 2: S7
            Seq. Thesis 3: S8
            Seq. Thesis 4: S9
            Seq. Thesis 5: S10
            Seq. Thesis 6: S11
        Comment: Coordinate ¶
            Thesis 1: S12
            Thesis 2: Comment ¶
                Thesis:     S13
                Comment:  S14
```

Figure 9.1. Paragraph analysis of "How to make an index," stage 4

The two main sequential theses are marked by sequence signals *now* and *then* in S1 and S2. The rest of the paragraph amplifies the sorting and alphabetizing thesis given in S2. The amplification is made by a comment paragraph which consists of three parts: introduction in S3 (with the expression, *in several stages*, previewing the following sequential theses), thesis in S4–11, and comment in S12–14. The thesis is filled by a sequence paragraph of six sequential theses, in which sequential thesis 1 (*begin by sorting all main entries into five piles*) is another amplification paragraph, whose amplification comprises another embedded sequence paragraph with two sequential theses—the innermost, fifth layer of embedding—in S5 (*Five cards are placed on a table...*) and S6 (*Slips are tossed onto the piles*). *Then* at the beginning of S7 indicates sequential thesis 2, while *A third sort* and *a fourth sort* in S8 signal sequential thesis 3, a single sequential thesis grammatically; both sortings occur in one sentence with the two parts loosely connected by a semicolon. Semantically, however, there are two steps in S8.[4] Sequential thesis 4 again consists of two semantic steps (*fifth and sixth sortings*), which are shown this time by the coordinate noun phrase subject in a single clause structure. The last two sequential theses describe *further sortings* and the final, direct alphabetizing. The comment

---

[4] Since these two steps are joined by a semicolon, one can alternatively divide the sentence into two, corresponding to the semantic division of the two steps. The fifth and sixth sortings described in S9, however, cannot be divided in this way.

is filled by a coordinate paragraph with two theses, and the last sentence, S14, functions as the comment to the second thesis in S13.

Thus, stage 4 describes two basic steps: slicing slips in S1 as sequential thesis 1, and sorting/alphabetizing in S2–14 as sequential thesis 2. As indicated by underlining, the sequential characteristic of procedural discourse appears in the use of sequence marking adverbs and explicit numbers for ordering. The last four sentences start with initial adverbial clauses with *when* or *if*, and one sentence ends with a final *until*-clause.

Paragraph analysis can be illustrated by considering several English procedural texts. A typical recipe in (53), from the *Jungle Camp Cook Book* (1980:436–437), has sentences in the imperative, giving steps in preparing and cooking the dish.

(53) "Oriental mixed vegetables"

Seq. Thesis 1: Sequence ¶
   Seq. Thesis 1: **Select** 3 or 4 different vegetables.
   Seq. Thesis 2: **Prepare** same as for regular vegetables, except **dice** each vegetable in small cubes and **keep** each vegetable separate before cooking.
Seq. Thesis 2: Sequence ¶
   Seq. Thesis 1: **Cook** the vegetables that require the longest cooking first (such as green beans).
   Seq. Thesis 2: **Add** the other vegetables according to the amount of cooking time they require <u>so that all the vegetables will become tender at the same time</u>.
Seq. Thesis 3: **Serve** as mixed vegetables.
Terminus: May also cook vegetables and serve as for Cuban Salad.

The recipe consists of a sequence paragraph with three sequential theses and a terminus. The first two sequential theses consist of an embedded sequence paragraph each, providing sub-procedures for preparing vegetables and cooking them (in two sentences each). The final sequential thesis simply instructs the addressee to *serve*. Typical of procedural discourse, imperatives occur without person specified, implying *you* or anyone who can follow the procedure. The clauses have simple activity verbs and objects in the patient role. The postposed purpose clause with *so that* indicates the goal orientation. The final sentence, which is not in the imperative but still lacks the subject, provides added information functioning as the terminus.[5]

The sequence paragraph text in (54) below is similar in structure to the recipe in (53), although very different in content. It is a text advising one how to stop worrying.

---

[5] Perhaps due to its brevity, this recipe text does not yield very well to macrosegmentation. The slot of problem/need is assumed and unstated. The first main sequential thesis might be related to preparatory procedures, while the second one to the main efficient procedures. We might consider the sentence in sequential thesis 3 as the concluding or utilization procedure.

(54) "How to stop worrying" (Carnegie 1976:88–89)

1. **Get** the facts.
2. **Remember** that Dean Hawks of Columbia University said that "half of the worry in the world is caused by people trying to make decisions before they have sufficient knowledge on which to base a decision."
3. <u>After carefully weighing all the facts,</u> **come** to a decision.
4. <u>Once a decision is carefully reached,</u> **act**!
5. **Get** busy carrying out your decision—and **dismiss** all anxiety about the outcome.

This text can be analyzed as having three sequential theses, but with embedded comment (or, alternatively, reason) and amplification paragraphs, as in figure 9.2.

> Seq. Thesis 1: Comment (or Reason) ¶
>   Thesis: S1
>   Comment (or Reason): S2
> Seq. Thesis 2:   S3
> Seq. Thesis 3: Amplification ¶
>   Thesis: S4
>   Amplification: S5

Figure 9.2. Paragraph analysis of "How to stop worrying"

Although there are three main steps (*get the facts, come to a decision,* and *act*), the global theme of worrying is buried in the non-mainline sentences 2 and 5 (*the worry* and *all anxiety*), which are a comment (or reason) and an amplification of sequential theses 1 and 3. Notice also the lexical repetition of *the facts* in S1 and 3, and of *decision* in S2–5. Before the main verbs are stated for sequential theses 2 and 3, we find adverbial expressions: S3 *After carefully weighing all the facts,* and S4 *Once a decision is carefully reached.* They underscore the importance of the action verbs in the main clauses by giving a preparatory step toward them and stating what is expected in the script. These same adverbial expressions are what make the sequentiality explicit, alerting the reader to the following step (sequential thesis). Furthermore, the *after-*clause in S3 also serves to tie in the sentence to S1, after a digression in S2.

The theme of this text, however, shows that it is notionally a hortatory discourse in intent, which tries to influence conduct and behavior, but it is cast in procedural type in its surface structure form.

The next text in (55) is another variation; it is rather humorous since what can be serious advice is cast in a typical recipe form.

9.1 Segmentation of English procedural discourse

(55) "How to preserve a husband" (Ann Landers 1994)[6]

1. <u>First,</u> **use** care in selection.
2. **Get** one that is not too young, but tender and healthy.
3. <u>If you choose one recklessly,</u> it may not keep.
4. **Don't put** in hot water.
5. <u>This</u> makes them turn sour.
6. **Sweeten** with smiles, and **spice** with patience.
7. All varieties will respond.
8. <u>To ensure a wonderful consistency,</u> **stir** gently over a low flame and **don't leave** unattended for long periods of time.
9. <u>To add a delicious flavor,</u> **sprinkle** generously with praise and appreciation.
10. The poorest specimen may be improved <u>if you follow these instructions</u> and will keep for an unlimited number of years in any climate.
    (Tested by Yours Truly)
    (I'd like to add one small suggestion: Ann's addition):
11. Frequent exposure to cold temperatures has been known to damage this dish permanently.
12. **Keep** a small, steady flame going at all times.

This text is analyzed in figure 9.3 as consisting of two main sequential theses and a terminus. Landers' addition is semantically an amplification of S8.

```
Seq. Thesis 1: Reason ¶
    Thesis: Amplification ¶
        Thesis:        S1
        Amplification: S2
    Reason:  S3
Seq. Thesis 2: Coordinate ¶
    Thesis 1: Reason ¶
        Thesis:  S4
        Reason:  S5
    Thesis 2: Comment ¶
        Thesis:        S6
        Comment:  S7
    Thesis 3:  S8
    Thesis 4:  S9
Terminus:   S10

Amplification of S8: Reason ¶
    Reason:  S11
    Thesis:  S12
```

Figure 9.3. Paragraph analysis of "How to preserve a husband"

---
[6] Reprinted by permission of Esther P. Lederer Trust and Creators Syndicate, Inc.

There is an explicit sequencing given by the expression *First* in S1 concerning selection. Other activities after the selection are not in sequence, but they are items (theses) in coordination (hence a coordinate paragraph). The conditional clauses (in S3 and 10) add cohesion across sentences, and the purpose clauses (in S8 and 9) reflect the goal orientation of procedural discourse. It is noteworthy that a husband is variously referred to as *one, it, them, all varieties, the poorest specimen,* and *this dish*. But also noteworthy is the fact that many times the reference is left implicit, even with a verb that is considered to require an overt object in the grammar of English, for example, *put, sweeten, spice,* and *leave*. This seems to be another characteristic of English recipes that strive for brevity.

While the recipe in (53) is a typical procedural text, the texts in (54) and (55) are not. They are notionally hortatory discourse giving advice but are skewed to be procedural discourse in surface structure. They illustrate the skewing of notional and surface discourse features "according to a hierarchy of degrees of vividness" from drama and narrative and procedural to expository and hortatory (Longacre 1996:15). Note that the texts (54) and (55) are made more vivid by taking on the surface features of procedural type. Note also that the sequentiality (corresponding to the contingent temporal succession parameter) is much weaker in these texts; that is, while the overall text is a sequence type with sequential theses, it is less pronounced in embedded structure than the earlier texts.

The procedural texts we have analyzed from English seem to group into two types: those with the surface structure of a recipe and one longer one without that form. The recipe type has action verbs in the imperative and the objects in patient roles. The non-recipe type has customary present tense verbs, which can be in the passive voice, often occurring with modals like *should, must,* and *could*. In both types, adverbial clauses of condition and purpose are common.

9.2 Characteristics of a Korean recipe

A simple Korean recipe (whose ingredients are not shown here) consisting of two sentences appears in (56) so that we may observe some language-specific characteristics of Korean procedural discourse. Each sentence consists of a chain of several short clauses connected by conjunctions suffixed to verbs, which mark the end of the clause in this language with the basic word order of SOV. The distinctive, inflected verb at the end of the chaining structure, however, is not in the imperative as in English recipes but in the present tense and declarative mood. Notice that no explicit subject occurs in any of the clauses, with the implication that it could be any person as indicated in free translation by 'one' as the implied subject.

(56) Oi Namul (Cucumber vegetable dish) (Kim and Hwang 1969:70)

1 *Kanun   oi-lul   twungkul-ko yalkkey   ssel-ese,*
  skinny   cucumber-ACC   round-and   thinly   slice-and

  sokum-ey 20 pun-kan   cyelyet-taka,   hengkep-ey kkok
  salt-at   minute-for   put.salt-after cloth-in   tightly

  cca.kaci-ko,   mulkki-lul   ppay-n-ta.
  squeeze-and   water-ACC   take.out-PRES-DECL

  'Slicing skinny cucumbers into thin and round shapes, leaving (them) for 20 min. with salt sprinkled (on them), squeezing (them) tightly in a cloth, (one) takes out water.'

2 *Penchel-ey   kilum-ul   neknekhi   pu-e,*
  frying.pan-at   oil-ACC   abundantly   pour-and

  pul-ey ollye.noh-ko,   oi-lul   ne-e,   salccak pokka-se,
  fire-at put.on-and   cucumber-ACC   put.in-and   lightly   stir.fry-and

  cepsi-ey   tam-ko,   sil-kochwu-lul   ppuli-n-ta.
  dish-in   put-and   thread-red.pepper-ACC   sprinkle-PRES-DECL

  'Pouring plenty of oil into a frying pan, putting (it) on the fire, putting the cucumbers into (the pan), stir-frying (them) lightly, putting (them) on a dish, (one) sprinkles red pepper strings (on top).'

Instead of choppy sentences with imperatives as in English recipes, these sentences are long with four and six clauses each in a chain. As is very common for verb-final languages in Papua New Guinea, India, and South America, clause chaining is heavily used, with medial clauses loosely marked by suffixal conjunctions like *-e, -se, -ko, -taka, -mye*, etc. Clauses in the chain are still choppy, often with only an object or an adverb of manner and the verb. Instead of imperatives with implied 'you', Korean recipes simply omit the subject (generic agent implied) and the sentences end with *-ta*, the plain speech level form of declarative ending. Remarkably, the *-ta* form achieves the same detached, impersonal function as the English imperative. It seems any form of imperative (used at the sentence final position in Korean) would imply some sort of social relationship (from intimate and informal to distant and formal). Therefore, instead of imperatives, declarative present forms are used (similar to those found in Pike's "How to make an index" in English).

A cursory look at some other Korean recipes reveals a frequent use of conditional, purpose, and temporal clauses—similar to their frequent use in English recipes—as well as the use of modals of permission and necessity.

9.3 Toward a characterization of procedural discourse

Although how-to texts are generally considered procedural discourse, there are different types among them. There are those providing temporally sequential procedures (e.g., "How to conduct surveys: A step-by-step guide" and those discussed in sections 9.1–9.2). There are others in which temporal succession is not explicit although there is logical succession, giving advice on how to do something well. A lot of how-to texts are written by experts giving advice to those who might be interested in learning to do something. Are they a simple procedure (matter-of-fact, straightforward steps)? Or, are they more like an expository or hortatory text that explains or urges one to do something well? Is it a matter of degree, or is it a difference of author intent and focus? Some sample titles of how-to books and an article that may not be procedural are:

> *How to Be a More Successful Language Learner* (Rubin and Thompson)
> *How to Be Born Again* (Billy Graham)
> *How to Do Things with Words* (John Austin)
> *How to Learn a Foreign Language* (E. Cornelius)
> "How to Learn Martian" (C. Hockett)
> *How to Read the Bible for All Its Worth* (Fee and Stuart)

The procedural and hortatory type texts, which are diametrically opposed in terms of the two main parameter values (i.e., contingent temporal succession and agent orientation), may be similar in surface grammatical form in English. Both types may make use of imperatives, with or without the second person pronoun *you*. Both types are more commonly plus projection, possibly causing them to have similar surface forms. Thus, the pronoun is interpreted sometimes as minus agent orientation (impersonal, general in procedural) and other times as plus agent orientation (specific addressee in hortatory).

Hwang (1993) has analyzed a text called "Shop With Your Eyes Open" in (57) and classified it as hortatory. Seven (orthographic) paragraphs of the text are divided into macrosegments, each with a different discourse type:

1. Situation-Problem:	¶1 (Expository)
2. Command:	¶2 (Hortatory)
3. Motivation by example:	¶3–5 (Narrative)
4. Motivation with covert command:	¶6–7 (Expository-Hortatory)

(57) "Shop With Your Eyes Open" (*Reader's Digest*, August 1988)[7]

> ¶1 Supermarkets try to coax you to spend more . . .
>
> ¶2 <u>To beat supermarkets at their own game,</u> **clip** coupons, **buy** in quantity and **shop** with your wits about you.
>
> ¶3 We gave an identical shopping list to two staff members, asking one

---

[7] The text is in the August 1988 issue of *Reader's Digest*, and comes from a longer version, "How much money smart supermarket shopping can save." Copyright 1988 by Consumers Union of U. S., Inc., Yonkers, New York 10703–1057. Excerpted by permission from *Consumer Reports*. March 1988. In (57) only part of the embedded narrative in ¶3–5 is shown.

9.3 Toward a characterization of procedural discourse

to choose items regardless of cost and the other to look for low prices. (Two more sentences are omitted here, as well as ¶4 and ¶5.)

¶6 Shopping the way our careful staffer did, you would be able to save $2500 a year buying for a family of four. <u>If you used coupons and shopped for specials</u>, you would save even more.

¶7 Sometimes, brand-name items are better quality. Sometimes they're more convenient. Nonetheless, we guarantee you: <u>if you shop with your eyes open</u>, you'll save money.

The imperatives occur in ¶2 (*clip, buy, shop*), but the last two verbs do not denote actions in a temporal sequence. As in typical procedural discourse, preposed purpose and conditional clauses are found in this text, but perhaps as a reflection of hortatory type these subordinate clauses may be viewed as disguised commands, for example, *If you used coupons and shopped for specials* may signal 'Use coupons and shop for specials' (and *you would save even more*). Also note the modal *would* used twice in ¶6. Thus, while there are some surface features in this text that are similar to procedural, the main problem in classifying this text as procedural is due to the fact that there is no contingent temporal succession among constituents. (The plus value of contingent temporal succession is found only in the embedded narrative in ¶3–5, not shown here.) Apparently, there are some how-to texts in which temporal succession is not in focus or even implicit.

The following text is another how-to text explaining how to care for and maintain wood stoves.

(58) Care and Maintenance (Gehring 2008:267)[8]

1. Wood stoves are not difficult to maintain.
2. The most important task is to empty the ash pit *daily*; <u>if the ashes get too high</u>, they can choke the fire and damage the grate through overheating.
3. **Do not throw** the ashes away.
4. <u>If they are kept dry</u>, they can be plowed into the garden to sweeten the soil or scattered over the garden to deter slugs.
5. They can <u>also</u> be used for making soap.
6. **Clean** the stovetop *after each meal* by rubbing it with a handful of newspapers.
7. **Sprinkle** salt or baking soda on messy spills, and **use** a scraper to remove the residue.
8. Some cooks wipe their iron stoves or stovetops with waxed paper or an oiled rag *once a week* to keep the surface shiny and rust free.
9. Enameled stoves can be washed with warm water and detergent.

---

[8] Reprinted by permission of Skyhorse Publishing, Inc.

10. *About every two weeks,* **clear out** soot and ashes from beneath the oven and under the lids.
11. The cleaned surfaces will conduct heat more effectively.
12. Wood stoves are fitted with clean-out doors so that hard-to-get-at spots can be reached with special L- or T-shaped cleaning rods.
13. A wire clothes hanger can be made to serve almost as well.
14. <u>After the bulk of the ashes have been removed,</u> **use** a vacuum cleaner to pick up the last traces.
15. Stove black should be applied to cast-iron stoves *occasionally* to improve the stove's appearance and to retard rust.
16. Stove black is sold in most hardware stores.
17. It comes either as a paste or a liquid.
18. The liquid is easier to apply, especially on highly ornate surfaces.
19. Minor cracks, chips, and gaps between parts can usually be plugged with oven putty, available at stove suppliers.
20. <u>If a crack is too large to be repaired,</u> **replace** the damaged part.
21. A few companies still supply spare parts for some old stoves, and a number of others will cast new parts for you <u>if you send them the damaged part as a pattern.</u>
22. For more information on stove care, **see** *Heating with Wood,* pp. 86–93.

At the discourse level it has five main points and an introduction and terminus at the two ends. Each point here is not in succession to or contingent upon the one before it, but explains things to do at different intervals of time. The sequential feature in this text only occurs embedded in point 3, and is expounded by a sequence paragraph, whose explicit expression of sequence is in S14, that is, *After the bulk of the ashes have been removed.*

Introduction:	S1
Point 1:	S2–5 (*daily*)
Point 2:	S6–9 (*after each meal* and *once a week*)
Point 3:	S10–14 (*about every two weeks*)
Point 4:	S15–18 (*occasionally*)
Point 5:	S19–21 (implied time: 'whenever cracks, chips, and gaps occur')
Terminus:	S22

The text in (58) is clearly an instructional, how-to-do-it text, but it involves no temporal sequence, and expressions such as *daily and once a week* are primarily concerned with frequency. Unlike the text in (57), however, it does not seem to be hortatory.

In classifying texts into discourse types, we can apply basic parameter criteria, but we may need to add the perspective of the prototype, as used in other areas of categorization (see Lakoff 1987, Hopper and Thompson 1984). Thus, a prototypical procedural text would be minus agent orientation and plus contingent temporal succession, but these values, while they form discrete categories for typical texts, may vary by degree in borderline cases. In fact, narrative might be considered to be most strongly plus contingent temporal succession, with procedural following next. Some instructional texts may be quite low in this value and may take on the feature of logical succession more strongly so as to be classified as expository or hortatory.[9] The text in (58) may be expository in the notional structure (as is *How to Do Things with Words* by John Austin, or *How to Read the Bible for All Its Worth* by Fee and Stuart), in that it explains different points necessary in maintaining wood stoves.

9.4 Conclusions

Procedural discourse in English has the following characteristics: (1) Tense/aspect/mode: imperative or customary present tense verbs are on the mainline of procedure, sometimes with modals, such as, *should, must, can*; (2) voice: passives may be frequent, often with unspecified agent; (3) person: second, or it may also be third, but generally person-less as in imperative for the non-specific agent; (4) objects occur in patient roles, and tools in instrument roles; (5) verbs are of the activity-action type; and (6) adverbial clauses are common, especially the conditional *if* for hypotheticality of conjecture about the future, the temporal *when, before, until* related to plus contingent temporal succession, and the purpose *(in order) to, so that*, signaling the goal or target orientation. A Korean recipe displays some procedural discourse features that contrast with those in English. The sentences are long, consisting of several clauses in the chain (Korean using a clause-chaining structure), and the verbs in the final clause are in the plain speech level form of declarative mood rather than imperative. Since any argument that is assumed to be known may be freely omitted from the Korean clause, the clauses are short and subjectless—equivalent to subjectless imperatives in English.

Procedural discourse is minus agent orientation and plus contingent temporal succession in the two basic parameter values. These values may be considered a matter of degree for those texts that are borderline cases. Thus, while prototypical how-to-do-it instructional texts are procedural, other instructional texts may be expository or hortatory when they do not have the feature of temporal succession but only logical succession.

---

[9] Virtanen (1992a:329) proposes a scale of text types ranging from "texts that are typically arranged temporally to others that rather conform to a temporally iconic, logical succession in discourse (cf. the all-pervasiveness of time in our lives), with several types in between": Narration–Instruction–Description–Exposition–Argumentation, with overlapping borders between adjacent types.

9.5 Exercises

Do procedural texts occur naturally in the target language? If not, are they easy to elicit? What subjects or topics might call for a procedural text? Remember that procedural texts may be how it was done, how it is done, or step-by-step instructions for doing or making something.

Chapter 10

Hortatory Discourse

According to our text typology (chapter 3), hortatory discourse is a subtype of behavioral discourse, which is plus agent orientation and minus contingent temporal succession. Agent orientation in behavioral discourse may refer to the addressee, who is potentially a specific agent if the text is to produce the impact that it is aiming for, or it may refer to the person being eulogized. Temporal organization is not important; rather, logical connection of the parts of the text is. A good behavioral text will present persuasive argumentation in order to influence beliefs, values, and conduct of the hearer. While hortatory discourse is plus projection toward future behavior, eulogy is minus projection because it deals with a person's conduct in the past. In this chapter, we deal with the hortatory type, with only passing remarks on the eulogy type, which is restricted to specific occasions.

Hortatory discourse can "range from sermons, to pep talks, to addresses of generals to the troops on the eve of an important battle" (Longacre 1996:13). Although not as well studied as narrative, it is also a cultural universal and basic to our daily communication. It is difficult to imagine a culture or a family in which somebody with experience does not give advice to somebody else less experienced, however covert, mitigated, or disguised it may be. Many stories such as folktales, in fact, are told to transmit values that are important to a cultural group. In this sense, we might argue that hortatory discourse is more basic to human communication than narrative, at least in terms of the notional intent of a speaker. In surface structure, however, the hortatory type would appear less frequently, since we normally do not like to be told to change our values, beliefs, and behaviors. We tend to like to hear entertaining and amusing stories of other people's experiences rather than to listen to admonitions and advice. Thus, narrative discourse may be the primary mode of human communication in terms of frequency in surface structure, but hortatory discourse may be primary in terms of the communicator's intent in notional structure (Virtanen 1992b). This split, dual primacy is due to human nature and can be considered to be a case of skewing between surface and notional discourse types, for example, a notional hortatory text can be presented in surface structure as a narrative text.

In terms of influencing conduct, procedural discourse might be similar to hortatory, but the intent is clearly different (Lowe 1986). The intent of a procedural type is on *how* (to follow a procedure), while that of a hortatory is on *why* (one should behave in a certain way). On the surface, mainline forms may converge into the same form, as in the case of imperatives in English recipes (procedural) and words of advice (hortatory).

There has been some effort to distinguish hortatory and persuasive as two separate text types, the hortatory trying to "effect an action" and the persuasive trying to "effect a change in belief and values systems" (Terry 1995:81). Terry notes that in Koine Greek, imperative verbs and other command forms serve as the mainline forms only in hortatory texts, although both hortatory and persuasive text types have motivational material, unlike expository texts. His arguments thus come from both notional structure intent and surface structure linguistic features.

Setting up a persuasive discourse type, however, as distinct from the hortatory and expository types, leads to a prototype or continuum approach to text typology, with persuasive straddling between hortatory and expository (Hwang 2005). A prototypical expository text may try to make us understand with our mind, a prototypical persuasive text attempts to influence what we believe, and a prototypical hortatory text attempts to affect our behavior. Mind, heart, and action can all be integrated in one hortatory discourse. At the expository end of the continuum, there is no agent orientation, that is, the discussion or explanation is directed toward a general audience, not any specific individuals. As we move toward the middle of the continuum, persuasive discourse influences individuals to modify their beliefs, and then at the hortatory end, they are led to change their personal conduct. Less prototypical types of texts may have skewing or mismatch between surface and notional types or extensive embedding of different discourse types.

Our view here is that persuasive texts belong to the hortatory type overall, but that some may occasionally turn out to be expository on the surface structure, depending on their text-internal linguistic features. If static and low-transitivity verbs in the indicative mood dominate the mainline, it is best to classify it as expository although there may be an unstated intent to influence the beliefs of the addressee. If command forms and modals feature in the mainline (see section 10.4), we can classify the text as hortatory. Seen from this view, most of the epistles from the New Testament are hortatory texts.

10.1 The hortatory template

A hortatory template (or schema) is somewhat more varied, and often more disguised, than the narrative template. Giving advice or issuing commands to one's fellow human beings often characterizes social relations. The advice-giver may be motivated by benign concerns for others or by the desire to dominate or by some combination of the two. Since our fellow human beings may not like to receive advice, the line of exhortation may be mitigated or somewhat disguised. For these reasons the analysis of hortatory discourse may present more challenges than the analysis of narrative. Before getting into these matters further, it is helpful to examine the hortatory template.

We fall back here on everyday conversation to present this template. Suppose someone in the family or workplace comes up to you and says, "I've got something I need to talk to you about." There has to be some sort of precipitating situation to provoke this person to talk to you this way. Furthermore, the advice-giver is gambling (in terms of personal relations) that you will feel disposed to listen; a miscalculation here may impair a relationship! Here, two elements of the hortatory template emerge: (1) the situation out of which the exhortation springs, and (2) the authority of the advice-giver (the exhorter); what right does he/she have to give advice to the advice-recipient (the exhortee)? Two further elements enter into the hortatory template: (3) the command element proper (however mitigated and disguised) and (4) motivation cited for obeying the command.

Thus, analogous to notional structure slots for narrative template, such as exposition, climax, and denouement, the hortatory template has the following slots (Longacre 1992a:110; 1996:34):

1. the authority and credibility of the text producer,
2. indication of the problem/situation,
3. one or more command elements—which may be brusque or mitigated, and
4. motivation for obeying (essentially threats or promises).

While these four slots are specific to the hortatory type and usually found, the command slot is minimal and basic to the type. The first two slots may be implicit, but the motivation is usually necessary for compliance. Unlike the narrative and procedural discourse types, in which the slots are sequentially ordered reflecting the value of contingent temporal succession, the slots in hortatory (or expository) template do not necessarily follow the order from (1) to (4) as given above. Even when all four elements are present, they can be arranged differently, for example, the motivation can come before the command, as long as there is a plausible logical succession in presenting the textual materials. The indication of a problem or undesirable situation, however, would normally come before a command to change the situation.

10.2 Text organization

Hortatory discourse may be segmented in its overall structure in different ways depending on the text. The primary division may follow the functional units from the template, or it may follow the topics. See Longacre's analysis of a fund-raising letter (1992a), which divides the body of the letter into three points, corresponding to the slots of the credibility claim, problem, and motivated appeal, respectively. Note that a given text may combine two slots together into one structural unit, as shown by the label, *motivated appeal*.

The epistle of Ephesians, as shown by Breeze (1992), displays an overall structure with a slight variation in the use of the template. It has two main sections, one largely with commands and the other with supportive information. The first three chapters include supportive information (situational, motivational, credential, and enabling)[1] regarding the truth of the Christian beliefs, but chapters 4–6 contain Paul's exhortation on unity, purity, and mutual love and submission, interspersed with motivational material. Breeze's analysis shows that while Ephesians is organized in two sections (supportive information versus mainline of exhortation), motivational information is scattered throughout the book.

In some hortatory texts, the slots may be found at a lower level of organization. In the epistle of 1 John, Longacre (1983a:3) finds that "the schema is repetitive and recursive and runs through component sentences of the text instead of determining three major sections." The three major sections are: a lengthy introduction about why John is writing (chapters 1–2), the main body urging the reader to believe in Jesus and love one another (3:1–5:12), and the conclusion (5:13–21). The introduction and the body are further broken down into points.

A text may be organized by topics. Romans, as analyzed by Longacre and Wallis (1998), shows that the topic of soteriology has three sections: preparatory exhortation in chapters 1–5, central exhortation in chapters 6–8, and resultant exhortation in chapters 12–15. The topic of eschatology is found in chapters 9–11. For Malachi, Clendenen (1993:340) presents three main movements or topics of the book, each of which has elements of situation, change (corresponding to commands), and motivation. In 1 Peter, Wendland (2000) observes that the overall arguments are in three major parts, each on a different topic and in three types of information: problems, motivations, and appeals.

What then? A hortatory text may have an overall structure of its own, which may be according to the template, the topics, or some other criteria. Since hortatory texts are organized logically, rather than temporally, the presentation order of main units and the resulting overall organization are not strictly bound to occur sequentially in the template. Narrative discourse, on the other hand, tends to develop from stage exposition and inciting moment to climax and denouement, following the ordering in the template. It is especially crucial in the analysis of hortatory discourse to find the natural seams or boundary markers (e.g., the vocatives in 1 John) as they relate to other surface structure features and the thematic unity of the constituents of the text.

---

[1] Enabling information refers to what has been done already to help the reader keep the commands.

10.3 Peak

The concept of peak has proved very helpful, especially in the analysis of narrative texts, to explain irregular features in morphosyntax and phonology. That is, the notional tension at the climax or denouement is reflected in unusual surface features, for example, rhetorical underlining, crowded stage, shift in tense and aspect, shift in person, etc. (Longacre 1996, 1985). Peak is less well studied in non-narrative texts, but Longacre points out that there are similar structures in them as well. How does it help in the analysis of hortatory discourse? It not only helps to explain unusual surface features, but also points out the main thrust of some texts. If a text is organized according to the hortatory template, the peak unit may correspond to the motivation or command, where the speaker may have the greatest struggle convincing the hearer of the soundness of the advice and to launch into action.[2]

A meaningful cumulative thrust in some hortatory texts may correlate with a marked surface structure peak, such as rhetorical underlining, and a shift to dialogue and eventually to drama in a sermon. In 1 John, Longacre (1992b:279–280) finds dual peaks both in the introduction and the body. In the introduction, an ethical peak (Do not love the world, in 2:12–17) precedes a doctrinal peak (warning that it is the last hour, in 2:18–27). In the body, the doctrinal peak (4:1–6) occurs first, and then the ethical peak (4:7–21) with two paragraphs (Longacre 1996:49). The first short paragraph (4:7–10) makes three points: let us love, love is of God, and God proved His love by sending His only Son to die for us. The second paragraph (4:11–21) elaborates the three points in greater detail with recapitulation and paraphrase, displaying rhetorical underlining: for example, John writes,

(59) we ought to love one another (v. 11)
    we have seen and bear witness that God sent His Son to be the Savior of the world (v. 14)
    we have known and believed the love that God has toward us (v. 16a)
    God is love, and the one who dwells in love dwells in God, and God dwells in him (v. 16b)

Longacre (1992b:281) further argues that "the peaks of a book are often especially relevant to the macrostructure," with "macrocstructure" defined as a summary or précis or abstract that gives the central thrust (van Dijk 1980). Thus, in 1 John both the doctrinal peak and ethical peak are featured in the macrostructure, which is overtly stated twice in the book (3:23 and 5:1): "that we should believe on the name of His Son Jesus Christ and love one another."

In their analysis of Romans, Longacre and Wallis (1998) posit multiple peaks corresponding to different sections. There are three peaks in the three sections on soteriology: 3:21–31 in preparatory exhortation in chapters 1–5,

---

[2] It is also conceivable to envision high tension or struggle in the problem/situation slot that requires change, or in the authority/credibility when it is at stake. If it is marked by unusual surface forms, it may be the peak.

chapter 8 in central exhortation in chapters 6–8, and 12:9–21 in resultant exhortation in chapters 12–15. These peaks are marked by unusual features, such as a concentration of prepositional phrases and noun phrases, a rhetorical question and answer, a lyric with almost hymn-like quality, reiterated command element, and a chiastic structure. In the interwoven section on eschatology in chapters 9–11, the peak occurs in 11:33–36 as the "exquisitely crafted doxology" (1998:382) with key words (riches, wisdom, knowledge), which are later echoed in reverse order (know, counselor, and give/repay).

Terry (1995) gives a statistical approach to the peak features, such as constituent order of clauses and verbless clauses, found in 1 Corinthians, chapters 12–15. The peak areas, he notes, include "topics about which Paul felt and showed a marked increase in emotion" (1995:124), and they correspond to the themes mentioned in the opening thanksgiving in the book. (See also Alaichamy (1999) for the peak features in Colossians.)

10.4 Mainline and supportive information

10.4.1 Mainline of exhortation

Command forms are central to hortatory discourse, because the command slot is basic and minimal to the type. The central mainlines of other discourse types are marked by verbs with a distinct tense and aspect, such as past tense or perfective aspect with action verbs in narrative and present tense with static and relational verbs in expository (Aaron 1999). In contrast, hortatory texts (and possibly procedural texts like recipes) make use of modality, that is, they use imperative verbs and modals for mainline information. Command forms include not only second-person imperatives but also "hortatives ('let us love'), jussives ('let him love his brother also'), and 'ought' forms" (Longacre 1992b:278). Typically, however, hortatory texts include only a small percentage of command forms, leaving many verbs in the indicative mood. Hortatory discourse tends to have extensive embedding of expository or even narrative material. In the study of 1 John, for example, Longacre finds only 9 percent of main clause verbs to be in command forms and 58 percent in relational and static verb forms, which are more typical of expository type. The overall discourse type, however, is hortatory because the command forms are central to the text, which moves from disguised and MITIGATED commands to overt commands at peaks. Regarding 1 John, he thus states: "By *count*, expository-type verbs predominate, but as to *weight*, hortatory-type verbs predominate" (1992b:279).

As a discourse type that is least vivid in the hierarchy of degrees of VIVIDNESS from drama to narrative, procedural, expository, and to hortatory (Longacre 1996:15), it is not surprising to find explicit command forms to be statistically less frequent than other verb forms in hortatory discourse. A sermon with an embedded story is more vivid and thus palatable and remembered longer by the congregation. Jesus frequently used parables for exhortation. While they are narratives in internal structure, they are hortatory texts—with a moral statement at the end—spoken in the presence of the Pharisees, disciples, or multitude of people (Hwang and Lathers 2002). If a preacher were to bombard a congregation with commands throughout the sermon, the listeners may want to flee or ignore his message and fall asleep. Thus, it is a distinct feature of many hortatory texts that the mainline forms of commands are not predominant in frequency counts. Embedding of other types higher on the vividness hierarchy with their characteristic verb forms is expected to be common. Likewise, there may be skewing; for example, a text may be expository on the surface but hortatory in the notional structure. In hortatory, embedding and skewing of discourse types are means of mitigation.

10.4.2 Salience ranking scheme of verb forms

Hortatory discourse includes not only the mainline of exhortation but also other types of information. Similar to the salience ranking scheme of verb forms in narrative discourse (see chapter 5), a salience scheme can be posited for hortatory discourse. Longacre (2003a:121) posits such a scheme for Biblical Hebrew (as found in the Joseph story in Genesis 37 and 39–48) from the primary line of exhortation to the setting/problem, with some explanations added in figure 10.1.

Band 1: Primary line of exhortation
    1.1   Imperative (2 person) (unranked)   'do X'
    1.2   Cohortative (1 person) (unranked)   'let me/us do X'
    1.3   Jussive (3 person) (unranked)   'let him do X'

Band 2: Secondary line of exhortation
    2.1   ʾal 'not' + jussive/imperfect   negative commands
    2.2   Modal imperfect   'should/must'

Band 3: Results/consequences (Motivation)
    3.1   w (consecutive) perfect   positive results
    3.2   lôʾ/p̄en + imperfect   negative results
    3.3   (Future) perfect   as part of conditional construction

Band 4: Setting (Problem)
    4.1   Perfect (of past events)   problem arising from the past
    4.2   Participles   '-ing'
    4.3   Nominal clauses   verbless

Figure 10.1. Salience scheme for hortatory discourse in Biblical Hebrew[3]

---

[3] While the sub-types in Band 1 are unranked, those in Bands 2–4 are sub-ranked within each given band.

On the scale, command forms mark the primary line of exhortation while negative commands and modal uses of the imperfect mark the secondary line. Band 3 is no longer filled by command forms but by results or consequences of obeying commands, and Band 4 includes other static, expository-like elements. Analogous ranking schemes are presented for Koine Greek by Terry (1995:95) based on 1 Corinthians, and by Alaichamy (1999:49) on Colossians. Wendland's gradient of "relative directness, urgency, or degree of mitigation" shows a similar ranking (2000:58).

10.4.3 The importance of sociolinguistic dynamics

Closely related to the issue of mainline of the exhortation are the sociolinguistic dynamics in different social contexts. Hortatory discourse spoken by a socially higher or dominant person to his subordinates may have more blunt imperatives compared with that spoken by a subordinate to a supervisor or a subject to a king. There are also texts between people of more or less the same status.

Longacre (2003a: chapter 5) finds that linguistic structures of hortatory discourse in the Joseph story in Genesis reflect differing social situations. Speaker dominance is exemplified by Jacob's speech to his sons in Genesis 43:11–14, where unmitigated imperatives are freely used. The dominance of the addressee is shown in Genesis 40:14–15, when Joseph speaks to the chief cupbearer after the interpretation of the dream. The mainline of exhortation is completely mitigated so that instead of the imperative Joseph uses the future perfect as in predictive discourse ("you will do me a favor, you will remember me to Pharaoh, you will get me out of this prison"). In Genesis 41:33–36 when Joseph speaks to Pharaoh, second person imperatives are avoided and deferential jussives are used instead ("let Pharaoh find a wise man" and "let him set him over the land of Egypt"). Similar uses of the jussive occur in the book of Esther, for example, when advice is given to the king in 1:19: "if it pleases the king, let him issue a royal decree…, let it be written in the laws…, let the king give her royal position to someone else."[4]

10.5 Sample text analyses

Three short texts—two English and one Korean—are used to show the characteristic features of hortatory discourse, and analysis of hortatory texts at the discourse and paragraph levels.

---

[4] This deferential use of *the king* as a term of address, rather than the second person pronoun, is similar to Korean, in which a nominal form like *mother, teacher,* or *pastor* is proper and the second person pronoun of any kind is impolite in speaking to a socially dominant or older person.

10.5 Sample text analyses

10.5.1 English texts

The first text comes from the *Dallas Morning News* (Fairbank 2004), with the headline in an imperative, "Prepare to be bugged, bitten" (see Hwang 2005). A box in the middle of the article has its own headline in capital letters, with four bulleted items:

(60) Tips on Reducing Problems

- **Get rid** of standing water—**overturn** containers, **change** the water in pet dishes frequently, **cover** trash cans and repair leaking plumbing or exterior faucets.
- **Maintain** door, porch and window screens to keep mosquitoes out.
- **Wear** long-sleeved shirts and long pants when outdoors, and **spray** clothing with repellents containing permethrin or DEET because mosquitoes may bite through thin clothing.
- **Stay** indoors at dawn, at dusk and in the early evening.

With every sentence in the imperative mood (boldfaced), we are told what to do (the command slot) to avoid being *bugged* and *bitten*, which is a motivation universally shared and thus implied. At the paragraph level, each of the four points functions as a thesis in a (hortatory) coordinate paragraph. All four theses are on the mainline of exhortation.

The main body of the article, in (61), surrounds the box and follows an indicative sentence as the sub-headline: *Wet, cool spring is expected to bring more bloodsucking critters.*

(61)

[a] The recent storms are going to bring swarms.
[b] "It's going to be pretty much perfect for insects through the summer. We had one of those springs that was wet and coolish, but never got horrible. Everybody remembers it as pleasant," said <u>Dr. Roger Gold, an urban entomologist</u> ... "So did the bugs."
[c] The repercussions of the wet, temperate weather will be felt for months to come. Mosquitoes, ticks, chiggers and fleas are expected to bite their way into our lives. "Tons of people already have been coming in with complaints of out-of-control flea infestations in their homes and their yards," said <u>Kendall Sheffield, a vet technician</u> ... "The fleas have taken over their animals."
[d] People **need to protect** themselves and their pets from the coming scourge since some pests carry disease. Insect repellent containing DEET is recommended.
[e] Mosquitoes can carry West Nile virus, which can sicken people and horses. They also carry heartworms, which can be fatal for dogs and

cats. "The more mosquitoes you have, the more opportunity you have for disease," said <u>Dean Brown</u>, <u>a master gardener</u>...

[f] Creepy crawlers, such as slugs, snails and cockroaches, will have a banner year also. Unfortunately, when the summer heats up, they'll want to move inside where it's air-conditioned. "They just love us to death," <u>Dr. Gold</u> said.

The text primarily presents problems and undesirable situations, except [d], which adds a mitigated command (with a modal form *need* and a recommendation). The text includes quotations from three people (underlined above), whose areas of expertise are related to the issue (an urban entomologist, a vet technician, and a master gardener), thereby giving the authority or credibility to the article. This text aims at influencing the reader's conduct, and has all four slots of the template: authority, problem/situation, command, and motivation. The implicit motivation is to avoid getting bugged and bitten. The predicted negative conditions provide explicit motivation to act now.

After the introductory thesis statement in [a], the quoted speech in [b] explains how the wet and coolish spring was pleasant for both human beings and bugs. Then three groups are pointed out which can create undesirable situations: fleas, mosquitoes, and creepy crawlers. The warnings about West Nile virus and heartworms associated with mosquitoes in [e] are threats, used as motivation. The mitigated command in [d] and the motivation in [e] function together as the motivated appeal/command, which may be argued to be the peak of this rather short text.

Another text comes from the Business section of the *Dallas Morning News* (Yip 2003) and carries the headline "Don't get bit." In the upper right-hand corner there is a section with five bulleted points. Only this section is presented in (62) and analyzed for its paragraph structure. The entire article on investment spans two pages of the newspaper, too long to reproduce here.

(62) Guarding against fraud: Here are ways to protect against investment fraud.[5]

> 1 Always **check out** the investment and the person promoting it.
> 2 **Don't invest** in something you don't understand.
> 3 **Take** your time learning about the investment.
> 4 **Don't be pressured** into turning over your money immediately.
> 5 If something sounds too good to be true, it probably is.
> 6 **Don't invest** based solely on the recommendation of a member of a organization or religious or ethnic group to which you belong.
> Source: *Dallas Morning News* research

The thesis of this short text is stated in S1: *Always check out the investment and the person promoting it*. The negative sentence in S2 is a paraphrase of the thesis. S3–4 amplifies the thesis regarding the time factor ('take time'), and

---

[5] Sentence numbers are added for ease of reference.

10.5 Sample text analyses

S6 further amplifies the thesis regarding personal relationship. The generic, common sense statement in S5 may be viewed as a reason for S6, which gives the second amplifying command in negative form.[6]

> Thesis: Negated Antonym Paraphrase ¶
>   Thesis: 1   **Always check out** the investment and the person promoting it.
>   Paraphrase: 2   **Don't invest** in something you don't understand.
> Amplification 1: Negated Antonym Paraphrase ¶
>   Thesis: 3   **Take your time** learning about the investment.
>   Paraphrase: 4   **Don't be pressured** into turning over your money immediately.
> Amplification 2: Reason ¶
>   Reason: 5   If something sounds too good to be true, it probably is.
>   Thesis: 6   **Don't invest** based solely on the recommendation of a member of an organization or religious or ethnic group to which you belong.

Figure 10.2. Analysis of "Guarding against fraud"

There are two positive commands, *check out* and *take your time*, and three negative commands, *don't invest* twice and *don't be pressured*. The paraphrase relations between S1 and S2, and between S3 and S4 can be called Negated Antonym Paraphrases (NAP) in a broad sense.[7] Negatives function here to paraphrase and reinforce what is given in positive command. That is, S2 and S4 do not deny what precedes them, but say the same things, in a different way, using negatives. These negative sentences, however, may occur on their own without the positive command sentences, in which case they would function to deny or warn against careless behavior, that is, investing in things that we don't understand. Note that the negative imperatives may strike the reader more strongly and vividly than the theses in positive forms. That is, the reader may take more notice of the paraphrases in negative form. S6 certainly is a strong warning against the common tendency to trust someone in our own group.

Let us compare the following two extracts of this text, with only the positives in (63) and with only the negatives in (64).

---

[6] Depending on the role S5 plays in the overall structure, alternative analyses are possible, but we believe this analysis is plausible and simple for our purpose. As the only indicative sentence in the stream of imperatives, S5 may be viewed as a reason for or a comment to S3–4, S2–4, or even the whole text.

[7] Longacre (1996:78) describes NAP as "one of the closest possible varieties of paraphrase" with examples like *poor* and *not rich*, and *short* and *not tall*.

(63) Guarding against fraud: Here are ways to protect against investment fraud.

- Always check out the investment and the person promoting it.
- Take your time learning about the investment.
- If something sounds too good to be true, it probably is.

(64) Guarding against fraud: Here are ways to protect against investment fraud.

- Don't invest in something you don't understand.
- Don't be pressured into turning over your money immediately.
- Don't invest based solely on the recommendation of a member of an organization or religious or ethnic group to which you belong.

Even without considering the third point in each group, which are not paraphrases, negative commands may be more weighty and informative. A similar point is made in Jordan (1998) about a negative statement. In certain contexts, as in *The captain was NOT drunk last night*, he states that "a clear negative statement had much more power than the positive, because it implied that the positive (the captain's drunkenness) is the usual or normal situation" (1998:706), and that it "contains more information" (1998:707). The negative imperatives in our text may similarly have "more power." It is noteworthy that negatives contribute to the mainline of exhortation in hortatory discourse in a crucial way that is not parallel to other types of discourse (Hwang 2004).

10.5.2 A Korean text

The Korean text entitled "The Working Person" comes from a newspaper column article written by Rev. Kyung-Jik Han, one of the best-known preachers from Korea. The text compares diligent workers who feel satisfaction with their work, and sluggards who are full of complaints and dissatisfaction, thus making work for others. Although sluggards are in the minority, they make noise and create disturbances. There should be more 'working people' and less 'work-making people' for the country to do well and for people to feel satisfaction with their lives. The last sentence, S28, of the text quotes 2 Thessalonians 3:11–12.

The first twenty-one sentences (S1–S21) present and compare two types of people. On the surface, the text seems to be expository with stative verbs in the timeless present tense and with no verbs in command forms. Sentences 22–23 contain the first overt indication of this text being hortatory, with verbs having a deontic modal 'should', arguing that there should be more people who work. Then in S24–26 the expository form is resumed. He states that although the world is not perfect, those who are devoted to their work know the value of life. The last two sentences lead the reader to the biblical

10.5 Sample text analyses

passage, which overtly gives a command in the imperative mood. In its template, the text is analyzed as having the following units (Hwang 1992):

Situation/Problem: S1–21
Motivation: S22–26
Command/Authority: S27–28

Notice that the motivation slot precedes the command, and the latter is combined with authority.

For the analysis at the paragraph level, the text is given in a literal English translation to reveal the structural features of Korean to a certain extent. The first word of each sentence in the Korean text appears in capital letters to show the presentation of sentence topics. See appendix 10 for the paragraph structure in a tree diagram.

The situation/problem is expounded by an (expository) contrast paragraph, consisting of an introduction in figure 10.3, thesis in figure 10.4, and antithesis in figure 10.5. The introduction has two sentences, with the second one identifying the two kinds of people stated in S1.

Introduction: Identification ¶
    Thesis: 1 In ANY organization or society (there) are generally two kinds of people.
    Identification: 2 ONE is people who work and the other is people who make work.

Figure 10.3. Analysis of introduction to Situation/Problem (Slot) of "The working person"

The thesis lists three characteristics of working type people in a coordinate paragraph. The second and third theses of the paragraph display embedded paragraphs of amplification and paraphrase, as shown below in the form of indentations.

```
Thesis: Coordinate ¶ (On working people)
    Thesis 1:               3 The FORMER are quiet.
    Thesis 2: Amplification ¶
       Thesis: Paraphrase ¶
          Thesis:           4 To MY(=their own) work (they) completely
                              devote mind and body.
          Paraphrase:       5 (They) do not meddle with OTHER's work.
       Amplification:       6 To fulfill (their) OWN assumed responsibility
                              (they) pour energy.
    Thesis 3: Paraphrase ¶
       Thesis:              7 ALSO in the work itself (they) feel satisfac-
                              tion.
       Paraphrase:          8 THAT IS, through work (they) feel happiness
                              and taste the value of life.
```

Figure 10.4. Analysis of thesis of Situation/Problem (Slot) of "The working person"

The antithesis, which presents the core problem, is about sluggards, and it is much longer (S9–21). It has two main parts: a thesis expounded by a reason paragraph with a reason and a thesis (S9–17), and a comment expounded by a concession paragraph with a concession and a thesis (S18–21). The list of characteristics of this group of people occurs in an embedded coordinate paragraph (S9–15) as the reason in a reason paragraph. The thesis is stated in S16–17 that sluggards create work.

```
Antithesis: Comment ¶ (On sluggards)
    Thesis: Reason ¶
       Reason: Coordinate ¶
          Introduction:     9 BUT people of a different kind are exactly the
                              opposite from the former.
          Thesis 1:        10 COMMONLY, (they) are talkative.
          Thesis 2:        11 (They) like to meddle with OTHER's work.
          Thesis 3: Reason ¶
             Reason: Coordinate ¶
                Thesis 1: 12 If (things) do not fit (their) own minds even
                              A LITTLE, (they) complain right away.
                Thesis 2: 13 In (their) OWN work (they) cannot feel
                              satisfaction.
                Thesis 3: 14 ESPECIALLY, if the work does not come out
                              well, (they) think that the responsibility lies
                              not with (them)selves but with others.
             Thesis:       15 THEREFORE, always (they) are full of com-
                              plaints and dissatisfaction.
```

```
            Thesis: Paraphrase ¶
              Thesis:          16 SO, (they) are bound to make work.
              Paraphrase:      17 (They) make the atmosphere such that (it) is
                                  difficult for OTHERS to work also.
        Comment: Concession ¶
          Concession: Paraphrase ¶
              Thesis:          18 What is (reason to be) THANKFUL is, (I)
                                  regard that the number of this kind of people
                                  is not high.
              Paraphrase:      19 (They) are the MINORITY.
          Thesis: Exemplification ¶
              Thesis:          20 BUT (they) make big noises.
              Example:         21 SOMETIMES (they) even come out to the street
                                  running.
```

Figure 10.5. Analysis of antithesis of Situation/Problem (Slot) of "The working person"

The comment of the antithesis has two parts forming a concession paragraph: a concession with an embedded paraphrase paragraph (S18–19) and a thesis with an exemplification paragraph (S20–21).

The motivation slot in figure 10.6 is expounded by a (hortatory) coordinate paragraph made up of two theses, which each have an embedded paragraph. Although this Korean text is also quite short (as are the two previous English texts), we might argue that this section is the peak. There is a shift in perspective from the two types of people to their relevance to the country and even the world. Especially note S25 where the society, the place of work, and the country are mentioned, and they occur with a reference to 'I' (*nay*) in all three clauses. Korean is a pro-drop language in which an overt reference to the subject, object, or any other argument may be omitted as long as it is identifiable in the context. Such omissions are shown in the English translation in parentheses, since they are needed for a correct understanding in English. We may consider this multiple reference to 'I' to be an excessive reference corresponding to the rhetorical underlining at the high point of the text. A note of interest is that 'I' occurs five times in the text, four times in the motivation and once in presenting the situation in S4, and they are used only in referring to the working group. In S26, there are two forms of reference for the same people, namely, 'I' and 'those who devote to work'. The normal English reference to them as 'they' is supplied in parentheses in S26.

Motivation: Coordinate ¶
    Thesis 1: Paraphrase ¶
        Thesis: 22 In order for the COUNTRY to do well, (there) is no need to speak twice as to which kind of people (there) should be more of.
        Paraphrase: 23 (There) should be many WORKING people.
    Thesis 2: Concession ¶
        Concession: Amplification ¶
            Thesis: 24 The WORLD is not perfect.
            Amplification: 25 The society in which I live, the place where I work, or the country to which I belong is not perfect.
        Thesis: 26 BUT those who devote to work no matter what workplace I am (=they are) feel the value of life.

Figure 10.6. Motivation slot of "The working person"

The command and authority slots are joined in one (hortatory) quote paragraph in figure 10.7. The quote formula referring to the Bible signals authority, while the quoted biblical passages include command elements. Although there are no other command forms in the text, the use of the deontic modal 'should' in the motivation slot and the listing of the obvious undesirable qualities of sluggards clearly reflect the hortatory thrust of the text before its final sentence.

Command/authority: (Hortatory) Quote ¶
    Quote Formula: 27 The BIBLE advises:
    Quote: 28 "WE hear that among you (there) are fellows who act without plans, who do not work but only make work; (we) exhort such persons ... to work in quietness and eat their food." (2 Thessalonians 3:11–12)

Figure 10.7. Command/authority slot of "The working person"

10.6 Conclusions

Hortatory discourse aims at influencing beliefs, values, and conduct. The central element of its template is thus the command or exhortation, but other elements may occur either explicitly or implicitly: the authority or credibility, the indication of a problem/situation, and the motivation to follow the command. While these four elements may contribute to the organizational structure of a text, they could just be typical types of information in hortatory discourse. The text organization may be based on topics as in Romans, 1 Peter, and Malachi, with schematic elements found recursively for each topic.

In several aspects we may note that hortatory texts are quite distinct from narratives and all other types of discourse. Hortatory differs from other types in using modals and command forms on its mainline, rather than using unique tense and aspect forms. In a way, the interaction between the text producer and the hearer/reader is more direct and tighter compared to other discourse types. The text producer is an exhorter trying to influence the exhortee's behavior, unlike a narrator or an expositor who can be somewhat detached or step aside from the participants involved in action. This is why the sociolinguistic dynamics are more important in hortatory texts than other types, sometimes resulting in differing linguistic forms, such as, blunt commands, mitigated forms of indicative mood, or deferential use. Peaks in narrative may encode mainline information as fast moving events, but it is very common for stories to stop the action progression altogether at peaks to exhibit the notional tension in paraphrases and parallelism along with a shift in tense/aspect/mood. So the eventline or storyline may stall at the climax, and background information of a stative or negative nature may dominate the peak episode, as we saw in the "Hans" text in chapter 4. In hortatory texts, several studies have noted that the unusual peak features correlate with the main cumulative thrust, sometimes especially relevant to the macrostructure. The peak in hortatory may thus include the mainline of exhortation.

Negatives, which tend to encode background information in all types of discourse, may also encode the mainline in hortatory when the command is given in negative form as in a prohibition of a certain behavior. The text in (62) on investment exemplifies the use of negatives to give a warning, perhaps more strongly than using only affirmative forms.

10.7 Exercises

(1) Consider again the speeches of Joseph (Gen. 42:18–20 and Gen. 45:9–13) as considered in the exercise at the end of chapter 3. In general, what are some ways to mitigate or make exhortation less pointed and sharp in the target language?

(2) If you have translated or will soon be translating the First Epistle of John in the New Testament, how is exhortation mitigated there in your target language, that is, when are straight commands given and when is another wording used?

Appendix 10. Paragraph structure of "The Working Person"

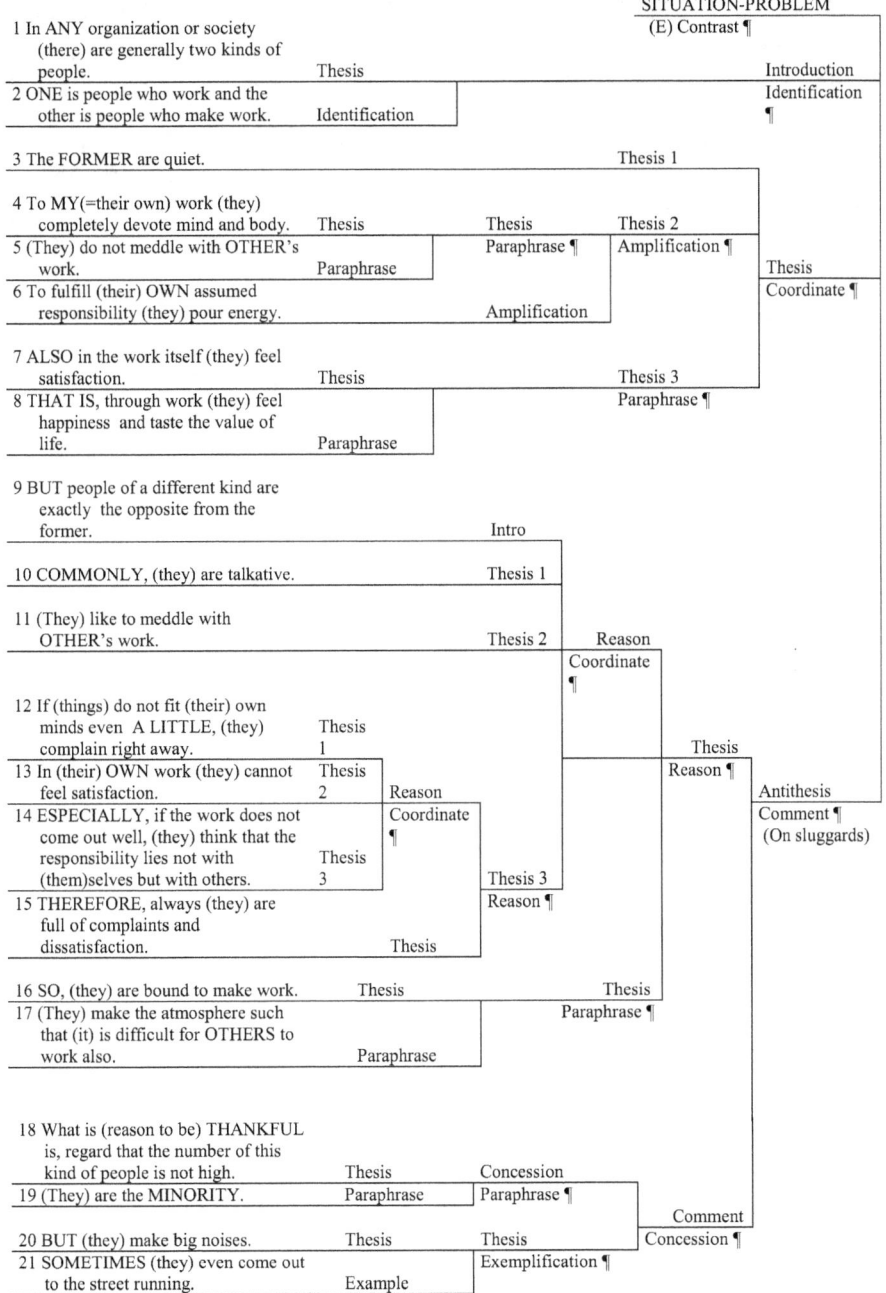

		MOTIVATION
		(H) Coordinate ¶
22 In order for the COUNTRY to do well, (there) is no need to speak twice as to which kind of people (there) should be more of.	Thesis	Thesis 1
23 (There) should be many WORKING people.	Paraphrase	Paraphrase ¶
24 The WORLD is not perfect.	Thesis	Concession
25 The society in which I live, the place where I work, or the country to which I belong is not perfect.	Amplification	Amplification ¶
		Thesis 2
26 BUT those who devote to work no matter what workplace I am (=they are) feel the value of life.	Thesis	Concession ¶

		COMMAND-AUTHORITY
27 The BIBLE advises:	Quote Formula	(H) Quote ¶
28 "WE hear that among you (there) are fellows who act without plans, who do not work but only make work; (we) exhort such persons … to work in quietness and eat their food." (2 Thessalonians 3:11-12)	Quote	

Chapter 11

Expository Discourse

Expository discourse has logical organization, instead of contingent temporal organization, and thematic orientation, instead of agent orientation. It has explanations and descriptions of salient themes (Jones 1977) on its mainline of development as against other supportive material. The most static verb forms tend to be used in explanations and descriptions, so expository discourse can be regarded as the antithesis of narrative discourse. We can turn the salience ranking scheme for narrative discourse (chapter 5) upside down, so to speak, so that one of the lower bands of narrative discourse, the setting, becomes the highest band in expository discourse. The bands beneath setting in narrative, namely, irrealis and evaluation, can still be retained in the new expository scheme. In scientific discourse, hypotheses are proposed and evaluated, so that irrealis (the tentative positing of schemes) and evaluation of those schemes are very much a part of the picture. Other elements of the now demoted upper bands of narrative, such as storyline along with its attendant background and flashback, can be found in anecdotes and illustrations in expository discourse.

For Biblical Hebrew, for example, Longacre (2003a:111) suggests a tentative ranking of verb forms for expository discourse: nominal (verbless) and existential ('there is' and 'there isn't') at the highest level, followed by copulative 'be', stative/denominative verbs, participials, and finite verbs. For expository discourse in Ecclesiastes, Hays (1995) presents a similar ranking of Biblical Hebrew verb forms in three levels: from nominal, existential, and participles (for statements of present reality) to imperfect (for supporting observations), and to perfect (for statements of past experience).

The sharp contrast in salience ranking scheme between expository and narrative discourse is also shown by the transitivity values (Hopper and Thompson 1980) of mainline clauses in the two types of discourse. Hwang

(2009) reports low transitivity values in expository mainline clauses in comparison to those of narrative, roughly at the ratio of 1:3. While narrative texts have events on its mainline with high action kinesis and telic aspect, expository mainline verbs are non-action, atelic, and non-volitional, which are low in transitivity. Thompson and Hopper (2001) also find that conversation in English is very low in transitivity, noting that everyday conversation is mostly about how things are from our perspective, describing states, revealing attitudes, ascribing properties to people and situations, and giving assessments of situations and behavior. Much of what they describe is expository material that is found in conversation.[1] The correlation between high transitivity clauses and foregrounding (mainline), as originally presented by Hopper and Thompson (1980), is restricted to a specific discourse type, that is, narrative, and their hypothesis can now be referred to as a *narrative discourse transitivity hypothesis*.[2]

Analogous to the plot structure or narrative template that includes inciting moment and climax, expository discourse may use a template comprising problem, solution, supporting argumentation, and evaluation (Longacre 1996:34). Hoey (1983) presents a similar schema: situation-problem-solution-evaluation.[3] This schema would suggest a scientific or a linguistic paper. On the other hand, expository discourse without such problem-solution tension, that is, one that is more descriptive, may largely use setting information in a simpler structure.

We first present an analysis of Psalm 23 in tree structure, which follows the general approach and methodology characterizing this volume or *The Grammar of Discourse* (1996) on which this volume is based. A radically different sort of analysis of expository discourse, based on the lexical structure of information, makes up the second section of this chapter. This further approach to expository discourse can be shown, however, to be relatable to that illustrated in the first section.

11.1 Analysis of Psalm 23 in tree structure

In illustrating the first and more conventional approach, we resort to a piece of expository discourse of high antiquity and devotional value, the Hebrew text of the 23rd Psalm. In expository discourse in Hebrew, the dominant mainline constructions are verbless clauses, which may on occasion have an overt copula. The participial clause is next in dominance. Clauses with all other verb forms are of less salience. While Psalm 23 belongs to this structure, there are instances in Biblical Hebrew of Psalms which fit the Hoey schema, for example, Psalm 73 (as given in chapter 8 of Longacre and Bowling, to appear).

---

[1] In terms of transitivity values, expository text may show the lowest of all discourse types. Although lower than narrative, mainline of procedural texts, being organized in contingent temporal succession, may show a correlation with high transitivity.

[2] Cumming and Ono (1997) refer to it as *discourse transitivity*, rather than simply *transitivity*, but we propose to call it *narrative discourse transitivity*. Even in narratives, those with detached perspectives show a better correlation with foregrounding (Hopper 1997 and Hwang 2009).

[3] Watson (1984) presents binary structuring of Pacoh expository texts, with two subtypes of evaluation and syllogism schemes of logical relationships.

11.1 Analysis of Psalm 23 in tree structure

In the following tree representation, Psalm 23 is displayed as a cyclic expository (E) result paragraph. It is cyclic in that the beginning of the psalm is echoed in its last verse. It is a result paragraph in that the results of having Yahweh as one's shepherd are largely what the psalm is all about. We do not give the text of this psalm separately; it is given in the tree indentation diagram.[4]

Title

מִזְמוֹר לְדָוִד [1]

"A Psalm of David."

Cyclic (E) Result ¶
  Thesis:

יְהוָה * רֹעִי

(v.1) Yahweh # my shepherd

Result: (progressively weighted) (Procedural) Amplification ¶
  Thesis:

לֹא אֶחְסָר:

I shall not want/lack [yqtl]

Amplification 1: (Procedural) Coordinate ¶
  Thesis 1:

בִּנְאוֹת דֶּשֶׁא יַרְבִּיצֵנִי [2]

(v.2) In green pastures he makes-lie.down-me [yqtl]

  Thesis 2:

עַל־מֵי מְנֻחוֹת יְנַהֲלֵנִי:

by waters of rest he-leads-me [yqtl]

Amplification 2: (Procedural) Coordinate ¶
  Thesis 1:

נַפְשִׁי יְשׁוֹבֵב [3]

(v.3) My soul he restores [yqtl],

  Thesis 2:

יַנְחֵנִי בְמַעְגְּלֵי־צֶדֶק לְמַעַן שְׁמוֹ:

he-leads-me [yqtl] in paths of righteousness for his name's sake.

---

[4] The implied copulas in verbless clauses are marked by * in the data line and # in translation. Verb tenses are indicated in brackets: *yqtl* is imperfect, *qtl* is perfect, and *wqtl* is *waw*-perfect.

Amplification 3: (Procedural) Reason ¶
   Thesis:

גַּם כִּי־אֵלֵךְ בְּגֵיא צַלְמָוֶת לֹא־אִירָא רָע ⁴

(v.4) Even though I walk *[yqtl]* a valley of deep darkness, I will not fear *[yqtl]* evil.

  Reason: (E) Paraphrase ¶
   Thesis:

כִּי־אַתָּה * עִמָּדִי

For you *[attah]* # with-me.

  Paraphrase:

שִׁבְטְךָ וּמִשְׁעַנְתֶּךָ * הֵמָּה יְנַחֲמֻנִי׃

Your rod and your staff # they *[hemmah]* comfort-me *[yqtl]*.

Amplification 4: (progressively weighted) (E) Coordinate ¶
   Thesis 1:

תַּעֲרֹךְ לְפָנַי ׀ שֻׁלְחָן נֶגֶד צֹרְרָי ⁵

(v.5) You set *[yqtl]* a table before-me in the presence of my enemies.

  Thesis 2:

דִּשַּׁנְתָּ בַשֶּׁמֶן רֹאשִׁי

You've-anointed *[qtl]* my head with oil

  Thesis 3:

כּוֹסִי * רְוָיָה׃

My cup # saturation/well-filled.

Thesis': (Predictive) Reason ¶
  Reason:

אַךְ ׀ טוֹב וָחֶסֶד יִרְדְּפוּנִי כָּל־יְמֵי חַיָּי ⁶

(v.6) Surely goodness and mercy shall-accompany-me *[yqtl]* all the days of my life

  Thesis:

וְשַׁבְתִּי בְּבֵית־יְהוָה לְאֹרֶךְ יָמִים׃

And I shall dwell *[wqtl]* in the house of Yahweh forever.

Figure 11.1. Psalm 23

This psalm turns on the metaphor announced in a verbless clause in verse 1: יְהוָה * רֹעִי 'Yahweh # my shepherd'. The result is expressed in a *yqtl* clause: לֹא אֶחְסָר 'I shall not want'. This is amplified in verse 2 with the metaphors of בִּנְאוֹת דֶּשֶׁא 'in green pastures' and מֵי מְנֻחוֹת 'waters of rest', in clauses with *yqtl* forms. In verse 3 clauses employing the same verb form constitute a second amplification with reference to restoration and leading in the paths of righteousness. In verses 2–4 the prevalence of *yqtl* clauses is best explained by assuming that they constitute embedded procedural (how-God-does-it) paragraphs. Amplification 3 in verse 4, however, although continuing to employ *yqtl* forms in its thesis, is a marked structure by the occurrence of the free pronouns *'attah* 'you' and *hemmah* 'they'. The former is found in a verbless clause, and the latter is found in a clause with a finite verb, where pronouns do not normally occur.

Amplification 4, in verse 5, has a progressive weighting in terms of the hierarchy of expository elements, *yqtl* ... *qtl* ... # (verbless clause), and exploits the basic structures of lyric expository poetry. Noticeably דִּשַּׁ֖נְתָּ בַשֶּׁ֥מֶן רֹאשִׁ֗י 'You've anointed my head with oil', with its *qtl*, outweighs the previous *yqtl* clause, but on the other hand is outranked by the following verbless clause כּוֹסִ֥י * רְוָיָֽה 'My cup # saturation'.

Verse 6 is a predictive reason paragraph which recapitulates the original thesis of verse 1; its thesis is weighted by a *wqtl* clause: וְשַׁבְתִּ֥י בְּבֵית־יְ֝הוָ֗ה לְאֹ֣רֶךְ יָמִֽים 'And I shall dwell in the house of Yahweh forever'. This weighted thesis is not only marked by *wqtl* but by the accompanying switch reference which indicates result/promise.

In brief, there is a lot of craftsmanship in this psalm, craftsmanship which reinforces its central metaphor of Yahweh as shepherd with a detailing of His care for His people.

11.2 Analysis according to the structure of information

The second main approach to expository discourse that is presented in this chapter is, in effect, Discourse Analysis as developed by Zellig Harris from the 1950's onward to the recent past (Harris 1952, 1963). In this approach and methodology, grammar is minimalized, and lexical (or as Pike and Pike 1982 would say, "referential") structure is exploited. It also ties into the interest in "collocations" in Great Britain.

Broadly speaking, expository discourse transmits information of a non-narrative sort by such statements as A=B (A equals B), A→B (A implies B), A ∧ B (A is associated with B), or A is constituted of B. Further relations such as A happens under B conditions are also encountered. We will illustrate Harris' approach to discourse analysis with portions of the first chapter of Paul's Epistle to the Ephesians (see appendix 11A) and with the medical discourse, "Amyloid Plaques and Neurofibrillary Tangles in Alzheimers Disease" by Margolis and Rabins (appendix 11B). We will show that one common approach can profitably be applied to these very different expository discourses, revealing the structure and meaning of both. As mentioned above, this approach is essentially what Harris first proposed in the 1950s and elaborated over the next several decades of his scholarly life, culminating in application to a medical text in collaboration with five colleagues (Harris et al. 1989).

Essentially, Harris's discourse analysis consists in tabulating a discourse in a columnar arrangement which shunts like-information into columns under controlled constraints, generalizes across columns, and presents the resultant structure as the information content of the discourse. Take the following illustrative piece:

(65)   1 John likes Mary. 2 He loves her big blue eyes. 3 He likes the very smell of her favorite perfume. 4 She has personality characteristics that also appeal to him. 5 He loves her enough to marry her 6 but he has no financial security to offer her. 7 Ed also loves Mary. 8 Ed is heir to a small fortune, 9 but Mary doesn't like him. 10a She really loves John 10b who appeals to her in every way.

Let us try tabulating the above discourse. We will need J, L, and M columns to start with (for John, Loves, Mary).

Table 11.1. Harris' discourse analysis applied to "John likes Mary" text

J(ohn)	**L(oves)**	**M(ary)**
1. John	likes	Mary
2. He	loves	her big blue eyes
3. He	likes	the very smell of her favorite perfume
4. *He	finds appealing	certain of her personality characteristics
5a. He	loves	her
5b. [enough to]	marry	her
7. Ed also	loves	Mary

Let us break our tabulation right here and offer a few comments. To begin with, *like* and *love* are seen to fall into the same column; or as we will henceforth say, the same equivalence chain. *John* and *he* are a regular equivalence by virtue of pronoun anaphora. Over in the third column, we find *Mary, her, the very smell of her favorite perfume* and *her big blue eyes*. But what about sentence 4? Here we resort—as Harris often did—to a grammatical transformation. Thus, *She has personality characteristics that appeal to him* can be transformed grammatically to "He finds appealing certain of her personality characteristics"; this can now be charted as above. This resort to a grammatical transformation, marked by an asterisk in tabulations, is in the interest of standardizing the text grammatically and thus minimizing grammatical differences with the intent of highlighting the lexical content.

11.2 Analysis according to the structure of information

We still have to account for the rest of our short text above. What do we do with the sentence, *But he has no financial security to offer her?* Here, in table 11.2, we can make a second tabulation with columns labelled J for John, $ for financial security, and M for Mary. The sentence *Ed also loves Mary* has already been relegated to the first tabulation; since *loves* is the same as L and *Mary* is the same as M, *Ed* proves to be in the same equivalence chain with *John*. Then in the second tabulation we can accommodate the sentence *Ed is heir to a small fortune*. Contrastive items often fall into the same equivalence chain, where *John* is –$ and *Ed* is +$.

Table 11.2. Second tabulation of "John likes Mary"

J(ohn)	[+/–] $	M(ary)
6. he	has no financial security	to offer her
8. Ed	is heir to a small fortune	

Finally, in our tabulation of the little text above we need an array in which M (Mary) is in the first column and L continues in the second column and J (John) is the third column. This array is the reciprocal of the first in that items are changed from first to third columns. Positive and negative values of L will occur:

Table 11.3. Third tabulation of "John likes Mary"

M(ary)	[+/–] L(oves)	J(ohn)
9. Mary	doesn't love	him (Ed)
10a. She	really loves	John
10b. *She	finds appealing in every way	John

The three tabulations in tables 11.1–11.3 make explicit the structure and meaning of the text.

We now turn our attention to the study of the content structure of the expository material found in the epistle of Paul to the Ephesians, chapter 1:3–14 (see appendix 11A). The study and tabulations will as a whole be based on the NIV translation—with occasional departures from that text as seen below.

Ephesians 1:3 is crucial to the content structure of much that follows: *Praise be to the God and Father of our Lord Jesus Christ, who has blessed us with the heavenly realms with every spiritual blessing in Christ.* Actually the Greek text implies a reciprocity which turns on the use of the same root in what is rendered *praise* and *blessing* here; that is, 'we bless God who has blessed us' but the divergent renditions *praise* and *bless* are more satisfactory for English. Our first tabulation focuses on the second half of the verse: *[God] has blessed us with every sort of blessing in the heavenly places in Christ.* This could be a rather hard-to-manage five column array, but we collapse *every spiritual blessing* with "blessed" and take God to be the intended actor in the whole proposition. Thus, we obtain a more manageable four-column array: GB (God has blessed), W (for 'us'), and CJ (Christ Jesus), over in column four. But what of column three? In this verse *in the heavenly realms* fits in column three, but more and very diverse material will fall into that column as we tabulate. In fact, so superlative is the expression in many sentences that we can entitle the whole column E (for 'extravagance'). The resultant columns will then be: GB, W, E, and CJ.

Table 11.4. First tabulation of Ephesians 1:3–14

G(od) B(lessed)	W(e)	E(xtravagance)	(in) C(hrist) J(esus)
3b. who has blessed… with all spiritual blessings	us	in the heavenly realms	in Christ
4a. For he chose	us	before the creation of the world…	in him
5. In love he predestined	us	to be adopted as his children	through Jesus Christ
6. (to the praise of) his glorious grace which he has freely given	us	[cf. column 1]	in the One he loves
7. *he has redeemed	us	through his blood	…in him
*he has forgiven sins	(our)	in accordance with the riches of God's grace	(in him)
8. he has lavished grace	on us	with all wisdom and understanding	
9. And he has made known	to us	the mystery of his will	
according to his good pleasure which he purposed	(for us?)		in Christ

11.2 Analysis according to the structure of information

G(od) B(lessed)	W(e)	E(xtravagance)	(in) C(hrist) J(esus)
10. *he will put into effect…to bring together	all things in heaven and earth ['all things' includes 'us']	when the times have reached their fulfillment	under one head, even Christ
11. *he chose	us		in him
*he predestined	(us)	according to the plan of him who works out everything in conformity with the purpose of his will	(in him)
13b. *God sealed 14a.	you	with promised Holy Spirit who is the guarantee of our inheritance	in him
14b. until *God will redeem	those who are God's possession		

Interwoven with the above is the further matter of our response to the divine extravagance. For this we have a further tabulation in table 11.5.

Table 11.5. Second tabulation of Ephesians 1:3–14

W(e)	P(raise/glorify)	G(od)
3. *(We)	praise be	to the God and father of our Lord Jesus Christ
4b. we	should be holy and blameless	in his sight
6. (we)	to the praise	of his glorious grace
12. In order that we, who first hoped in Christ,	might be for the praise	of his glory
14c. (we should be)	to the praise	of his glory

Still a further tabulation is needed for the further chain: "We believed in Christ."

Table 11.6. Third tabulation of Ephesians 1:3–14

W(e)	F(irst believed)	(in) C(hrist)
[From 12 above] *we	first hoped	in Christ
13a. …you also	were included	in Christ
when you	heard	the word of truth, the gospel of your salvation
(You)	having believed	(in him)
[for 13b see table 11.4]		

We can summarize tables 11.4–11.6 as the extravagance of God and our response to it. "God has blessed us extravagantly in Christ. We, in turn, should praise and glorify God. All this has come about in our believing in Jesus Christ." Here as in the medical text below the structure and meaning of the text emerge from the successive tabulations.

We now turn our attention to the medical article by Margolis and Rabins (see appendix 11B), a very different sort of expository discourse (see also Longacre 2007b). It is striking that essentially the same sort of analysis and tabulations prove as insightful here as in the study of the preceding biblical material. A brief abstract of the article follows. The article begins with mentioning that researchers, beginning with Alois Alzheimer, have studied structural abnormalities in the brains of people with Alzheimers Disease (AD) by autopsying the brains of people who displayed behavioral symptoms of the disease. Two sorts of abnormalities are described: amyloid plaques (AP) and neurofibrillary tangles (NT). The article also mentions that certain areas of the brain, the hippocampus and the entorhinal cortex, are especially associated with memory. These are the first areas of the brain to be affected by the disease, and are the most thoroughly affected by it. But the article, reverting to the perspective of the researcher, mentions that the correlation between the presence of AP and NT in the brain and the symptoms of Alzheimer Disease is only approximate. This is because, although AP and NT are present and dense in the brains of people with AD, they are also found in people who either have other mental impairments or have no behavioral symptoms at all.

All of this invites a three-fold tabulation of the information found in the discourse. The first tabulation involves three columns with *researchers/investigators/scientists* (and of course *Alois Alzheimer*) in the first column, such verbs as *report/find/concentrate (attention on)* in the second column, and AP/NT and the like in a third column. We tabulate these elements as in table 11.7, with O for a generic verb 'observe'. Sentence 1 has been grammatically transformed from passive to active to accommodate it within the tabulation; such a transformation is marked by an asterisk.

11.2 Analysis according to the structure of information

Table 11.7. First tabulation of medical text

	R(esearchers)	O(bserve)	X/ Y [where X= brain abnormalities, and X_1 = AP (Amyloid Plaques), X_2 = NT (Neurofibrillary Tangles), Y = behavioral & cognitive impairment]
1a.	*We	know much	about AD (Alzheimer Disease)
1b. because	*researchers	have studied	human brains obtained during autopsies
2. In 1907,	neurologist Alois Alzheimer	reported	damaged nerve cells and other abnormalities in the brain of a woman who displayed progressive behavioral and intellectual disturbances before her death
3. Since this report,	researchers	have sought to define	the role that these abnormalities play....
4a. Although	research	has not yet shown	that AP and NT cause cognitive impairment in people with AD
4b.	the study of these abnormalities	may one day lead to	better treatments for the disease
10a. However	researchers	consistently find	extensive plaque formations in certain brain areas...in AD
10b. but	(researchers)	(do) not (find)	(extensive plaques) in people with other brain diseases
14c.	many investigators	have concentrated their attention on determining	how plaques form and how to prevent them
15.	Mice genetically engineered to develop a high density of plaques...	show	memory deficits (Y) similar in people with AD

	R(esearchers)	O(bserve)	X/ Y [where X= brain abnormalities, and X_1 = AP (Amyloid Plaques), X_2 = NT (Neurofibrillary Tangles), Y = behavioral & cognitive impairment]
16.	Researchers	have developed	a vaccine....
20b. but	some scientists	believe	tangles hold the key to the primary cause of the disease $X_2 \rightarrow$ FB [see tabulation in table 11.8]
27.	*researchers	observe[a]	AD in a person's behavior Y when tangles X_2 begin to appear in the cerebral cortex [see tabulation in table 11.8]

[a] Here again a grammatical transformation proves strategic: 'Alzheimers disease becomes apparent in a person's behavior' is transformed to 'Researchers observe AD in a person's behavior.'

Several comments are in order regarding the above tabulation: (a) In the first column (R), there seems to be no problem in roughly equating *neurologist Alois Alzheimer, researchers, research, the study of these abnormalities,* and *some scientists*. Sentence 4b can be taken to indicate a particular type of research. S27 presents more of a problem but *AD becomes apparent* is still from the viewpoint of the research-observer. This sentence is transformed here and paraphrased to "researchers observe AD in a person's..." In S15 *genetically engineered mice* takes the place of the researcher. (b) The verbs in the second column (O) exhibit a general semantic similarity. (c) The more diffuse material in the third column (X) can all be summarized as *X (brain abnormalities)* and *Y (behavioral and cognitive impairment)*. In two instances, S20b and 27, an X→FB (X Forms in Brain) array is embedded in column three. (See table 11.8 for tabulation of X→FB.) (d) Sentence 16 presents us with a vaccine which can be considered to be a negative value to the references to AD, and to the symptoms of AD as well as to the references to plaques and neurofibrillary tangles in column three. In tabulating this sentence, *Researchers* goes in column one, and *have developed* in column two, with *vaccine* now finding its place in column three. But the rest of the material which qualifies *vaccine* is put, not in column three, but is charted in the second table. Actually, while *vaccine* as a remedy for AD can be considered to be a negation of AD, it is developed somewhat differently in the second tabulation.

11.2 Analysis according to the structure of information

A second tabulation in table 11.8 is one which puts X in the first column, *form/spread to,* and so forth, in the second column, and location of abnormality in the third column. *Vaccine* in S16b fits in here as the attempted negation of *plaques,* marked as *[–plaques].*

Table 11.8. Second tabulation of medical text

	X (brain abnormalities)	F(orm/spread)	B(rain)
2b.	damaged nerve cells and other abnormalities	(were found)	in the brain of a woman who displayed progressive behavioral Y and intellectual disturbances Y before her death
6a.	Amyloid plaques	are composed of	abnormal proteins
6b.	(abnormal proteins)	surrounded by	a layer of damaged nerve cell fragments
7.	these clusters	form	in the spaces between nerve cells
11a. Although	the density and distribution of plaques	varies	in the brains of people with AD
11b.	plaques	generally form first	in the entorhinal cortex...
12a. As	AD	progresses	
12b.	plaques	begin to form	in the hippocampus, an S-shaped structure that is seated deep in the middle of the brain adjacent to the entorhinal cortex
13. Later	plaques	spread to	the temporal, parietal, and frontal cortices
14a. Because	extensive plaque formations	are characteristic	of AD
14b. and because	they	form before	the accumulations of tangles

	X (brain abnormalities)	F(orm/spread)	B(rain)
16b.	A vaccine [= –plaques]	that reduces	the number of plaques in the brains of these mice
16c.	(a vaccine)	by stimulating the immune system	to eliminate the proteins that form plaques
17. Whether …is unknown	such a vaccine	would prevent	AD or improve memory in people with AD
20a.	Tangles	form later	
than	plaques	(form)	in the disease
20b. but some scientists believe that	tangles	hold the key	to the primary cause of the disease.
21.	The density and distribution of tangles in the brain	tend to follow a fixed pattern	with little variation among people with AD
22.	Tangles	are formed	from the collapse of brain cell microtubules
23. Overall,	the density of tangles in the brain	tends to correlate directly with	the severity of the dementia
24. but	tangles	are found	in the brains of people with other neurological diseases
25a. Like plaques,	tangles	can be found	in the brains of people without cognitive impairment
25b. particularly	(tangles)	can be found)	in the hippocampus and entorhinal cortex
26a.	A high density of tangles....	does not prove that a person has AD	in these areas
26b. although	they first	occur	in these areas

	X (brain abnormalities)	F(orm/spread)	B(rain)
27b. when	tangles	begin to appear	in the cerebral cortex
28. At this point	tangles	form	in the inferior temporal cortex, an area of the cerebral cortex near the hippocampus and the entorhinal cortex
29. In more advanced stages of AD	tangles	begin to appear	in other areas of the cerebral cortex

The tabulation in table 11.8 is lengthier than the first but perhaps more straightforward. *Plaques* and *tangles* occur in the first column, or some semantic elaboration of them, for example, *these clusters* and *extensive plaque formation*. *Tangles* occurs in the same contexts as *plaques* (e.g., with the verb *form*), but this is elaborated in phrases such as, *the density of tangles* and *the density and distribution of tangles*, and *a high density of tangles*. The verbs in the center column (F) include *form, are composed of, appear, occur, can be found* and the like. But in several instances this reporting stance gives way to metalanguage: *hold the key, tends to correlate with,* and *does not prove*. Sentence 20 is especially crucial in relating the first tabulation to the second. The items in the last column (Brain) are mainly locative. A medical research problem is indicated here in S22 to 25 in table 11.8, where it is stated that tangles as well as plaques can occur in the brains of people either with neurological diseases other than AD or with no cognitive impairment—even though the entorhinal cortex and the hippocampus are heavily affected. The information about a possible vaccine in S16 and 17 is absorbed into this tabulation but is tentative (note the modal in S17) both structurally and on the research front. Here again the text structure mirrors the reality being described.

Still a third tabulation is needed to capture the association of certain areas of the brain with memory. We label the three columns H, Λ (is associated with), and M in table 11.9.

Table 11.9. Third tabulation of medical text

	H(ippocampus)	Λ (is associated with)	M(emory)
11.	the entorhinal cortex, an area	known	for its involvement in memory
12.	the hippocampus, an S-shaped structure that is seated deep in the middle of the brain adjacent to the entorhinal cortex	is also known	for its important role in memory

The structure and meaning of the text can now be seen and summarized as in table 11.10.

Table 11.10. Summary of structure and meaning of medical text

R(esearchers)	O(bserve)	X /Y/ XFB
Researchers	observe	X
Researchers	observe	Y
Researchers	observe	XFB
Researchers	try to correlate	X, Y, and XFB

The crux of the matter is seen in a summary of the second (table 11.8) and third tabulations (table 11.9), in table 11.11.

Table 11.11. Summary of second and third tabulations of medical text

	X	F(orm)	B(rain of AD patients with Y)
	X_1 Plaques	form	in brains of people with AD
	X_2 Tangles	form	in brains of people with AD
	X (AP and NT)	become dense	in brains of people with AD
	X (AP and NT)	first affect	H, i.e., hippocampus and entorhinal cortex
But	X	may form	in brains of people with other neurological diseases
And	X	may form	in brains of people without Y, i.e., without cognitive impairment
	[H(ippocampus)	Λ (is associated with)	Memory (Brain)]

This leads to the conclusion:

∴ **Researchers (approximately) correlate X with Y.**

Tabulations in tables 11.7–11.11 may possibly indicate a template for such discourses as this: (a) Researchers observe one set of phenomena X; (b) researchers observe a second set of phenomena Y; (c) researchers have reason to try to correlate the two; (d) on studying the phenomena in detail, the attempted correlation proves to be only approximate but the attempted correlation is instructive.

In turn, however, this template is similar to the Hoey (1983) schema: situation-problem-solution-evaluation. In fact, the ad hoc template suggested here may simply be a variant of the more inclusive Hoey schema.

We suggest that the malleability of expository discourse to tabulation as illustrated here may in itself be a characteristic of this discourse type. Expository discourse is static and invites a flat tabulation or even a more advanced tabulation in more than two dimensions. In this respect it presents a contrast to the dynamism of narrative. Narrative discourse has a vertical storyline defined by chronological sequence which clearly sets it apart from expository discourse.

11.3 Conclusion

We have illustrated two possible lines of analysis for expository texts. The first line of analysis tracks along well from the analysis of other discourse types in terms of backgrounding and foregrounding. In brief, what is backgrounded in narrative is foregrounded in an expository text. The structure of the Hebrew text of Psalm 23 was rather meticulously presented according to this line of analysis. The second line of analysis says in effect: "Forget grammar. Minimalize it by transformations that give a grammatically homogeneous text. Then see what collocates with what. The structure of the text and its meaning will emerge from the endeavor."

11.4 Exercises

(1) Are exposition (explaining a topic) and description the same or different in the target language?

(2) Make a guess at ways of handling a complex expository text such as the first chapter of the Epistle to the Ephesians. How would you break up Paul's long sentence in that chapter?

Appendix 11A. Ephesians 1:3-14 (NIV)

3 Praise be to the God and Father of our Lord Jesus Christ, who has blessed us in the heavenly realms with every spiritual blessing in Christ. 4 For he chose us in him before the creation of the world to be holy and blameless in his sight. 5 In love he predestined us to be adopted as his sons through Jesus Christ, in accordance with his pleasure and will—6 to the praise of his glorious grace, which he has freely given us in the One he loves. 7 In him we have redemption through his blood, the forgiveness of sins, in accordance with the riches of God's grace 8 that he lavished on us with all wisdom and understanding. 9 And he made known to us the mystery of his will according to his good pleasure, which he purposed in Christ, 10 to be put into effect when the times will have reached their fulfillment—to bring all things in heaven and on earth together under one head, even Christ.

11 In him we were also chosen, having been predestined according to the plan of him who works out everything in conformity with the purpose of his will, 12 in order that we, who were the first to hope in Christ, might be for the praise of his glory. 13 And you also were included in Christ when you heard the word of truth, the gospel of your salvation. Having believed, you were marked in him with a seal, the promised Holy Spirit, 14 who is a deposit guaranteeing our inheritance until the redemption of those who are God's possession—to the praise of his glory.

Appendix 11B. Alzheimer disease text

Sentences of the text are numbered for ease of reference (Margolis and Rabins 2002:3).[5]

1 Much of what we know about Alzheimer disease (AD) stems directly from studies of human brains obtained during autopsies. 2 In 1907, neurologist Alois Alzheimer first reported the presence of damaged nerve cells and other abnormalities in the brain of a woman who displayed progressive behavioral and intellectual disturbances before her death. 3 Since this report, researchers have sought to define the exact role that these abnormalities—called amyloid plaques and neurofibrillary tangles—play in the development and progression of AD. 4 Although research has not yet shown that plaques and tangles cause cognitive impairment in people with AD, the study of these abnormalities may one day lead to new treatments for the disease.
  5 Amyloid Plaques
  6 Amyloid plaques are composed of abnormal proteins surrounded by a layer of damaged nerve cell fragments. 7 Also called senile plaques, these clusters form in the spaces between nerve cells. 8 Exactly how they affect nerve-cell function is unclear. 9 At autopsy, the brains of most older people—even those without cognitive decline—show accumulations of amyloid plaques. 10 However, researchers consistently find extensive plaque formations in certain brain areas (specifically the cerebral cortex and hippocampus) in AD but not in people with other brain diseases.
  11 Although the density and distribution of plaques varies in the brains of people with AD, plaques generally form first in the entorhinal cortex, an area known for its involvement in memory. 12 As AD progresses, plaques begin to form in the hippocampus, an S-shaped structure that is seated deep in the middle of the brain adjacent to the entorhinal cortex and is also known for its important role in memory. 13 Later, plaques spread to the temporal, parietal, and frontal cortices.
  14 Because extensive plaque formations are characteristic of AD, and because they form before the accumulations of tangles, many investigators have concentrated their attention on determining how plaques form and how to prevent them. 15 Mice genetically engineered to develop a high density of plaques (but not tangles) show memory deficits similar to those in people with AD. 16 Researchers have developed a vaccine that reduces the number of plaques, in the brains of these mice by stimulating the immune system to eliminate the proteins that form plaques. 17 Whether such a vaccine would prevent AD or improve memory in people with AD is unknown. 18 (For more information on the Alzheimer vaccine, see the feature on pages 20–21.)
  19 Neurofibrillary Tangles
  20 Tangles form later than plaques in the disease, but some scientists believe that tangles hold the key to the primary cause of AD. 21 The density and

---

[5] Included by permission of Johns Hopkins University Health Publishing/Medletter Associates, Inc.

distribution of tangles in the brain tend to follow a fixed pattern with little variation among people with AD.

22 Tangles are formed from the collapse of brain cell microtubules (an internal structure that helps transport substances within the cell). 23 Overall, the density of tangles in the brain tends to correlate directly with the severity of dementia, 24 but tangles are found in the brains of some people with other neurological diseases.

25 Like plaques, tangles can be found in the brains of people without cognitive impairment, particularly in the hippocampus and entorhinal cortex. 26 A high density of tangles in these areas does not prove that a person has AD, although this is the first place they occur as AD develops.

27 Alzheimer disease becomes apparent in a person's behavior when tangles begin to appear in the cerebral cortex. 28 At this point, tangles form in the inferior temporal cortex, an area of the cerebral cortex near the hippocampus and entorhinal cortex. 29 In more advanced stages of AD, tangles begin to appear in other areas of the cerebral cortex. 30 The dots in the illustration above depict the location and density of both amyloid plaques and neurofibrillary tangles in the advanced stages of AD.

Glossary

action peak. refers to specially marked surface structure episode correlating with climax or denouement

adverbial clause. a clause with subordinating conjunctions like *when*, indicating time, purpose, reason, etc.

agent orientation (AO). a notional parameter used in discourse typology, agent reference occurring frequently throughout the discourse

agglutinative. words formed by several morphemes with discrete boundaries

alternation. disjunctive combination of propositions with a notional structure *or* relationship

amplification. the relationship between propositions in which a proposition is repeated and additional information is given

anaphoric. referring backward to an item mentioned earlier, as in *John left. He ran away.*

ancillary. not dominant; accessory, auxiliary

answer (A). resolves a question

antithesis. thesis that is in contrast to the main thesis

antithetical. directly opposed, as expressed by the conjunction *but*

antonym. dictionary antonyms, as in *good/bad*; includes clearly opposed roles, as in *husband/wife*, binary temporal or spatial oppositions, as in *day/night, this/that,* and situational and contextual opposites

aperture. formulaic opening to a discourse, an abstract overview, as in *I'm going to talk about...* or *Once upon a time...*

argument. participant required by a particular verb

aspect. kind of action in relation to time; quality of action indicated in verb, as in perfective, progressive, punctiliar, completive, repetitive, etc.

attribution. the relationship between propositions that includes speech attribution (*say, talk, whisper,* etc.) or awareness attribution (*think, see, know, hear,* etc.) and the content of that speech or awareness

awareness attribution. attributing cognitive/sensory content to a conscious subject, as in *She knew that she made a mistake.*

awareness formula. the part stating who is aware of the cognitive content, such as *John realized*

backbone. main events, mainline, foreground information, eventline, storyline, main points

background. in narration, explanations regarding participants, props, actions, events or even places, times and circumstances; minor events; usually expository in tone and structure; some happenings (in pluperfect) and some activities (in progressive); also used broadly to refer to all nonevents, including setting, comments, and irrealis information (in opposition to foreground information)

backreference. onset clause of a succeeding sentence refers in some way to preceding sentence; recapitulation, as in *He ate. Having eaten, he...*

bands of information. levels reflecting the salience of information in any particular type of text; these are primarily reflected in the tense, aspect, and mood of a language, but also can be handled through word order changes, conjunctions, particles, and other surface structure markings; salience ranking scheme; spectrum

base. functional subunit in nuclear unit (clause or sentence) in a sentence

behavioral. discourse type such as hortatory and eulogy

blocking circumstance. a notional proposition that hinders or prevents the expected proposition from happening in a frustration (counter-expectation) type combination of propositions

cataphoric. referring forward to an item to be identified later, as in *When he is in a good mood, John sings a song.*

central participant. main participant around whom a narrative revolves; protagonist and antagonist

central exhortation. the overall main exhortation of a hortatory discourse

chaining. series of contiguous nuclear clauses in a sentence where medial or consecutive clauses (with dependent and not fully inflected verbs) are linked to final or initial clauses (with independent and fully inflected verbs, for tense, aspect, and/or mood)

chiasmus, chiastic. symmetry by reversal in lexical reference of two otherwise parallel constituents, as in *We walked, talked, and chuckled. We giggled, gabbed, and strolled.* a b c c' b' a'

chronological linkage. seen in surface structure; some or most events follow previous events in time

chunking. separating a text or a paragraph into its natural parts

circumstance. relationship of weak causation between propositions, as with *since, in that, in view of the fact that*

clause combination. the different strategies of presenting information by putting together more than one clause in a sentence or clause; juxtaposed, coordinated, subordinated, or merged

climax. notional structure slot of a narrative where tension is highest; very high interest, drama, or complication

close-knit. closely related together in some way grammatically and/or semantically

Glossary

closure. bounded; definite or specific beginning and end; usually introducers, setting, and terminus mark closure in a paragraph; explanatory summary; concluding unit to a discourse

cognitive events. sensory happenings, punctiliar, mainline, as in *John suddenly realized that...*

cognitive states. non-punctiliar, durative, off-line, as in *John knew all along that...*

coherence. the logical and semantic connection between lexical elements; a text is understandable if it is coherent. Languages have various ways to tie together lexical items of different semantic domains or explain culturally unexpected information

cohesion. the unifying parts of a discourse on surface structure; agreement between constituents, use of conjunctions; information in the lowest band in narrative in adverbial/participial/nominal clauses in back-referential function

cohortative. verb form of first person plural inclusive (of the hearer); used for encouragement or exhortation, as in *Let's go!*

combination of propositions. the notional structure unit of relationships between propositions. These often map to sentences and paragraphs in surface structure. Cues for the relationships can come from the conjunctions, clauses, and discourse contexts.

comment. author intrusion into a text to address assumed questions of audience; or, the non-topic, new information of a clause

complement clause. embedded clauses functioning as an argument in another clause (as S, O)

completive aspect. verb marking, indicating the action as being finished at the time of the speech situation

complex dialogue. second speaker wants to evade or moderate the force of the previous speaker's utterance and so extends the dialogue in some way using the continuing utterance (CU)

compound dialogue. surface structure paragraph consisting of two or more linked exchanges of simple or complex dialogue

conclusion. notional slot corresponding to closure in narrative discourse, where resolution is made and discourse is brought to an end

conditionality with universal quantifier. combining propositions where something is implied based on some universal statement, as in *Whoever goes there should be careful.*

conjoining. relationship of coupling, contrast, and comparison between propositions; joining together

consecutive verb. lesser inflected verb in a head-initial chaining language

contingent temporal succession (CTS). a notional parameter used in discourse typology; some or most events, which occur in sequence, hinge on previous events or doings

continuing utterance (CU). after IU, instead of resolving the dialogue exchange with a RU, a counter token is used: counter-question (c-Q), counter-proposal (c-Pro), or counter-remark (c-Rem)

contraction paraphrase. paraphrase relationship between propositions where part of the second proposition is elided or reduced

contrafactual. contrary to fact, as in *If she had thought of him, she would have gone to him for help.* (The fact is: She didn't think of him and she didn't go to him.)

contrast. relationship between two propositions or larger units, where there is at least two opposed pairs of lexical items; conjoined with *but* in English

contrast by exception. relationship between propositions where one or a few members of a universal set are opposite to the rest of the group, as shown in English by *except, apart from,* or *all but*; subtype of contrast

coordinate paragraph. sentences or embedded paragraphs linked in a coordinated (notional *and*) way with slots of Thesis 1, 2, 3, etc.

coordinate sentence. clauses or embedded sentences linked by coordinating conjunction (*and*)

coordination. constructions that join two nuclear independent units with conjunctions like *and, but,* and *or*

copula. a linking or equative verb used in nonactive clauses, like *be.*

co-ranking. base clauses in a sentence are usually independent and inflected, linked by coordinating conjunctions; margins may precede or follow the nuclear clauses

counter-expectation. reversal or different from expected events; frustration

coupling. relationship of coordination between propositions with a non-temporal *and* relationship

cyclic. a paragraph type where the first part of paragraph is repeated again at the end of that paragraph; similar to chiasmus

declarative. mood of a statement asserting information

definitivization. use of articles, as in indefinite: *a, an,* or as in definite: *the*

deictics or deixis. identificational or contrastive pointing to person, place, and time, as in *this, that, here, there, I, you*

demonstrative. grammatical class or word specifying or pointing out particular referent(s) like *this, that*

demotion. moving information down the salience ranking scale, less eventline, less mainline, as using a durative adverb like *all along* or a relative clause as a demotion device

denouement. from French 'loosen' or 'untie it'; notional slot of narrative discourse after climax where a crucial event happens making possible a resolution or a way out of a difficulty

deontic. a mood expressing obligation and/or permission

dependent clause. subordinated, non-main clause of a sentence; adverbial clause

depictive. describe vividly, portray or characterize in words; descriptive

descriptive clause. affirming a characteristic or quality of something, as in *Her hair is beautiful,* or *John is old.*

Glossary

descriptive discourse. a type of expository discourse mainly describing some thing or situation

developing conflict. notional slot of narrative discourse where situation intensifies or deteriorates before climax

dialogue. presentation of the exchanges of a sequence of speakers

different subject. switch reference code that indicates that the next, or some other, clause subject is different from that of the current clause

discourse. unit of entire speech event, monologue if one speaker, or dialogue if more than one speaker, as in joke, conversation, sermon, or story; whole texts take into account the context

discourse-level slots. surface and notional structure constituents in specific type of discourse; for example, surface slots in narrative: title, aperture (formulaic phrase or sentence opening a text often indicating the genre), stage (expository), prepeak episodes, peak episode, postpeak episode, closure (summary or moral), finis (formulaic phrase or sentence); and notional slots: exposition, inciting moment, developing conflict, climax, denouement, and conclusion

drama. dialogue form without quote formulas

durative. over a period of time; non-punctual

echo question. a sentence nucleus that has a fully inflected confirmation question clause added at the end, as in *You like ice cream, don't you*?

efficient cause. cause that "pushes"; reason, as in *You didn't go because you feared the outcome*, or result, as in *You were afraid so you didn't go.*

embedding. recursion of a unit within another unit of the same hierarchical level; a discourse, paragraph, sentence, etc. may include within it another discourse, paragraph, sentence, etc.; a unit of a higher level inside a lower level unit, as in a relative clause in a NP

emic. the language-specific system of contrasting units

enablement. describing how the carrying out of a particular exhortation is aided or made possible

encoded. a notional structure realized by a surface structure, as in contrast encoded in an antithetical sentence with *but* or a coordinate sentence with *and*

episode. a surface slot or sub-unit of a narrative discourse filled by a paragraph or an embedded discourse (with more than one paragraph), unified by a theme or a particular set of participants who are in a certain general location or time; beginning and ending boundaries are often marked in some way

epistemic. a mood of knowledge describing an event as actual, possible, or probable

equational sentence. English sentence nucleus where two clauses are combined by a *be* verb, as in *His purpose in coming was so that he could confuse the issue.*

equative clause. a clause where the complement of the subject is a noun, affirming set-membership, as in *John is a preacher*

equivalence paraphrase. combines propositions that are logically equivalent, using synonyms

etic. raw data information, not necessarily related to a given language system; universal set of possible units across all languages

eulogy. behavioral text of past behavior, often given about a recently dead person

evaluation. narrator surfaces to make value judgments of participant, action, place, etc.; often involves shift to first person and present tense; adjectives, as in *good, worthy,* or *brave*

evaluation (Eval). in dialogue, evaluation resolves a remark (Rem)

eventline. any happening that pushes the narrative text forward; includes actions, motions, cognitive events (sudden realization), and contingencies (events with no volitional agents, as in *We had a flat tire*); backbone, mainline, storyline, foreground information

exception. type of contrast relationship between propositions where a predicate has one term contrasted with a universal set minus that one term, as in *John spoke up but nobody else did.*

exchange. dialogue pair, as in question-answer, proposal-response, or remark-evaluation

execution paragraph. one where a plan or idea is suggested by someone, and then carried out; it typically follows an utterance unit of a dialogue in which speaker states intention and then it is carried out

exemplification. illustration relationship between propositions; in English it can be indicated by *for example, for instance,* etc.

exhortation. a command or expression to bring about or change some behavior, conduct, or action

existential. establishing the existence of someone, something, or some event; in English it can be indicated by *there is, exists, it happened*

expectancy chain. situation where the result or cause of an event would be inferred or deduced from normal assumptions, as in *He left for New York and arrived there safely.*

explicit. marked on the surface structure

exposition. notional structure of stage, where time, place, participants, and circumstance are described; explanation

expository. discourse type that expounds, explains, sets forth, and describes, such as proposals, essays, scientific papers

final cause. cause that "pulls" (cf., efficient cause); teleological (toward); purpose, as in *We went outside in order to get some fresh air.*

final clause. the last clause of a sentence in head-final chaining language; it has independent, fully inflected verb

final suspense. notional slot of narrative discourse after denouement that works out details of resolution before the final conclusion

finis. formulaic final utterance signaling the end of discourse, as in *That's all. That's it. The end.*

first mention. introduction of a participant or theme

flashback. earlier event inserted into a current situation

Glossary 217

focus. essential new piece of information; main point of the sentence; focus may be an argument, the predicate, or the whole sentence
foregrounded. more salient, prominent; promoted to mainline
foregrounded frame. a frame that is already evoked in the text
foreshadowing. event sequence which indicates or suggests future actions placed forward in time
formulaic. stereotypical, very frequent way of saying something
frame. the typically expected idea or picture and the associated terms that come to mind with a word or phrase, as in a *restaurant frame*; we may picture *menu, waitress, food,* etc.
frustration. counter-expectation relationship between propositions; an expectancy chain of events or implication which does not come off as expected
generic-specific paraphrase. propositions are combined so that the first proposition is broader, more inclusive and general while the following one(s) are narrower and more limited in reference
grammatical relations. syntactic relations contracted between a NP and its predicate, such as subject, direct object, and indirect object
grammatical word order language. language where subjects and objects typically are in fixed positions relative to the verb
grammaticalization. the change of a lexical item from having meaning to more of a grammatical function. The infinitive *to* was historically derived from the conjunctive phrase *in order to*. The phrase *going to* is being grammaticalized to a slang contraction in American English *gonna* which is an auxiliary verb meaning 'intending to' as in *I'm gonna go now*. The historical sequence of grammaticalization is often from a noun or verb to a preposition to a conjunction
grounding. the presenting of information with various levels of salience so that certain information is more prominent to an audience
happenings. events such as actions, motions, cognitive and sensory events, and contingencies
head-final chaining. a language where only the last clause of a sentence has a fully inflected verb for tense, aspect, or mood; also called medial-final chaining
head-initial chaining. a language where only the first clause of a sentence has a fully inflected verb for tense, aspect, or mood; also known as initial-consecutive chaining
head-marking language. a language where the head is inflected with agreement information, as in case agreement markers on verbs and possessor information on possessed head nouns
hortatory. a discourse type of urging or exhortation, such as sermons, pep talks, advertisements; attempts to influence conduct
illustration. subtype of elaborated relations between propositions, comprised of simile and exemplification
imperfect. tense or aspect of an action uncompleted or with no endpoint, for example, past progressive, as in *was walking*

imperfective. aspect describing a situation/action with reference to its internal temporal structure; viewing a situation from within; cover term for ongoing aspects such as customary, habitual, continuative

implication. the relationship between two or more propositions that are organized logically; antecedent and consequence, as in *if-then* sequence

implicit. unmarked on the surface structure but implied or deducible from context

inciting incident or inciting moment. notional structure unit of narrative discourse where the planned and predictable is broken up; usually the first episode of a narrative

inclusio. construction whose boundary units have identical or similar forms or meaning, thus making a sandwich-like structure around the construction

independent clause. main, normal clause not marked to be dependent

indictment. an accusation of wrongdoing

induction. conclusion or thesis given at end; supported by evidence or observations

infinitive. typically a tenseless (non-finite) and uninflected form of the verb, as in *be* as opposed to *is* or *was*

information flow. the sequencing of linearly presented data to achieve a cohesive and coherent text

initial-consecutive chaining. a language where only the first clause of a sentence has a fully inflected verb for tense, aspect, or mood. The fully inflected clause is known as the initial clause, the rest are known as consecutive clauses. Found in VO languages of Africa, Indonesia

initiating utterance (IU). a remark, proposal, or question beginning a dialogue, normally responded to by resolving utterance (RU)

introducer. a non-clausal word or phrase beginning a sentence, often with a larger scope than the immediate clause, or a fronted element; can be a conjunction, prepositional phrase, adverb phrase, or noun phrase

irrealis. unrealized, potential actions/events which don't occur; marked by negatives and modals

jussive. a third person mild command form found in Biblical Hebrew and some other languages, as in *Let George do it!*

juxtapose. to place side by side without a linker or conjunction, as in sentences for paraphrase, recapitulation, or echo question

lead-in. prepare way for dialogue paragraphs, often reporting actions which precede the dialogue proper

macrosegmentation. chunking a text into major discourse level parts

macrostructure. the gist; germinal/global idea, or overall conception of a specific text; thrust of a text, its message

mainline information. mainline of development as against other supportive material: temporally sequential events in narrative discourse (storyline), procedures or steps in procedural discourse, exhortations in hortatory discourse, and explanations and descriptions of salient themes in expository discourse

major participant. character contributing greatly to the plot of a story, frequently performing mainline actions

margin. peripheral, less central role, supportive; it does not determine the construction type

marked. expressed or indicated by some form; or, exceptional, unusual, stands out in comparison with what is normal in its context

medial clause. base clause not last in a sentence of a chaining language; it is dependent in surface structure with a verb not fully marked for tense, aspect, and mood

medial-final chaining. a language where only the last clause of a sentence has a fully inflected verb for tense, aspect, or mood; also known as head-final chaining; mostly found in SOV languages

merged sentence. requires two verbs, one of which contains nonfinite form of the verb, e.g., infinitive or participial form, as in *He tried to move the chair. He found her moving his chair. He got his chair moved.*

metalanguage. language or system used to discuss, describe, or analyze another language or system

metaphor. surface structure variety of simile; shortened simile, as in *She is a rose.*

minor participant. character contributing only a little to the plot of a story, seldom or occasionally performing mainline actions, not acting throughout the story

mitigated. presenting a command or exhortation with forms that soften the intense social force

modal (modality). desire/intent, as in *want/will*; obligation/necessity, as in *must/should*; ability, as in *can/could*

mode. See *mood*

monologue. text where only one person is talking

mood or mode. function normally reflecting the intent of the communicator, such as declarative, interrogative, imperative, subjunctive; mood can be skewed for politeness, as in *Would someone open the door, please?*; the actuality of an activity can be also included in terms of either realis (actually happened, realized) or irrealis (not yet happened, unrealized)

morphosyntax. surface structure of grammar; morpheme, word, phrase, clause levels of grammar

mystery particle. a morpheme difficult to gloss, which has little or no meaning for an outsider but native speakers know where to use, and often carrying some kind of function at discourse level

narrative. discourse type such as a story or prophecy

negated antonym paraphrase. relationship between propositions where an antonym is negated in order to paraphrase, as in *It's not black, it's white.*

non-central major character. participants that go throughout the story but are antagonists or helpers of the antagonists or protagonists

nonevent. non-storyline information that supports eventline/storyline, such as non-punctiliar, non-sequential, non-dynamic, irrealis, author intrusions, or non-substantive information

non-finite. typically unmarked (or less marked) and without tense or aspect, like the infinitive

non-punctiliar. ongoing, durative activities

nonrestrictive relative clause. an appositive type relative clause which adds or elaborates information about the head noun, but does not necessarily identify or restrict the head noun

notional structure. structures found universally; generally expected to be found in all languages

nucleus. central and characteristic part of a unit, which is independent of the margin or periphery

obligation modality. mood that calls for some activity, as in *ought* or *should*

overlap. at some point in time an activity occurs simultaneously with another activity

paragraph. developmental unit of a discourse, typically filling the episode slot in narrative, argumentation or exhortation slot in hortatory; sub-unit of a discourse; composed of sentences and/or embedded paragraphs

parallelism. saying different things in similar patterns of grammar

paraphrase. saying approximately the same thing twice in alternate versions without changing meaning; saying one thing in different ways

participant. entity more agentive; not necessarily animate though usually so; more directly involved in the actions; tends to be more involved in the plot than props

participant reference. the words or phrases used to refer to a character or prop in a text

participial clauses. non-finite forms of verbs used in subordinated or embedded clauses, as in English *-ing* clauses

peak. an episode-like unit in a narrative set apart by special surface structure features and corresponding to climax or denouement in the notional structure; zone of turbulence grammatically; in non-narrative, surface marking is usually at the culminating exhortation, or argument, or the most adequate explanation

perfect. action already completed and currently relevant in respect to another action, as in past perfect *had left*

perfective. aspect viewing an event as a whole from outside, which is already finished, such as preterite or past tense; a feature of storyline information

persuasive discourse. discourse type trying to influence beliefs and values; presents a problem, proposes a solution, provides supporting argumentation, and appeals to adopt the belief or value, and may even state the implications for adopting the beliefs

plot. a coherent notional structure of narrative discourse parallel to the surface structure discourse

pluperfect. past perfect aspect, as in *had peeled*

postpeak episode. episode following the peak episode

postposed. constructions, e.g., adverbial clauses, occurring after the basic independent clause of a sentence

pragmatic word order language. using word order to indicate new or old information, as in Russian, where topic is placed sentence initially and new information is placed sentence finally

predicate nominal. a nominal element that functions as a predicate and may be connected by a copula. In the sentence, *He is a boy*, the predicate nominal is *a boy*.

prepatory exhortation. exhortation that leads up to and prepares the listener/reader for the central exhortation

prepeak episode. episode preceding the main action peak episode

preposed. constructions, e.g., adverbial clauses, occurring before the basic independent clause of a sentence; prenuclear

presentational construction. special construction typically used to introduce new participants or props into a text, as is the existential *there was...* in English

preterite. perfective aspect parallel to past tense action in English

procedural. discourse type such as a how-to text and recipe

profile. visual representation of the overall discourse progression from aperture, stage, prepeak, peak, postpeak to closure and finis; surface structure realization of mounting and declining tension within a discourse

progressive. aspect showing an action in process, as in *was reading*

projection (P). a notional parameter in discourse typology for a situation or action contemplated, enjoined, or anticipated but not realized; prophecy is a +Projection narrative

prominence. spotlighting, highlighting, or drawing attention to something

promotion. moving up the verb ranking scale, more eventline, more mainline; a punctiliar adverb like *suddenly* is a promotion device

prop. not necessarily inanimate though usually so; less directly involved in the actions and the plot; often an instrument or tool

proposal (Pro). a call to action; advice, suggestion, invitation, plan, request, threat, command

proposition. a notional underlying structure of a clause

prototype (prototypical). the most commonly thought of or ideal representation

pseudo-cleft. in English, a *be* verb construction where a phrase or clause beginning with a *wh-* word like *what* fills the subject slot, as in *What she does is teach children.*

pseudo-dialogue. talking to oneself or an absent/imaginary person, rhetorical questions; not truly direct dialogue

punctiliar. punctual; pertaining to a particular, definite point in time, a feature of mainline information in narratives

question (Q). true solicitation of information

quote formula. the part stating who is saying the quotation, such as *John said*

ranking of participants. classifying participants in a given narrative as to central, major, or minor participants

realis. marking an action as already realized as a fact

recapitulation. onset of a succeeding sentence refers in some way to preceding sentence; backreference; in surface structure of sentence, with a repetition of the verb or a verb having similar meaning

recursion (recursive). same level embedding, as a paragraph in a paragraph or phrase in a phrase, as in *the house of my father*

reference. a word or NP used to talk about referents or participants

referent. a participant or entity in any text

referential. word or phrase indicating a particular referent

reinstatement. restaging; mentioning again a participant at a new episode or paragraph boundary

relative clause. clause embedded in a NP; restrictive relative clauses help to identify the head noun, while nonrestrictive relative clauses give additional information

remark (Rem). declaration or comment, request for evaluation

remote past. a tense more distant in time than a simple past tense; in some languages, any time before yesterday is 'remote past', in other languages, this refers to time prior to the recollection of any person living today

reported speech or dialogue. narrator's report of direct and indirect speeches of the participants, e.g., quotes with quote formulas, as in *John said...*

resolution. the actions in a narrative that simplify or resolve the problems and difficulties

resolving utterance (RU). concludes dialogue paragraph; includes three possible notional types: answer (to question), response (to proposal), or evaluation (or remark)

response (Res). resolves a proposal

restaging. mentioning again a participant who has exited the stage of a story

restrictive relative clause. relative clause that is necessary to identify or restrict the head noun to a particular referent

resultant exhortation. exhortations logically or temporally following from the central exhortation

rheme. part of clause adding new information to the text

rhetorical questions. statements or exclamations posed as questions; not true questions seeking information or answers from the audience

rhetorical underlining. elaboration and use of extra words similar in form and meaning, such as parallelism, paraphrase, and tautology

right dislocation. the backing of data to the final position in a clause or sentence, usually to maintain information flow of the core constituents of the clause, breaking up an NP as in *Everyone should walk daily who is able to walk*, or as in *He is a great guy, your brother.*

Glossary

salience ranking scheme. the ranking continuum of verbs and clauses in a text so as to reflect the salient (highly prominent) mainline information down through the lowest supportive information

same subject marking. clause/verb marking in a chaining language indicating that the next or final clause subject is the same as the one in this clause

schema. mental structure consisting of sets of expectations about the way in which discourse proceeds; plot, layout of a discourse, diagram, plan, scheme; any discourse level construction and its slot constituents

script. a predetermined, stereotyped sequence of actions that define a well-known situation, as in a 'Dining-out' script, we may expect the following sequence: registering and waiting to be seated, being escorted to the table, looking at the menu, waitress asking for orders, etc.

script predictable. when the topic being discussed concerns a sequence of events that is familiar to both the speaker and hearer

secondary storyline. narrative events less salient than the primary storyline, often more prepatory to or resultative from the primary storyline

segmentation. division of a construction into its parts

sentence. bundle of clauses making a cohesive construction unit; some clauses may be more important and nuclear than others

sequence signals. conjunctive elements or adverbial phrases that indicate a change in time or a particular logical relationship

setting. the circumstances of where and when, and conditions under which a paragraph occurs; stage/setting (introductory sentences) of discourse or paragraph; non-dynamic existential, equative, and descriptive clauses about the setting; *be* verbs (or nominal clause) and stative verbs

simile. illustration where two dissimilar things are paired by virtue of one point of similarity they share, as in *He is sly like a fox.*

simple dialogue. paired utterances; initiating utterance and resolving utterance

simple sentence. sentence made of only one clause in the nucleus

simple structure. a higher level unit composed of one lower level unit as in a one-sentence paragraph or a one-clause sentence

skewing. the surface structure may be different from the notional structure; out-of-phase encoding between notional structures and the expected surface structures

slot. functional position in a construction to be filled by a class or set

source language. the language you are translating from, e.g., Koine Greek in the New Testament

specific-generic paraphrase. propositions are combined such that information in the last clause is paraphrased in generic terms with a loss of information, as in *They dug for gold, they did some excavation.*

spectrum. cline of information ranging from most dynamic to most static; continuing strands (marked by verb tenses and aspects, word order, etc.) that unite a discourse and hierarchically distinguish the types of information in it; salience ranking scheme

speech attribution. attributing speech content to a speaker, as in *She said that she was happy.*

stage. discourse slot, setting out information of time, place, participants, and circumstances

step down. a sentence at end of dialogue, concluding a paragraph and representing an action taken at its conclusion

stimulus-response paragraph. the spoken plan of a participant is not answered nor carried out by the hearer, but rather the hearer does some action unexpected or counter to the plan

storyline. series of temporally successive and partially contingent events in a narrative

subjunctive. mood for actions not yet realized; doubtful, hypothetical, as in *If he were only here...*

subordination. unit marked to be lower status and dependent; can mark forms in VP or use conjunctions; includes adverbial clause, complement clause, and relative clause

summary paraphrase. propositions are combined such that information in the last clause summarizes the previous proposition(s)

supportive material. non-mainline information, as in background, collateral, comment, setting; descriptions and explanations in narrative

surface structure. the structure that corresponds with the actual form of a text in a given language

surrogate noun. substitute nouns for the name of a participant, especially the general nouns of kinship relationship *mother*, occupation *teacher*, or social role *king*

switch reference system. verbal affix relates and links the subject of that clause to the following or final clause subject, indicating subject referent as same subject (SS) or different subject (DS)

tail-head linkage. last clause of a sentence is recapitulated in the beginning of the following sentence, or last sentence of one paragraph cross-references to the first sentence of the following paragraph

TAM. acronym for tense, aspect, mood (modality)

target language. the language you are translating into, e.g., Mixtec, Totonac

target procedure. in procedural discourse, attaining the goal of the activity, as in finishing building a house, or serving a dinner after cooking it

telic. aspect with definite endpoint in an action like *fall, hit, kick, jump*

template. schema; the typical profile and schema of a particular discourse type constituent

temporal overlap. the relationship between propositions, where at some point in time an activity occurs simultaneously with another activity, as in *He glanced back once as he walked away.*

temporal succession. the relationship between propositions, where events follow one another in time

tension. a notional structure parameter in discourse typology; struggle or polarization of some (emotional) sort from the reader's perspective; discourses with climaxes, obstacles, or argumentation are plus tension

terminating utterance (TU). coda to a dialogue; an acquiescence or rejection forming an additional coda to the dialogue following the resolving utterance

tertiary storyline. script-predictable or habitual routine events

textlinguistics. study of the linguistic structures of texts; similar to discourse analysis

thematic participant. main participant discussed in a paragraph or discourse

thematic unity. construction with the same continuing participant, events, and/or topic

theme. in broader usage: what a paragraph or discourse is all about; or, part of the clause giving old information

thesis. the dominant, highest-weighted verb/clause/sentence within a paragraph; corresponds to the mainline base relative to the discourse type

topic. the referent selected as the subject or local theme; what the sentence or discourse is about

topicalization. to make something a topic by fronting to sentence-initial position, as in *Apples I like very much.*

tracking routinely. typical reference to continuing participants in normal, unmarked places in a text

tree diagram. pictorial representation with lines showing the relationships in the structure of a construction

typology. classification of types by use of characteristics

universal. applicable to every language

universal quantifier. reference of totality like *wherever, whomever, everyone*

unmarked. not expressed or indicated by some form; or, neutral, normal, common, basic in relation to something that stands out as different

utterance. unit bounded by what a single speaker says, bound by when he starts and stops talking

vantage point. view of observer, through whose eyes the story is told

vividness. psychological impact of high degree through a variety of grammatical features

vocative. name or kinship term to get someone's attention in a surface structure sentence

voice. a verb-marking showing the relation of subjects to agent or patient, as in active, passive, reflexive, causative, middle, benefactive, and antipassive

volitional. whether or not an action was done deliberately and consciously, on purpose

warning. a combination of propositions in which a specially inflected predicate of obligation (like *should* or *ought*) is paired with an implied or explicit potentially undesirable outcome

zero anaphora. deletion of any reference within a construction that can be deciphered from a previous reference to the same referent, as in *John soon arrived home, Ø running all the way.*

zone of turbulence. change from the expected, normal, or established grammatical structures which can indicate peak, peak prime, or thematic peak

References

Aaron, Uche. 1999. *Tense and aspect in Obolo grammar and discourse.* Summer Institute of Linguistics and the University of Texas at Arlington Publications in Linguistics, 128. Dallas: Summer Institute of Linguistics and the University of Texas at Arlington.

Alaichamy, Shalom. 1999. Discourse structure and hortatory information in Colossians. M.A. thesis. University of Texas at Arlington.

Anderson, Stephen R., and Edward L. Keenan. 1985. Deixis. In Shopen 3, 29–308.

Austin, John. 1975. *How to do things with words.* Cambridge, Mass.: Harvard University Press.

Benveniste, Emile. 1974. *Problèmes de linguistique générale* 2. Bibliothèque des Sciences Humaines. Paris: Gallimard.

Benveniste, Emile. 1977. *Problems in general linguistics.* Mary Elizabeth Meek, translator. Miami Linguistics Series 8. Coral Gables, Fla.: University of Miami Press.

Bergen, Robert D., ed. 1994. *Biblical Hebrew and discourse linguistics.* Dallas: Summer Institute of Linguistics.

Black, David Alan, ed. 1992. *Linguistics and New Testament interpretation: Essays on discourse analysis.* Nashville: Broadman Press.

Breeze, Mary. 1992. Hortatory discourse in Ephesians. *Journal of Translation and Textlinguistics* 5:313–347.

Burusphat, Somsonge. 1991. *The structure of Thai narrative.* Summer Institute of Linguistics and the University of Texas at Arlington Publications in Linguistics, 98. Dallas: Summer Institute of Linguistics and the University of Texas at Arlington.

Bybee, Joan. 2002. Main clauses are innovative, subordinate clauses are conservative: Consequences for the nature of construction. In Bybee and Noonan, 1–17.

Bybee, Joan, and Michael Noonan, eds. 2002. *Complex sentences in grammar and discourse: Essays in honor of Sandra A. Thompson.* Amsterdam: John Benjamins.

Cahill, Mike, compiler. 2002. Stories of linguistics and translation. Manuscript.
Callow, Kathleen, and John C. Callow. 1992. Text as purposive communication: A meaning-based analysis. In Mann and Thompson, 5–37.
Carnegie, Dale. 1976. How to stop worrying. In Jacqueline Berke, *Twenty questions for the writer: A rhetoric with readings*, 88–89. Second edition. New York: Harcourt Brace Jovanovich.
Chafe, Wallace L. 1994. *Discourse, consciousness, and time: The flow and displacement of conscious experience in speaking and writing*. Chicago: University of Chicago Press.
Christian, Imanuel. 1987. *Language as social behavior: Folk tales as a database for developing a beyond-the-discourse model*. Language Data, Asian-Pacific Series, 17. Huntington Beach, Calif: Summer Institute of Linguistics.
Chu, Chauncey C. 1998. *A discourse grammar of Mandarin Chinese*. Berkeley Models of Grammars 6. New York: Peter Lang.
Chung, Sandra, and Alan Timberlake. 1985. Tense, aspect, and mood. In Shopen 3, 202–258.
Clendenen, E. Ray. 1993. Old Testament prophecy as hortatory text: Examples from Malachi. *Journal of Translation and Textlinguistics* 6:336–353.
Cody, Iron Eyes. 1988. Words to grow on. *Guideposts*, July 1988:32–33.
Comrie, Bernard. 1976. *Aspect*. Cambridge: Cambridge University Press.
Comrie, Bernard. 1989. *Language universals and linguistic typology: Syntax and morphology*. Second edition. Chicago: University of Chicago Press.
Cornelius, Edwin. 1955. *How to learn a foreign language*. New York: Thomas Y. Crowell.
Cumming, Susanna, and Tsuyoshi Ono. 1997. Discourse and grammar. In Teun A. van Dijk (ed.), *Discourse as structure and process*. Discourse Studies: A Multidisciplinary Introduction 1, 112–137. Thousand Oaks, Calif.: Sage.
Davenport, J. 1973. Apartment fire tragedy. *Dallas Morning News*, April 20.
van Dijk, Teun A. 1980. *Macrostructures: An interdisciplinary study of global structures in discourse, interaction, and cognition*. Hillsdale, N.J.: Lawrence Erlbaum Associates.
Dooley, Robert A., and Stephen H. Levinsohn. 2001. *Analyzing discourse: A manual of basic concepts*. Dallas: SIL International.
Fairbank, Katie. 2004. Prepare to be bugged, bitten. *Dallas Morning News*, June.
Farr, Cynthia. 1999. *The interface between syntax and discourse in Korafe: A Papuan language of Papua New Guinea*. Pacific Linguistics Series C 148. Canberra: Australian National University.
Fee, Gordon D., and Douglas Stuart. 1982. *How to read the Bible for all its worth: A guide to understanding the Bible*. Grand Rapids, Mich.: Zondervan.

Firbas, Jan. 1966. On defining the theme in functional sentence analysis. *Travaux Linguistiques de Prague* 1:267–280.
Ford, Cecilia E. 1993. *Grammar in interaction: Adverbial clauses in American English conversations.* Studies in Interactional Sociolinguistics 9. Cambridge: Cambridge University Press.
Fox, Barbara A. 1987. *Discourse structure and anaphora: Written and conversational English.* Cambridge Studies in Linguistics 48. Cambridge: Cambridge University Press.
Gee, H. L. 1955. *Five hundred tales to tell again.* New York: Roy Publishers.
Gehring, Abigail R., ed. 2008. *Back to basics: A complete guide to traditional skills.* Third edition. New York: Skyhorse Publishing.
Genetti, Carol. 2005. The participial construction of Dolakha Newar: Syntactic implications of an Asian converb. *Studies in Language* 29:35–87.
George, Jacob, and Susan Jacob. 1990. Participant reference in Konda. *Occasional Papers in Translation and Textlinguistics* 4(1–2):95–113.
Givón, Talmy. 1983. Topic continuity in discourse: An introduction. In Talmy Givón (ed.), *Topic continuity in discourse: A quantitative cross-language study.* Typological Studies in Language 3, 3–41. Amsterdam: John Benjamins.
Givón, Talmy. 1987. Beyond foreground and background. In Tomlin 1987a, 175–188.
Givón, Talmy. 2001. *Syntax: An introduction* 2. Revised edition. Amsterdam: John Benjamins.
Graham, Billy. 1989. *How to be born again.* Dallas: Word Publishing.
Grimes, Joseph E. 1975. *The thread of discourse.* Janua Linguarum, Series Minor 207. The Hague: Mouton.
Gundel, Jeanette K., Nancy Hedberg, and Ron Zacharski. 1993. Cognitive status and the form of referring expressions in discourse. *Language* 69:274–307.
Hailey, Arthur. 1959. *The final diagnosis.* Garden City, N.Y.: Doubleday.
Haiman, John. 1978. Conditionals are topics. *Language* 54:565–589.
Haiman, John, and Pamela Munro, eds. 1983. *Switch reference and universal grammar: Proceedings of a symposium on switch reference and universal grammar, Winnipeg, May 1981.* Typological Studies in Language 2. Amsterdam: John Benjamins.
Haiman, John, and Sandra A. Thompson. 1984. "Subordination" in universal grammar. In Claudia Brugmann and Monica Macauley (eds.), *Proceedings of the Tenth Annual Meeting of the Berkeley Linguistics Society*, 510–523. Berkeley, Calif.
Haiman, John, and Sandra A. Thompson, eds. 1988. *Clause combining in grammar and discourse.* Typological Studies in Language 18. Amsterdam: John Benjamins.
Halliday, M. A. K., and Ruqaiya Hasan. 1976. *Cohesion in English.* English Language Series 9. London: Longman.

Harkins, Gerald. 2005. RST for Longacre: Diagrams used to show the results of an RST analysis are modified to portray analyses using Longacre's linguistic model. Manuscript.

Harris, Zellig. 1952. Discourse analysis. *Language* 28:1–30.

Harris, Zellig. 1963. *Discourse analysis reprints*. Papers on Formal Linguistics 2. The Hague: Mouton.

Harris, Zellig, M. Gottfried, T. Ryckman, P. Mattick, A. Daladier, and S. Harris, 1989. *The form of information in science: Analysis of an immunology sub-language*. Boston Studies in the Philosophy of Science 104. Dordrecht: Kluwer Academic Publications.

Haspelmath, Martin. 1995. The converb as a cross-linguistically valid category. In Martin Haspelmath and Ekkehard König (eds.), *Converbs in cross-linguistic perspective: Structure and meaning of adverbial verb forms*. Empirical Approaches to Language Typology 13, 1–56. Berlin: Mouton de Gruyter.

Healey, Phyllis, and Alan Healey. 1990. Greek circumstantial participles: Tracking participants with participles in the Greek New Testament. *Occasional Papers in Translation and Textlinguistics* 4:177–259.

Hays, J. Daniel. 1995. Verb forms in the expository discourse sections of Ecclesiastes. *Journal of Translation and Textlinguistics* 7:9–18.

Hemingway, Ernest. 1938. *The short stories of Ernest Hemingway*. New York: The Modern Library.

Hinds, John, and Wako Hinds. 1979. Participant identification in Japanese narrative discourse. In George Bedell, Kazuko Inoue, Eichi Kobayashi, and Masatake Muraki (eds.), *Explorations in linguistics: Papers in honor of Kazuko Inoue*, 201–212. Tokyo: Kenkyusha.

Hockett, Charles. 1955. How to learn Martian. *Astounding Science Fiction* 55:97–106.

Hoey, Michael. 1983. *On the surface of discourse*. London: Allen and Unwin.

Honda, Toshie. 1989. Participant reference in Japanese narratives. M.A. thesis. University of Texas at Arlington.

Hopper, Paul J. 1979. Aspect and foregrounding in discourse. In Talmy Givón (ed.), *Discourse and syntax*. Syntax and Semantics 12, 213–241. New York: Academic Press.

Hopper, Paul J. 1997. Dispersed verbal predicates in vernacular written narrative. In Akio Kamio (ed.), *Directions in functional linguistics*, Studies in Language Companion Series 36, 1–18. Amsterdam: John Benjamins.

Hopper, Paul J., and Sandra A. Thompson. 1980. Transitivity in grammar and discourse. *Language* 56:251–299.

Hopper, Paul J., and Sandra A. Thompson. 1984. The discourse basis for lexical categories in universal grammar. *Language* 60:703–752.

Horie, Kaoru, ed. 2000. *Complementation: Cognitive and functional perspectives*. Converging Evidence in Language and Communication Research 1. Amsterdam: John Benjamins.

Howard, Linda. 1977. Camsa: Certain features of verb inflection as related to paragraph types. In Longacre and Woods, 273–299.

Huang, Yan. 2000. *Anaphora: A cross-linguistic approach*. Oxford Studies in Typology and Linguistic Theory. Oxford: Oxford University Press.

Huttar, Lars A. 2003. Constituent charting for discourse analysis: Information model and presentation model. M.A. thesis. Graduate Institute of Applied Linguistics (Dallas).

Hwang, Shin Ja J. 1987. *Discourse features of Korean narration*. Summer Institute of Linguistics Publications in Linguistics 77. Dallas: Summer Institute of Linguistics and the University of Texas at Arlington.

Hwang, Shin Ja J. 1989. Recursion in the paragraph as a unit of discourse development. *Discourse Processes* 12:461–477.

Hwang, Shin Ja J. 1990a. Foreground information in narrative. *Southwest Journal of Linguistics* 9(2):63–90.

Hwang, Shin Ja J. 1990b. The relative clause in narrative discourse. *Language Research* 26:373–400.

Hwang, Shin Ja J. 1992. Analyzing a hortatory text with special attention to particle, wave, and field. In Ruth M. Brend (ed.), *The Eighteenth LACUS Forum*, 133–146. Lake Bluff, Ill.: Linguistic Association of Canada and the United States.

Hwang, Shin Ja J. 1993. Embedding and skewing of discourse types. In Peter A. Reich (ed.), *The Nineteenth LACUS Forum*, 153–162. Chapel Hill, N.C.: Linguistic Association of Canada and the United States.

Hwang, Shin Ja J. 1994. Relative clauses, adverbial clauses, and information flow in discourse. *Language Research* 30:673–706.

Hwang, Shin Ja J. 1996. The grammar and discourse of relative clauses. In Bates Hoffer (ed.), *The Twenty-second LACUS Forum*, 144–156. Chapel Hill, N.C.: Linguistic Association of Canada and the United States.

Hwang, Shin Ja J. 1997. A profile and discourse analysis of an English short story. *Language Research* 33:293–320.

Hwang, Shin Ja J. 2004. Negation in hortatory discourse. In Gordon D. Fulton, William J. Sullivan and Arle R. Lommel (eds.), *The Thirtieth LACUS Forum*, 367–377. Houston: Linguistic Association of Canada and the United States.

Hwang, Shin Ja J. 2005. Classifying hortatory and persuasive discourse. In Adam Makkai, William J. Sullivan and Arle R. Lommel (eds.), *The Thirty-first LACUS Forum*, 147–158. Houston: Linguistic Association of Canada and the United States.

Hwang, Shin Ja J. 2006. Clause combining in English narrative discourse. In Shin Ja J. Hwang, William J. Sullivan and Arle R. Lommel (eds.), *The Thirty-second LACUS Forum*, 313–323. Houston: Linguistic Association of Canada and the United States.

Hwang, Shin Ja J. 2007. Discourse operations and ranking in variable forms of participant reference. In Peter Reich, William J. Sullivan, Arle R. Lommel and Toby Griffen (eds.), *The Thirty-third LACUS Forum*, 179–190. Houston: Linguistic Association of Canada and the United States.

Hwang, Shin Ja J. 2009. Transitivity and expository discourse. In Patricia Sutcliffe, Lois Stanford, and Arle Lommel (eds.), *The Thirty-fourth LACUS Forum*, 93–102. Houston: Linguistic Association of Canada and the United States.

Hwang, Shin Ja J., and Jonathan Lathers. 2002. Discourse structure of two parables. In Ruth Brend, William Sullivan, and Arle R. Lommel (eds.), *The Twenty-eighth LACUS Forum*, 257–266. Houston: Linguistic Association of Canada and the United States.

Jones, Larry B. 1983. *Pragmatic aspects of English text structure*. Summer Institute of Linguistics Publications in Linguistics 67. Dallas: Summer Institute of Linguistics and the University of Texas at Arlington.

Jones, Linda K. 1977. *Theme in English expository discourse*. Edward Sapir Monograph Series in Language, Culture, and Cognition 2. Lake Bluff, Ill.: Jupiter Press.

Jordan, Michael P. 1998. The power of negation in English: Text, context and relevance. *Journal of Pragmatics* 29:705–752.

Kantor, Robert. 1976. Discourse phenomena and linguistic theory. Manuscript.

Keyes, Kenneth C. 2001. Word order and rhetorical organization in Qazaq. M.A. thesis. University of Texas at Arlington.

Kim, Byung-Sul, and Hei-Sung Hwang. 1969. *Yoli/yungyang* [Cooking/nutrition]. Seoul: Samjwung Dang.

Kim, Haeyeon. 1992. Clause combining in discourse and grammar: An analysis of some Korean clausal connectives in discourse. Ph.D. dissertation. University of Hawaii.

Kim, Yoon-Sook. 2000. Clause combining in Korean. M.A. thesis. University of Texas at Arlington.

Labov, William. 1972. The transformation of experience in narrative syntax. *Language in the inner city: Studies in the Black English vernacular*, 354–396. Philadelphia: University of Pennsylvania Press.

Lakoff, George. 1987. *Women, fire, and dangerous things: What categories reveal about the mind.* Chicago: University of Chicago Press.

Lakoff, Robin T. 1982. Persuasive discourse and ordinary conversation, with examples from advertising. In Deborah Tannen (ed.), *Analyzing discourse: Text and talk*. Georgetown University Round Table on Languages and Linguistics 1981, 25–42. Washington, D.C.: Georgetown University Press.

Lambrecht, Knud. 1994. *Information structure and sentence form: Topic, focus, and the mental representations of discourse referents*. Cambridge Studies in Linguistics. Cambridge: Cambridge University Press.

Landers, Ann. 1994. How to preserve your husband. *Dallas Morning News*, October 1.

Larson, Mildred L. 1978. *The functions of reported speech in discourse*. Summer Institute of Linguistics Publications in Linguistics 59. Dallas: Summer Institute of Linguistics and the University of Texas at Arlington.

Larson, Mildred L. 1984. The structure of Aguaruna (Jivaro) texts. In Robert E. Longacre (ed.), *Theory and application in processing texts in non-Indoeuropean languages*. Papiere zur Textlinguistik 43 (Papers in Textlinguistics 43), 153–209. Hamburg: Helmut Buske Verlag.

Levinsohn, Stephen H. 1976. Progression and digression in Inga (Quechuan) discourse. *Forum Linguisticum* 1:122–147.

Levinsohn, Stephen H. 2000. *Discourse features of New Testament Greek: A course book on the information structure of New Testament Greek*. Second edition. Dallas: SIL International.

Levinsohn, Stephen H. 2007. *Self-instruction materials on narrative discourse analysis*. Online at https://mail.jaars.org/~bt/narr.zip (accessed 11/2007).

Lewis, C. S. 1984. *Out of the silent planet*. New York: Macmillan Company.

Li, Charles N., and Sandra A. Thompson. 1981. *Mandarin Chinese: A functional reference grammar*. Berkeley: University of California Press.

London, Jack. 1945. To build a fire. *Best short stories of Jack London*, 9–22. New York: Doubleday.

Longacre, Robert E. 1968. *Discourse and paragraph structure: Discourse, paragraph, and sentence structure in selected Philippine languages* 1. Santa Ana, Calif.: Summer Institute of Linguistics.

Longacre, Robert E. 1970. Sentence structure as a statement calculus. *Language* 46:783–815.

Longacre, Robert E. 1976. "Mystery" particles and affixes. *Chicago Linguistic Society* 12:468–475.

Longacre, Robert E. 1981. A spectrum and profile approach to discourse analysis. *Text* 1:337–359.

Longacre, Robert E. 1982. Discourse typology in relation to language typology. In Sture Allén (ed.), *Text processing: Text analysis and generation, text typology and attribution: Proceedings of Nobel Symposium 51*. Data Linguistica 16, 457–486. Stockholm: Almqvist och Wiksell.

Longacre, Robert E. 1983a. *Exhortation and mitigation in First John*. Selected Technical Articles Related to Translation 9:3–44. Dallas: Summer Institute of Linguistics.

Longacre, Robert E. 1983b. Switch reference systems from two distinct linguistic areas: Wojokeso (Papua New Guinea) and Guanano (Northern South America). In Haiman and Munro, 185–207.

Longacre, Robert E. 1985. Discourse peak as zone of turbulence. In Jessica R. Wirth (ed.), *Beyond the sentence: Discourse and sentential form*, 81–98. Ann Arbor: Karoma.

Longacre, Robert E. 1989. Two hypotheses regarding text generation and analysis. *Discourse Processes* 12:413–460.

Longacre, Robert E. 1990. *Storyline concerns and word order typology in East and West Africa*. Studies in African Linguistics, supplement 10. Los Angeles: The James S. Coleman African Studies Center and Department of Linguistics, University of California.

Longacre, Robert E. 1992a. The discourse strategy of an appeals letter. In Mann and Thompson, 109–130.

Longacre, Robert E. 1992b. Towards an exegesis of 1 John based on the discourse analysis of the Greek text. In Black, 271–286.

Longacre, Robert E. 1994. *Weqatal* forms in Biblical Hebrew prose: A discourse-modular approach. In Bergen, 50–98.

Longacre, Robert E. 1995a. Building for the worship of God: Exodus 25:1–30:10. In Walter R. Bodine (ed.), *Discourse analysis of biblical literature: What it is and what it offers*. The Society of Biblical Literature Semeia Studies, 21–49. Atlanta: Scholars Press.

Longacre, Robert E. 1995b. Some interlocking concerns which govern participant reference in narrative. *Language Research* 31:697–714.

Longacre, Robert E. 1996. *The grammar of discourse*. Second edition. New York: Plenum Press.

Longacre, Robert E. 1998. A suggestion for the training of mother-tongue translators. *Notes on Translation* 12(1):39–43.

Longacre, Robert E. 1999a. Mark 5:1–43: Generating the complexity of a narrative from its most basic elements. In Porter and Reed, 169–196.

Longacre, Robert E. 1999b. A top-down, template-driven narrative analysis, illustrated by application to Mark's Gospel. In Porter and Reed, 140–168.

Longacre, Robert E. 2003a. *Joseph: a story of divine providence: A text theoretical and textlinguistic analysis of Genesis 37 and 39–48*. Second edition. Winona Lake, Ind.: Eisenbrauns.

Longacre, Robert E. 2003b. *Holistic textlinguistics*. SIL Electronic Working Papers. http://www.sil.org/silewp/2003/silewp2003-004.pdf (accessed 10/31/2008).

Longacre, Robert E. 2004. Holistic textlinguistics. In Carol L. Moder and Aida Martinovic-Zic (eds.), *Discourse across languages and cultures*. Studies in Language Companion Series 68, 13–36. Amsterdam: John Benjamins.

Longacre, Robert E. 2006. On the psycho-sociological reality of discourse templates. In Shin Ja J. Hwang, William J. Sullivan and Arle R. Lommel (eds.), *The Thirty-second LACUS Forum*, 343–353. Houston: Linguistic Association of Canada and the United States.

Longacre, Robert E. 2007a. Sentences as combinations of clauses. In Shopen 2, 372–420.

Longacre, Robert E. 2007b. The structure of information in expository discourse. In Peter Reich, William J. Sullivan, Arle R. Lommel, and Toby Griffen (eds.), *The Thirty-third LACUS Forum*, 349–358. Houston: Linguistic Association of Canada and the United States.

Longacre, Robert E., and Andrew C. Bowling. To appear. *Discourse modular grammar of biblical Hebrew*. Dallas: SIL International.

Longacre, Robert E., and Shin Ja J. Hwang. 1994. A textlinguistic approach to the biblical Hebrew narrative of Jonah. In Bergen, 336–358.

Longacre, Robert E., and Stephen Levinsohn. 1978. Field analysis of discourse. In Wolfgang U. Dressler (ed.), *Current trends in textlinguistics*. Research in Text Theory 2, 103–122. Berlin: Walter de Gruyter.

Longacre, Robert E., and Wilber B. Wallis. 1998. Soteriology and eschatology in Romans. *Journal of Evangelical Theological Society* 41:367–382.

Longacre, Robert E., and Frances Woods, eds. 1976–1977. *Discourse grammar: Studies in indigenous languages of Colombia, Panama, and Ecuador*, 3 vols. Summer Institute of Linguistics Publications in Linguistics and Related Fields 52. Dallas: Summer Institute of Linguistics and the University of Texas at Arlington.

Lowe, Ivan. 1986. Information distribution in hortatory discourse. In Benjamin F. Elson (ed.), *Language in global perspective: Papers in honor of the 50th anniversary of the Summer Institute of Linguistics 1935–1985*, 183–203. Dallas: Summer Institute of Linguistics.

Mann, William C., and Sandra A. Thompson. 1988. Rhetorical structure theory: Toward a functional theory of text organization. *Text* 8:243–281.

Mann, William C., and Sandra A. Thompson, eds. 1992. *Discourse description: Diverse linguistic analyses of a fund-raising text*. Pragmatics and Beyond New Series 16. Amsterdam: John Benjamins.

Mansen, Richard, and Karis Mansen. 1976. The structure of sentence and paragraph in Guajiro narrative discourse. In Longacre and Woods, 147–258.

Margolis, Simeon, and Peter Rabins. 2002. Amyloid plaques and neurofibrillary tangles in Alzheimer disease. *Memory*. The Johns Hopkins White Papers 3. Baltimore: The Johns Hopkins Medical Institutions.

Marchese, Lynell. 1987. On the role of conditionals in Godié procedural discourse. In Tomlin 1987a, 163–180.

Matthiessen, Christian, and Sandra A. Thompson. 1988. The structure of discourse and "subordination." In Haiman and Thompson, 275–329.

McArthur, Harry S. 1979. The role of aspect in distinguishing Aguacatec discourse types. In Linda K. Jones (ed.), *Discussion: Discourse studies in Mesoamerican languages 1*. Summer Institute of Linguistics Publications in Linguistics 58, 97–122. Dallas: Summer Institute of Linguistics and the University of Texas at Arlington.

McEvoy, Richard Steven. 2008. Grammar of narrative discourse in Migabac, a Papuan (Non-Austronesian) language. M.A. thesis. Graduate Institute of Applied Linguistics (Dallas).

Mushin, Ilana. 2005. Narrative functions of clause linkage in Garrwa: A perspective analysis. *Studies in Language* 29:1–33.

Myhill, John, and Junko Hibiya. 1988. The discourse function of clause-chaining. In Haiman and Thompson, 361–398.

Noonan, Michael. 2007. Complementation. In Shopen 2, 52–150.

Ono, Tsuyoshi. 1994. *Te, I,* and *Ru* clauses in Japanese recipes: A quantitative study. *Studies in Language* 14:73–92.

Paredes, J. Anthony, and Marcus J. Hepburn. 1976. The split brain and the culture-and-cognition paradox. *Current Anthropology* 17:121–127.

Pike, Kenneth L. 1967. *Language in relation to a unified theory of the structure of human behavior.* Janua Linguarum Series Maior 24. The Hague: Mouton.

Pike, Kenneth L. 1968. How to make an index. *PMLA* 83:991–993.

Pike, Kenneth L. 1977. Linguistic complexity in a two-page instruction sheet. Paper presented at the Third Annual Convention of the Kentucky Interdisciplinary Conference on Linguistics, Eastern Kentucky University, April 1, 1977.

Pike, Kenneth L. 1982. *Linguistic concepts: An introduction to tagmemics.* Lincoln: University of Nebraska Press.

Pike, Kenneth L., and Evelyn G. Pike. 1982. *Grammatical analysis.* Second edition. Summer Institute of Linguistics Publications in Linguistics 53. Dallas: Summer Institute of Linguistics and the University of Texas at Arlington.

Porter, Stanley E., and Jeffrey Reed, eds. 1999. *Discourse analysis and the New Testament: Approaches and results.* Sheffield, England: Sheffield Academic Press.

Prince, Ellen F. 1981. Toward a taxonomy of given-new information. In Peter Cole (ed.), *Radical pragmatics*, 223–255. New York: Academic Press.

Pu, Ming-Ming. 1997. Zero anaphora and grammatical relations in Mandarin. In Talmy Givón (ed.), *Grammatical relations: A functionalist perspective.* Typological Studies in Language 35, 281–321. Amsterdam: John Benjamins.

Rand, Sharon. 1993. *The French imparfait and passé simple in discourse.* Summer Institute of Linguistics and the University of Texas at Arlington Publications in Linguistics 116. Dallas: Summer Institute of Linguistics and the University of Texas at Arlington.

Reeder, JeDene. 1998. Pagibete, a Northern Bantu Borderlands language: A grammatical sketch. M.A. thesis. University of Texas at Arlington.

Ricoeur, Paul. 1985. *Time and narrative* 2. Kathleen McLaughlin and David Pellauer, translators. Chicago: University of Chicago Press.

Roberts, John R. 1987. *Amele.* Croom Helm Descriptive Grammars Series. London: Croom Helm.

Rubin, Joan, and Irene Thompson. 1994. *How to be a more successful language learner: Toward learner autonomy.* Second edition. Boston: Heinle and Heinle.

Rudolph, Elisabeth. 1987. Connective relations—connective expressions—connective structures. In János Petöfi (ed.), *Text and discourse constitution: Empirical aspects, theoretical approaches.* Research in Text Theory 4 (Untersuchungen zur Texttheorie 4), 97–133. Berlin: Walter de Gruyter.

Scancarelli, Janine. 1992. Clause-combining constructions. In William Bright (ed.), International Encyclopedia of Linguistics 1, 267–269. New York: Oxford University Press.

Shopen, Timothy, ed. 1985. *Grammatical categories and the lexicon*. Language typology and syntactic description 3. Cambridge: Cambridge University Press.
Shopen, Timothy, ed. 2007. *Complex constructions*. Language typology and syntactic description 2. Second edition. Cambridge: Cambridge University Press.
Shopen, Timothy, ed. 2007. *Language typology and syntactic description*. 3 vols. Second edition. Cambridge: Cambridge University Press.
Southgate, Vera, reteller. 1965. *The three little pigs*. Well Loved Tales 5. Loughborough, England: Ladybird Books.
Staley, William. 2007. *Referent management in Olo: A cognitive perspective*. SIL e-Books 5. Dallas: SIL International. http://www.sil.org/silepubs/abstract.asp?id=48757.
Terry, Ralph Bruce. 1995. *A discourse analysis of First Corinthians*. Summer Institute of Linguistics and the University of Texas at Arlington Publications in Linguistics 120. Dallas: Summer Institute of Linguistics and the University of Texas at Arlington.
Terry, Ralph Bruce. 1996. Patterns of discourse structure in 1 Corinthians. *Journal of Translation and Textlinguistics* 7(4):1–32.
Thompson, Sandra A. 1978. Modern English from a typological point of view: Some implications of the function of word order. *Linguistische Berichte* 54:19–35.
Thompson, Sandra A. 1985. Grammar and written discourse: Initial vs. final purpose clauses in English. *Text* 5(1–2):55–84.
Thompson, Sandra A. 1987. 'Subordination' and narrative event structure. In Tomlin 1987a, 435–454.
Thompson, Sandra A. 2002. 'Object complements' and conversation: Towards a realistic account. *Studies in Language* 26(1):125–163.
Thompson, Sandra A., and Paul J. Hopper. 2001. Transitivity, clause structure, and argument structure: Evidence from conversation. In Joan Bybee and Paul Hopper (eds.), *Frequency and the emergence of linguistic structure*, Typological Studies in Language 45, 27–60. Amsterdam: John Benjamins.
Thompson, Sandra A., Robert E. Longacre, and Shin Ja J. Hwang. 2007. Adverbial clauses. In Shopen 2, 237–300.
Tomlin, Russell. 1985. Foreground-background information and the syntax of subordination. *Text* 5(1–2):85–122.
Tomlin, Russell, ed. 1987a. *Coherence and grounding in discourse: Outcome of a symposium, Eugene, Oregon, June 1984*. Typological Studies in Language 11. Amsterdam: John Benjamins.
Tomlin, Russell. 1987b. Linguistic reflections of cognitive events. In Tomlin 1987a, 455–479.
Tracy, Hubert P., and Stephen H. Levinsohn. 1977. Participant reference in Ica expository discourse. In Longacre and Woods, 3–23.
Twain, Mark. 1964. *A Connecticut Yankee in King Arthur's court*. New York: Airmont Publishing Co.

Van Otterloo, Roger. 2011. *A descriptive grammar. The Kifuliiru language 2*. Publications in Linguistics 147. Dallas: SIL International.

Van Valin, Robert D. 1993. A synopsis of role and reference grammar. In Robert D. Van Valin (ed.), *Advances in role and reference grammar*. Amsterdam Studies in the Theory and History of Linguistic Science. Series IV, Current Issues in Linguistic Theory 82, 1–164. Philadelphia: John Benjamins.

Van Valin, Robert D., and Randy J. LaPolla. 1997. *Syntax: Structure, meaning and function*. Cambridge Textbooks in Linguistics. Cambridge: Cambridge University Press.

Virtanen, Tuija. 1992a. *Discourse functions of adverbial placement in English: Clause-initial adverbials of time and place in narratives and procedural place descriptions*. Åbo: Åbo Akademis Förlag.

Virtanen, Tuija. 1992b. Issues of text typology: Narrative—a "basic" type of text? *Text* 12(2):293–310.

Watson, Richard. 1984. Scheme and point in Pacoh expository discourse. In Robert E. Longacre (ed.), *Theory and application in processing texts in non-Indoeuropean languages*. Papiere zur Textlinguistik 43 (Papers in Textlinguistics 43), 113–151. Hamburg: Buske.

Weinrich, Harald. 1964. *Tempus: Besprochene und erzahlt Zeit*. Stuttgart: W. Kohlhammer.

Weinrich, Harald. 1973. *Le Temps: Le récit et la commentaire*. Michele Lacoste, translator. Paris: Seuil.

Wendland, Ernst R. 2000. 'Stand fast in the true grace of God!': A study of 1 Peter. *Journal of Translation and Textlinguistics* 13:25–102.

Wiesemann, Ursula, and Kent Spielmann. 2002. *Grammar by means of discourse analysis*. Dallas: SIL International. (LinguaLinks Library)

Woods, Frances. 1980. The interrelationship of cultural information, linguistic structure, and symbolic representations in a Halbi myth. Ph.D. dissertation. University of Texas at Arlington.

Yip, Pamela. 2003. Don't get bit. *Dallas Morning News*, June 9.

Language Index

Afar (Cushitic, Ethiopia) 115
Africa, languages of xii, 76, 94, 115, 155, 156, 218
Aguacatec (Mayan) 39–42
Aguaruna (Peru) 5, 13, 40, 7

Bantu languages 2, 155

Camsa (Colombia) 3–4, 40
Chinese 4–5, 83, 90
Czech 2

Dibabawon (Philippines) 38
Dravidian 5, 94

Ethiopia, languages of 115

Fore (Papua New Guinea) 5
French 3, 77, 132

Garrwa (Australia) 235
German 3
Godié (Cote d'Ivoire) 156
Greek 6, 83–84, 195
Guajiro (Colombia) 9–10
Guanano (Northern South America) 233
Gujarati (Indo-Aryan) 76–77

Halbi (Indo-Aryan) 75

Hebrew, Biblical xii, 5, 40, 42, 75, 155, 175, 189–193
Hungarian 2

Ibaloi (Philippines) 118, 120
Ica (Colombia) 10–11
Indo-Aryan languages 75, 76–77
Indo-European languages 6, 94
Inga (Colombia) 10

Japan, languages of 83, 94
Japanese 83

Kazakhstan, languages of 94
Kifuliiru (Bantu, DRC) 2
Koine Greek 84, 100, 103, 170, 176
Konda (Dravidian) 5
Koorete (Omotic; Ethiopia) 115
Korafe (Papua New Guinea) 96
Korean 7, 47, 83, 96, 103, 107–115, 154, 162–163, 167, 176, 180–184

Latin 3

Migabac (PNG) 93, 103–107, 115
Mixtec (Mexico) 7

Obolo (Nigeria) 227
Olo (PNG) 237
Oto-Manguean (Mesoamerica) 96

Pacoh (Austro-Asiatic, Viet Nam, Laos) 190
Pagibete (Northern Bantu, DRC) 155
Papua New Guinea, languages of 5, 94, 108, 163
Philippines, languages of 38, 118, 120

Quechuan languages 10

Russian 221

Sabaot (Eastern Sudanic, Kenya) 78–79
South America, languages of 94, 163
Southern Nilotic 78–79
Spanish 5–7, 75, 83

Thai (Thailand) 71
Totonac (Mexico) 5
Trique (Mexico) 6, 8, 46

Wik-Munkan (Australia) 120
Wojokeso (Papua New Guinea) 233

Index

A

action peak 54–55, 211
adverbial clause(s) 4, 7–8, 24, 46, 49, 74–75, 94–95, 101–102, 107, 115, 156, 159, 162, 167, 211
Afar (Cushitic, Ethiopia) 115
affixes 82–83
Africa, languages of xii, 76, 94, 115, 155, 156, 218
agent orientation 37, 42–43, 153, 164, 167, 169–170, 189, 211
agglutinative 3–4, 211
Aguacatec (Mayan) 39–42
Aguaruna (Peru) 5, 13, 40, 76
alliteration 27
alternation 117–118, 211
American English 7
amplification 119, 135–145, 211
antithesis 28, 55, 123, 136–137, 181–182, 211
antithetical 123, 211
aperture 53, 88, 211
article(s) 6, 82–84, 86–92
aspect ix, 40–41, 52–53, 94, 167, 185, 211
   completive 77, 213
   imperfect 75, 78–79, 218
   imperfective 78, 218
   perfective 52, 58, 71, 77, 174, 220–221

pluperfect 78–79, 138, 221
progressive 17–18, 58, 73, 75, 77, 139, 221
punctiliar 17, 58, 77, 221
assonance 27
attribution 120, 211
   awareness attribution 120, 211
Australia, languages of 120, 235
awareness 28
   awareness formula 28–29, 212

B

backbone 36, 38, 212
background 22, 74, 77–79, 101–102, 115, 185, 189, 205, 212
backreference 7–8, 74, 212
Bantu languages 2, 155
behavioral 37, 169, 212
Biblical Hebrew xii, 5, 40, 42, 75, 155
   expository 189–193
   hortatory 175

C

Camsa (Colombia) 3–4, 40
chaining x, 5, 13, 95, 100, 212
   chaining structure(s) 94, 96, 103, 115, 162, 167
   initial-consecutive 76, 78
   medial-final 76

chiasmus 89
  chiasmus, chiastic 212
  chiastic structure 59–60, 174
Chinese 4–5, 83, 90
circumstance 119, 212
clause chaining 163. See also chaining.
  Korean 107–115
  Migabac 103–107
clause combining 47–49, 93, 108, 115–116, 212
  English 96–103
climax 11, 53–55, 59, 72, 87, 91, 99, 115, 132, 171–172, 185, 190, 212
clitics 82–83
closure 53, 98, 114–115, 134, 213
cognitive event(s) 17–18, 27–28, 72–73, 213
cognitive state(s) 73, 213
coherence 23–26, 81, 213
cohesion 23–26, 52, 74, 78, 81, 162, 213
cohesive 8, 57, 101, 103, 115
Colossians 174, 176
command(s) 37, 170–181, 184
comment(s) 28, 74
  author comment(s) 78–79, 84
comparison 117
complement clause(s) 46–47, 63, 95–96, 98, 103, 108, 213
concession 182–183
concessive sentence 124
conclusion 53–54, 57, 97, 213
conditionality with universal quantifier 118, 213
conjunction(s) xi, 8–9, 51–52, 57, 73, 89–90, 100–101, 162–163
  coordinate 46, 95, 99
  subordinate 47–49, 94–95, 107
connectives 23, 35, 43, 107
constituent charting 46–53, 64–70
contingency 118

contingent temporal succession 35–37, 42–43, 153, 162, 164, 167, 213
contrafactual/contrafactuality 119, 124, 214
contrast 55, 93, 117, 137, 214
coordinate 99–100, 103
  conjunction. See conjunctions, coordinate.
  paragraph 28, 135, 159, 162, 181–183, 214
  sentence 47, 96, 123, 214
coordination 95–96, 99–101, 115, 136, 214
co-ranking 115, 214
  co-ranking structures 94
Corinthians, First Epistle 174, 176
counter-expectation 93, 100
coupling 100, 117, 214
Czech 2

D
deictics/deixis 6–7, 82–83, 214
demote/demotion 73, 75, 116, 189, 214
denouement 12–13, 53–55, 57, 97, 132, 171–173, 214
descriptive 17, 37–41, 73–74
descriptive discourse 13, 37, 39, 215
developing conflict 53–55, 215
dialogue 5, 10, 84, 141, 146–148, 151, 173, 215
dialogue paragraph 132
  complex 146–148, 151, 213
  compound 133–134, 147–148, 151, 213
  simple 141, 144–145, 147–148, 151, 223
Dibabawon (Philippines) 38
direct quotation(s) 5, 9, 49, 58, 63, 90, 124
discourse operations 84–86, 90–92
discourse type(s) 35–42, 132, 166, 171, 174, 185
drama 37, 215

Dravidian 5, 94

E
Ecclesiastes 189
efficient cause 119, 215
embedded/embedding 46–48, 148, 215
   clauses 47, 95–96, 102–103, 114
   discourses 39, 43, 60, 73, 75, 132–134, 170, 174–175
   paragraphs 28–29, 73, 134, 136–138, 140, 142–143, 146, 158–160, 181–183, 193
emic 13, 35, 38–40, 153, 215
English 4, 6–8, 11, 29, 38, 47–48, 98–100, 103–104, 108, 115, 123, 125, 163–164, 167, 170, 195
   expository 198–205
   hortatory 177–180
   narrative 55–60, 74
   participant reference 82–92
   procedural 154–162
   salience scheme 72–75
   sample texts 42–44
Ephesians 172, 195–198, 207
episode(s) xi, 13, 39, 41, 45, 49, 53–55, 57–59, 215
equational 124, 215
equative 5, 78–79, 215
equivalence paraphrase 119, 142, 216
Esther 176
Ethiopia, languages of 115
etic 35–36, 40, 42, 216
eulogy 36, 169, 216
evaluation 19, 74, 84–86, 91, 189–190, 216
eventline 9–10, 58–59, 84, 97, 99, 216
exemplification 120, 216
existential 40, 216
Exodus 155
expectancy chain 7, 216
exposition 53–54, 57, 97, 172–173, 216
expository 37, 73–74, 81, 133–134, 153, 164, 167, 170, 174, 180, 189–205, 216

F
final cause 119, 121, 216
final suspense 53–54, 216
finis 53, 132, 134, 216
first mention 6, 84, 86–87, 90, 92, 216
flashback(s) 19, 73–74, 78–79, 189, 216
focus 2, 101, 156, 217
focus-presupposition 82
followability xii, 4, 71
Fore (Papua New Guinea) 5
foreground 29, 102, 115, 205, 217
   foregrounded frame 6, 91
   foreground information 96–97
   foregrounding 190
foreshadowing 58, 217
frame 24–25, 29–30, 217
French 3, 77, 132
frustration 121, 217

G
Garrwa (Australia) 235
Genesis 5, 44, 60, 175–176, 185
German 3
Godié (Cote d'Ivoire) 156
grammaticalization 115, 217
grammaticalized conjunctions 8
grammatical word order 2
   grammatical word order language 217
Greek 6, 83–84, 195. See also Koine Greek
Guajiro (Colombia) 9–10
Guanano (Northern South America) 233
Gujarati (Indo-Aryan) 76–77

H

Halbi (Indo-Aryan) 75
happening(s) 20, 71, 73, 75–76, 79, 217
head-final chaining languages 47, 94, 217
head-initial chaining languages 94, 217
head-marking languages 83
Hebrew. See Biblical Hebrew
hortatory 7–8, 37, 127–128, 130–132, 153, 160, 164, 167, 169–185, 218
Hungarian 2
hypotheticality 118

I

Ibaloi (Philippines) 118, 120
Ica (Colombia) 10–11
iconicity 81
idiomatic phrase 22
imperative(s) 37, 156–159, 162–165, 167, 170, 174–177, 180–181
implication 118, 124, 218
inciting incident/inciting moment 53–55, 57–58, 97, 133–134, 172, 190, 218
inclusio 85, 218
indentation diagram 28–29, 130–132, 191
indirect quotations 49, 124
Indo-Aryan languages 75, 76–77
Indo-European languages 6, 94
information flow 81, 218
Inga (Colombia) 10
initial-consecutive 76, 94, 218
introducer(s) 46–57, 218
irrealis 18, 23, 74, 189, 218

J

Japan, languages of 83, 94
Japanese 83
John, First Epistle 172–174, 185
juxtaposed/juxtaposition 25, 39, 59, 95, 99, 115, 123, 218

K

Kazakhstan, languages of 94
Kifuliiru (Bantu, DRC) 2
Koine Greek 84, 100, 103, 170, 176
Konda (Dravidian) 5
Koorete (Omotic; Ethiopia) 115
Korafe (Papua New Guinea) 96
Korean 7, 47, 83, 96, 103, 154, 167, 176. See also clause chaining, Korean.
   hortatory 180–184
   procedural 162–163

L

Latin 3
logical connection 169
logical succession 42, 164, 167, 171

M

macrostructure 173, 185, 218
macrosegmentation 45, 53–61, 155–156, 159, 219
macrosegments 54, 60, 164
mainline(s) 1, 4, 22, 40–42, 71, 96, 132, 154, 218
   expository 189–190
   hortatory 170, 172, 174–177, 180, 185
   procedural 167
Malachi 172, 184
Mandarin Chinese. See Chinese
medial-final 76, 96, 115, 218. See also chaining.
Migabac (PNG) 93, 103–107, 115. See also clause chaining, Migabac.
mitigated forms 37
Mixtec (Mexico) 7
modal(s) 18, 58, 74, 163, 167, 170, 176, 180, 184–185, 203, 219
modality 52–53, 71, 107, 115, 156, 174, 219
mode 17, 169, 221
mood 172, 177, 181, 185, 219

Index 245

mystery particle(s) 9–11, 35, 52, 219

N
narrative(s) 7, 9, 45–61, 92, 134, 153, 167, 169, 173–175, 185, 190, 205, 219
  salience scheme 74–79
negated antonym paraphrase 23, 27, 119, 142, 179, 219
negative(s) 18, 23, 58, 74, 175, 179–180, 185
New Testament 170
New Testament Greek. See Koine Greek
Non-Indo-European languages 4
notional structure x, 54, 58, 96–97, 117, 146, 151, 167, 169–171, 220
noun(s) 20–22, 49, 53, 74, 82, 87, 90–91

O
Obolo (Nigeria) 227
Olo (PNG) 237
Oto-Manguean (Mesoamerica) 96

P
Pacoh (Austro-Asiatic, Viet Nam, Laos) 190
Pagibete (Northern Bantu, DRC) 155
Papua New Guinea, languages of 5, 94, 108, 163
parallelism 24, 26, 134, 185, 220
paraphrase(s) 24, 26, 99, 119–120, 142, 173, 179, 185, 220
participant(s) 27, 40, 48, 52–53, 55, 57, 77, 85–86, 100, 103, 135, 220
  central/principal 20, 23, 83, 85, 90, 92, 97, 133, 212
  main/major 83–84, 88, 90–92, 98, 219
  minor 83–84, 90–92, 219
  ranking. See ranking of participants
  thematic 5, 11, 225
participant reference(s) 4–5, 20, 22, 27, 50, 52, 54, 81–92, 220
participial clause(s) 8, 48, 74, 85, 87, 97–102, 115, 190, 220
participle(s) 18, 74
particles 9, 38, 76
peak 13, 27, 53–54, 60, 97–98, 100, 107, 133–134, 173–174, 178, 183, 185, 220
  peak episode 55, 57, 59, 114–116
persuasion 37, 39
persuasive discourse 37, 170, 220
Peter, First Epistle 172, 184
Philippines, languages of 38, 118, 120
pivotal event(s) 40, 77
poetry 27
postpeak 98–99
  postpeak episode(s) 53, 59, 97, 100, 221
postposed clauses 47, 87, 101–102, 116
pragmatic word order 2. See also grammatical word order.
pragmatic word order language 221
predicate nominal 85
prepeak 97
  prepeak episode(s) 53, 55, 57, 98–100, 221
presentational construction 82, 84, 87, 98, 221
procedural discourse 4, 36–38, 40, 41–42, 75, 153–167, 170–171, 174, 221
procedure(s) 41, 44, 156
profile 54–55, 57, 59, 221
projection 36–37, 43, 153, 164, 169, 221
promoted/promotion 75, 221
pronoun(s) 5–6, 53, 81–92, 163, 176, 193–194

prop(s) 27, 52, 83–85, 90–92, 103, 221
prophecy 36–37
propositions 93–96, 100–101, 115, 117, 221
Proverbs 127–129, 142
Psalm 23 190–192, 205
Psalm 73 190
pseudo-cleft 41, 222
pseudo-dialogue 58, 222
purpose clause(s) 41, 47, 159, 162

Q

Quechuan languages 10
quotation(s) 9, 48, 103, 120, 124, 146, 178
  quotation formula 72
quote 90, 144, 146
  quote formula 9, 48, 103, 184, 222

R

ranking of participants 20–23, 82–83, 90, 92, 222
ranking of verbs 17–20, 22–23, 141, 154, 175, 189. See also salience scheme.
recapitulate/recapitulation 7, 24, 173, 222
recursion 135, 222
reference(s) 20–22, 29, 162, 183, 222
referring expressions 82
relative clause(s) 46, 49, 52, 63, 78, 81, 87–88, 90, 95–97, 102, 108, 116, 222
reported speech 9–10, 39, 103, 222
resolution 54, 132, 146, 222
restaging 84–86, 91, 222
rheme 2, 222
rhetorical question(s) 57, 98–99, 174, 222
rhetorical structure theory 129, 135
rhetorical underlining 54, 173, 183, 222

Romans 172–173, 184
Russian 221

S

Sabaot (Eastern Sudanic, Kenya) 78–79
salience (ranking) scheme 74, 76, 78–79, 154–155, 223
  Biblical Hebrew 175
  hortatory 175
  narrative 74–79
schema(s) xi, 53–54, 132, 154, 170, 190, 205, 223
script(s) 24–26, 30, 223
script predictable 78, 223
sentence fragments 13
sequence signals 8, 156, 158, 223
serialization 96
serial verb construction 104
setting 28, 73–74, 134, 137, 139, 189, 223
simile 19, 120, 223
skewed/skewing xi, 100, 102, 115, 223
  of discourse types 39, 170, 175
slot xi, 45, 53, 54–55, 57, 60, 97, 115, 154, 171–172, 174, 178, 181–184, 223
source language x, 223
South America, languages of 94, 163
Southern Nilotic 78–79
Spanish 5–7, 75, 83
spectrum 19. See also salience scheme.
speech attribution 120, 224
stage 53–54, 57, 77, 98–99, 115, 132, 172, 224
storyline 1, 4, 19, 22, 25, 29, 52–53, 72–76, 115, 185, 189, 205, 224
  in chaining language 76–79
  primary 40, 75
  secondary 40, 75
  tertiary 75

subjunctive 9, 224
subordinate/subordination 75, 95, 115, 224
   clause(s) 51, 96, 102, 157, 165
   conjunction(s). See conjunction(s), subordinate
surface structure x, 38, 45, 54, 93, 96, 151, 160, 162, 169–170, 172–173, 224
surrogate noun 82, 224
switch reference x, 5, 83, 94, 103–104, 107, 193, 224

T

tail-head linkage 7, 104, 107, 224
target language x, 44, 61, 79, 116, 148, 168, 185, 224
template(s) xi, 53, 132, 154, 170–172, 181, 184, 190, 205, 224
temporal overlap 118, 224
temporal succession 38, 93, 100, 118, 169, 190, 225
tense(s) ix, 17, 53, 71, 94–95, 107, 114–115, 167, 185, 191
   future 42
   past 17–18, 43, 52, 58, 72–73, 75, 78–79, 83, 139, 174
   present 42, 83, 156, 162, 174, 180
tension 36–37, 42–43, 153, 225
Thai (Thailand) 71
thematic participant. See participant
thematic peak 54–55
theme(s) 2, 4, 36, 38, 225
thesis xi, 28, 55, 123, 129, 131–132, 139, 181–182, 225
Thessalonians, Second Epistle 180, 184
topic-comment 40, 82
topic(s) 3, 10, 81, 83, 153, 156, 168, 171, 181, 184, 225
Totonac (Mexico) 5
tracking of participants 84, 86–87, 91, 225
Trique (Mexico) 6, 8, 46

U

utterance 15
   continuing 146, 151, 213
   initiating 144, 151, 218
   resolving 144, 151, 222
   terminating 144, 151, 225

V

vantage point 58, 225
verb(s) 4, 7, 27, 47, 98, 139, 141, 154, 156, 189, 200, 203
   compound 77
   consecutive 76
   final 76
   in narrative 17–19
   initial 76
   medial 76–77
   non-finite 85, 94
   stative 58, 73, 180
verb-final languages 94, 163
verb-initial languages 94
vividness 44, 54, 174, 225
vocative 55, 225
voice 225
   active 156
   passive 78, 156

W

warning 119, 185, 226
Wik-Munkan (Australia) 120
Wojokeso (Papua New Guinea) 233
word order 1–3, 49–50, 82, 87, 90, 94, 162

Z

zero anaphora/reference 4, 35, 52, 83–85, 89–90, 226

www.ingramcontent.com/pod-product-compliance
Lightning Source LLC
Chambersburg PA
CBHW071819300426
44116CB00009B/1370